D0377152

THE INTERNET GALAXY

Please
return
materials
on time

WITHDRAWN
Highline College Library

HIGHLINE COMMUNITY COLLEGE
LIBRARY
P.O. BOX 98000
DES MOINES, WA 98198-9800

DEMCO

'A readable, articulate and persuasive account of why the internet's most powerful impacts on the shape of business, politics and society may be yet to come. Castells . . . is the nearest thing the internet has to a founding philosopher. . . . One of Castells' great strengths is his ability to combine academic rigour with an appetite to engage with current social and economic trends. He brings to this task an impressive array of knowledge about cities, labour markets, business history and technology. As a result his writing combines a sense of excitement and energy, with the sage judgment needed to resist glib simplifications and address the complex factors driving the internet.' *Financial Times*

'[An] excellent, readable, nontechnical summary of the history, social implications and likely future of Internet business.' *Publishers Weekly*

'A compelling analysis of the influence of the Internet, considering topics as diverse as individual communication and freedoms, the new dynamics of social movements, business networks in the new economy, and geographic development patterns such as metropolization and digital divide . . . Castells addresses the network society from a rich set of perspectives, taking into account both social and economic theory.'
Erkki Liikanen, European Commissioner for
Enterprise and Information Society

'Among technology's intelligentsia Castells has quickly earned a reputation as a pioneer, someone who has hacked out a logical, well-documented, and coherent picture of early 21st century civilization, even as it rockets forward largely in a blur.' *The Christian Science Monitor*

'A superb guide to the workings of the internet and its wider implications. . . . [Castells] brings a sociologist's understanding of the importance of culture in business to his analysis of the internet. . . . stands supreme as a wise and insightful guide to the web.' *Management Today*

'The Internet is shaping society and in turn being shaped by society. It takes a scholar of Manuel Castells's range to do justice to this phenomenon. His book is learned without being pompous, and insightful without being impenetrable. If we ever get a discipline of Internet studies, this will be one of its founding texts.'
John Naughton, author of
A Brief History of the Future: The Origins of the Internet

'Manuel Castells has proved once again that he has an unmatched synoptic capacity to make sense of the complexities of a networked world, and here writes with clarity and insight about everything from the history of the technology to the subcultures that have done so much to shape it.'
Geoff Mulgan, author of
Communication and Control and *Connexity*;
Head of the Prime Minister's Forward Strategy Unit,
Number 10, Downing Street

'Thoroughly researched . . . [and] truly global in scope. Castells provides balanced coverage of e-business and the new economy; the politics of the Internet, including privacy and freedom; and the geography of the Internet. . . . Highly recommended for academic libraries.' *Library Journal*

WITHDRAWN
HIGHLINE COLLEGE LIBRARY
Highline College Library

THE
INTERNET
GALAXY

*Reflections on the Internet,
Business, and Society*

Manuel Castells

OXFORD
UNIVERSITY PRESS

OXFORD

UNIVERSITY PRESS

Great Clarendon Street, Oxford OX2 6DP

Oxford University Press is a department of the University of Oxford.
It furthers the University's objective of excellence in research, scholarship,
and education by publishing worldwide in

Oxford New York

Auckland Bangkok Buenos Aires Cape Town Chennai
Dar es Salaam Delhi Hong Kong Istanbul Karachi Kolkata
Kuala Lumpur Madrid Melbourne Mexico City Mumbai Nairobi
São Paulo Shanghai Taipei Tokyo Toronto

Oxford is a registered trade mark of Oxford University Press
in the UK and in certain other countries

Published in the United States
by Oxford University Press Inc., New York

©Manuel Castells 2001

The moral rights of the author have been asserted
Database right Oxford University Press (maker)

First published 2001

Published new as paperback 2002

All rights reserved. No part of this publication may be reproduced,
stored in a retrieval system, or transmitted, in any form or by any means,
without the prior permission in writing of Oxford University Press,
or as expressly permitted by law, or under terms agreed with the appropriate
reprographics rights organization. Enquiries concerning reproduction
outside the scope of the above should be sent to the Rights Department,
Oxford University Press, at the address above

You must not circulate this book in any other binding or cover
and you must impose the same condition on any acquirer

British Library Cataloguing in Publication Data

Data available

Library of Congress Cataloging in Publication Data

Data available

ISBN 0-19-924153-8 (hbk)
ISBN 0-19-925577-6 (pbk)

10 9 8 7 6 5 4 3 2 1

Typeset by Florence Production Ltd, Stoodleigh, Devon
Printed in Great Britain
on acid-free paper by
Biddles Ltd., *www.biddles.co.uk*

To my grandchildren
Clara, Gabriel, and Sasha

Contents

Acknowledgments

This book grew out of the 2000 Clarendon Lectures in Management at Oxford University. My first acknowledgment, therefore, goes to those who invited me to give this lecture series: the Oxford University Saïd Business School, and Oxford University Press. I also thank Linacre College for extending a concurrent invitation, and providing hospitality during my visit to Oxford. A special word of gratitude goes to David Musson, commissioning editor at Oxford University Press, and the inspirer of this book. Without his enthusiasm for this project, and his support and advice during its elaboration, this book would not have been written.

Emma Kiselyova-Castells has continued to be a fundamental source of personal support, intellectual advice, and substantive collaboration. I particularly thank her for the many informal conversations we have had during the past few years on the meaning and use of the Internet. She always makes me see what I did not see in the first instance. I am also grateful for her patience in our daily life during the intense periods of work that were necessary to research and write this book.

I am deeply indebted to a number of colleagues who read and commented on successive drafts of this book, providing additional material, correcting mistakes, suggesting interpretations, and ultimately transforming the form and content of the volume in a very substantial way. Many of them put so much work into this effort that it can be said that the book has been produced by a network of researchers and experts from different fields, working in the spirit of "open source" that is the root of the Internet world. Naturally, I assume sole responsibility for the errors and misunderstandings still remaining in the text, but I want to emphasize the collective

Acknowledgments

endeavor in whatever contribution this book may represent. My belated thanks go to: Jerry Feldman, Patrice Riemens, Ilkka Tuomi, Steven Cisler, Matthew Zook, Bernard Benhamou, Blanca Gordo, Barry Wellman, Claude Fischer, Pekka Himanen, William Dutton, Paul Di Maggio, Steve Jones, Anna L. Saxenian, William Mitchell, Christos Papadimitriou, David Lyon, Lisa Servon, Fritjof Capra, Martin Carnoy, Erin Walsh, Regis McKenna, Stuart Henshall, Shujiro Yazawa, and Marty Hearst.

I was also fortunate to be able to present and discuss the ideas leading to this book at a number of meetings and seminars around the world. This exchange was an essential part of the intellectual process that produced the analysis presented here. I would like to highlight two exceptional events of a very different character. One was the First Conference of the Association of Internet Researchers which was held at the University of Kansas, in Lawrence, in September 2000. Here I experienced the beginning of a new field of academic research, learned a great deal from the meetings, and was able to contrast my hypotheses with well-informed researchers from many areas, particularly with those of the younger cohorts: there is clearly an Internet research generation in the making. The other intellectual environment that shaped my views on the Internet world was the series of seminars in South Africa organized by the Center of Higher Education Transformation in June–July 2000. These seminars were not about the Internet, but about the relationship between information technology, globalization, development, and social change. Yet the content of these discussions changed my view of the world, and thus of the Internet. I therefore want to thank publicly the organizers of these seminars, Nico Cloete, Shireen Badat, and Johan Muller.

A number of lectures, debates, and meetings in institutions around the world were also influential in forming the analysis presented here, and I therefore wish to thank the colleagues who invited me and, even more, the participants in these debates at the following institutions: Universitat Oberta de Catalunya (Barcelona), University of Southern California, University of California at Los Angeles, University of California at San Diego, University of Washington, Santa Clara University, Intel Museum,

Acknowledgments

SITRA (Helsinki), Virtual Society Program (United Kingdom), Centre Européen des Mutations et des Reconversions Industrielles (Longwy, France), Higher School of Economics (Moscow), Universidad de Guadalajara (Mexico), Massachusetts Institute of Technology, and Columbia University (New York).

Special thanks, as always in my work, go to my students, who are key contributors to my thinking and research. I want to mention especially Chris Benner, Matthew Zook, Blanca Gordo, Elsie Harper-Anderson, Miriam Chion, Grace Woo, Manuel Suarez, and Madeleine Zayas. Three Berkeley seminars were particularly influential in the exchange that led to this analysis: the Seminar on the Information Society in the Department of Sociology; the Seminar on the Internet and Economic Development in the Department of City and Regional Planning; and the Seminar on Information Technology and Social Values co-taught with my colleague Jerry Feldman in the Computer Science Department. I would like to express my gratitude to all the students in these seminars. My special thanks go to the members of our private seminar at Berkeley on the social implications of information technology, whose ideas, in their contradictory diversity, are present in this book.

I also wish to reiterate my debt to my copy-editor, Sue Ashton, whose dedication and professionalism are the key link between this author and you, the reader.

Manuel Castells

Berkeley, California, April 2001

The Network is the Message

The Internet is the fabric of our lives. If information technology is the present-day equivalent of electricity in the industrial era, in our age the Internet could be likened to both the electrical grid and the electric engine because of its ability to distribute the power of information throughout the entire realm of human activity. Furthermore, as new technologies of energy generation and distribution made possible the factory and the large corporation as the organizational foundations of industrial society, the Internet is the technological basis for the organizational form of the Information Age: the network.

A network is a set of interconnected nodes. Networks are very old forms of human practice, but they have taken on a new life in our time by becoming information networks, powered by the Internet. Networks have extraordinary advantages as organizing tools because of their inherent flexibility and adaptability, critical features in order to survive and prosper in a fast-changing environment. This is why networks are proliferating in all domains of the economy and society, outcompeting and outperforming vertically organized corporations and centralized bureaucracies. However, in spite of their advantages in terms of flexibility, networks have traditionally had to reckon with a major problem, in contrast to centralized hierarchies. They have had considerable difficulty in coordinating functions, in focusing resources on specific goals, and in accomplishing a given task, beyond a certain size and complexity of the network. For most of human history, unlike biological evolution, networks were outperformed as tools of instrumentality by organizations able to muster resources around centrally defined goals, achieved through the implementation of tasks in rationalized, vertical chains of command and control. Networks were primarily the preserve of private life; centralized hierarchies were the fiefdoms of power and production. Now, however, the introduction of computer-based information and communication technologies, and particularly the Internet, enables networks to deploy their flexibility and adaptability, thus asserting their evolutionary nature. At the same time, these technologies allow the coordination of tasks, and management of complexity. This results in an unprecedented combination of flexibility and task performance, of coordinated decision-making and decentralized execution, of individualized expression and global, horizontal communication, which provide a superior organizational form for human action.

In the last quarter of the twentieth century, three independent processes came together, ushering in a new social structure predominantly based on networks: the needs of the economy for management flexibility and for the globalization of capital, production, and trade; the demands of society in which the values of individual freedom and open communication became paramount; and the extraordinary advances in computing and telecommunications made possible by the micro-electronics revolution. Under these conditions, the Internet, an obscure technology without much application beyond the secluded worlds of computer scientists, hackers, and countercultural communities, became the lever for the transition to a new form of society—the network society—and with it to a new economy.

The Internet is a communication medium that allows, for the first time, the communication of many to many, in chosen time, on a global scale. As the diffusion of the printing press in the West created what MacLuhan named the 'Gutenberg Galaxy', we have now entered a new world of communication: the Internet Galaxy. The use of the Internet as a communication system and an organizing form exploded in the closing years of the second millennium. At the end of 1995, the first year of widespread use of the world wide web, there were about 16 million users of computer communication networks in the world. In early 2001 there were over 400 million; reliable forecasts point to about 1 billion users in 2005, and we could be approaching the 2 billion mark by 2010, even taking into consideration a slowing down of diffusion of the Internet when it enters the world of poverty and technological retardation. The influence of Internet-based networking goes beyond the number of users: it is also the quality of use. Core economic, social, political, and cultural activities throughout the planet are being structured by and around the Internet, and other computer networks. In fact, exclusion from these networks is one of the most damaging forms of exclusion in our economy and in our culture.

Yet, in spite of the pervasivenes of the Internet, its logic, its language, and its constraints are not well understood beyond the realm of strictly technological matters. The speed of transformation has made it difficult for scholarly research to follow the pace of change with an adequate supply of empirical studies on the whys and wherefores of the Internet-based economy and society. Taking advantage of this relative void of reliable investigation, ideology and gossip have permeated the understanding of this fundamental dimension of our lives, as is often the case in periods of rapid social change. Sometimes this has been in the form of futurological prophecies based on the simplistic extrapolation of social consequences from the technological wonders emerging from science and engineering; at other times, it appears as critical dystopias, denouncing the supposedly alienating effects of the Internet before even practicing it. The media, keen to inform an anxious public, but lacking the autonomous capacity to assess social trends with rigor, oscillate between reporting the amazing future on offer and following the basic principle of journalism: only bad news is worthy news.

The volatility of the stock market contributes to this ambivalent feeling toward the Internet. Once upon a time, before April 2000, any business related to the Internet was greeted by the market with staggeringly high valuation, regardless of its performance. By the beginning of 2001, most technology stocks were battered by the flight of investors, again without much discrimination between good and bad management and business prospects. The new financial markets are strongly influenced by crowd psychology and information turbulences, rather than by a sound evaluation of the relatively new conditions under which business currently operates. The effect of these developments is that we are entering, full speed, the Internet Galaxy in a state of informed bewilderment.

And yet, while we do not know enough about the social and economic dimensions of the Internet, we know something. This book presents some of this knowledge, and reflects on the meaning of what we know. In the pages that follow you will find no predictions about the future, since I think we barely understand our present, and I deeply distrust the methodology underlying these predictions. You will not find moral admonitions either—or, for that matter, policy prescriptions or management advice. My purpose here is strictly analytical since I believe that knowledge should precede action, and action is always specific to a given context and a given purpose. But I hope that by rooting my reflection in observations concerning various domains of the practice of the Internet I will be able to shed some light on the interaction between the Internet, business, and society. Furthermore, I hope that this will help to illuminate the path to better our society and to stabilize our economy—since volatility, insecurity, inequality, and social exclusion go hand in hand with creativity, innovation, productivity, and wealth creation in these first steps of the Internet-based world. The improvement of our condition will depend on what people do, including you and me. But in this book, as the academic researcher I am, my job, and indeed my responsibility, is to provide you with the best possible intellectual tools I can, within the limits of my knowledge and experience.

The point of departure of this analysis is that people, institutions, companies, and society at large, transform technology, any technology, by appropriating it, by modifying it, by experimenting with it. This is the fundamental lesson from the social history of technology, and this is even more so in the case of the Internet, a technology of communication. Conscious communication (human language) is what makes the biological specificity of the human species. Since our practice is based on communication, and the Internet transforms the way in which we communicate, our lives are deeply affected by this new communication technology. On the other hand, by doing many things with the Internet, we transform the Internet iself. A new socio-technical pattern emerges from this interaction.

Moreover, the Internet was purposely designed as a technology of free communication, for historical and cultural reasons that I will present in this book. It is not the result of this project that we are free at last thanks to the Internet—as I hope I will be able to show: it all depends on context and process. But it follows that the Internet is a particularly malleable technology, susceptible of being deeply modified by its social practice, and leading to a whole range of potential social outcomes—to be discovered by experience, not proclaimed beforehand.

Let me provide some examples to illustrate this statement. Take the new economy. If e-business is understood as the commercialization of the Internet by dot.com firms, this would be an interesting, innovative, and sometimes profitable business, but rather limited in its overall economic impact. If, as I shall argue, the new economy is based on unprecedented potential for productivity growth as a result of the uses of the Internet by all kinds of business in all kinds of operations, then we are entering, probably, a new business world. A world that does not cancel business cycles or supersede economic laws, but transforms their modalities and their consequences, while adding new rules to the game (such as increasing returns and network effects). In one perspective, the new economy is the economy of Internet industry. In another approach, we observe the growth of a new economy from within the old economy, as a result of the use of the Internet by business, for its own purpose and in specific contexts.

Consider a very different issue. I believe that the Internet is a fundamental instrument for development in the Third World. And so do some of the people who can really make a difference, such as Kofi Annan, Thabo Mbeki, and Ricardo Lagos. However, this does

5

not mean that by diffusing the Internet without altering the context of its appropriation we can reverse the current situation, in which about 50 percent of humankind barely survives with less than two dollars a day.

Unless we act on a broader development strategy, we could find ourselves in the situation I found myself on landing in Bogotá in April 1999. I was initially thrilled by the headline of *El Tiempo*: "New uses of Internet in Colombia." I care very much about Colombia, so I was eager to see any small sign of light at the end of its tunnel of violence. Yet, it turned out that, confronted with the flight from Bogotá of the upper middle class, barricaded in its suburban gated communities, extortionists and kidnappers had resorted to the Internet to distribute their threats by the hundreds through electronic mailing lists; then had proceeded to selective kidnapping to enforce their threats, so cashing in on their Internet-based, mass-produced extortion business. In other words, some sectors of Colombian society were appropriating the Internet for their own purposes, their criminal practices, rooted in a context of social injustice, political corruption, drug economy, and civil war. The elasticity of the Internet makes it particularly susceptible to intensifying the contradictory trends present in our world. Neither utopia nor dystopia, the Internet is the expression of ourselves— through a specific code of communication, which we must understand if we want to change our reality.

This book proposes a number of ideas on the interaction between the Internet, the economy, and society, on the basis of selective observations. It does not exhaust the sources of available information because research cannot be completed when the object of the research (the Internet) develops and changes much faster than the subject (this researcher—or, for that matter, any researcher). It does not deal either with all the relevant themes, simply because I did not have the time or energy to write another encyclopedic book covering most dimensions of social life. I want to mention two particularly blatant omissions. I do not deal with the uses of the Internet in education, and particularly in e-learning, a key domain of activity that is transforming the world where I live; that is, the world of educational institutions. And, because of the complexity of the matter, I could not finish the work I had undertaken on gender and the Internet, although there are some remarks on this issue in different passages of the book. I have vowed to myself (and to the reader) to continue working on this topic, and to have it ready for a possible second edition of this book.

The pages that follow simply try to anchor current discussion of the Internet in documented observation, thus laying the ground for further research in an open, interactive process. This observation is limited in terms of its social and cultural context. Most of the data and sources refer to North America. This is partly because it is where the practice of the Internet is most developed, and partly because it is the area about which we have most information. I have tried to compensate for this bias by gathering information on other countries, and by familiarizing myself, during 1998–2001, with discussions on the social and economic dimensions of the Internet in a variety of contexts, beyond my Californian hub, including Spain, England, Finland, France, The Netherlands, Sweden, Portugal, Germany, Ireland, Russia, Brazil, Argentina, Bolivia, Chile, Colombia, Mexico, and South Africa. I have not undertaken a systematic investigation in all these contexts, and so I do not have specific findings to report. However, by interacting with researchers, social actors, business managers, technologists, and politicians in these countries, and by asking them the questions I consider in this book, I was able to record a differential feedback, which I have tried to take into account when reaching my conclusions. The Internet is a global communication network, but its use and its evolving reality are the product of human action under the specific conditions of differential history. It is up to the reader to filter, interpret, and use, according to his or her own context, the analytical contribution I can offer on the basis of my own theory and observation.

The book is organized along a sequence of topics, covering some of the most important areas of Internet use. I start with the historical and cultural process of the creation of the Internet because it provides the clues to understanding what the Internet is, both as a technology and a social practice. Then I examine the role played by the Internet in the emergence of the new economy, considering the transformation of business management, capital markets, work, and technological innovation. Next, I invite the reader to move from economy to society by assessing the emergence of new forms of sociability on-line on the basis of available evidence. This will lead us to analyze the political implications of the Internet: first, by studying new forms of citizen participation and grassroots organizing, secondly, by analyzing the issues and conflicts related to liberty and privacy in the interplay between government, business, and Internet-based communication. In order to understand new communication patterns, I then probe the famed convergence between the Internet and multimedia, exploring the formation of a multi-modal hypertext. Then, down to earth: the Internet does have a geography. I will show you which one, and what are its implications for cities, regions, and our urban life. Finally, I will address the fundamental issue of inequality and social exclusion in the age of the Internet by analyzing the contours and dynamics of the digital divide in a global perspective.

So, let us depart on this intellectual journey. It is my hope that it will give the reader a better understanding of a significant dimension of our world, and our lives, at the onset of their transformation.

Chapter 1

Lessons from the History of the Internet

The story of the creation and development of the Internet is one of an extraordinary human adventure. It highlights people's capacity to transcend institutional goals, overcome bureaucratic barriers, and subvert established values in the process of ushering in a new world. It also lends support to the view that cooperation and freedom of information may be more conducive to innovation than competition and proprietary rights. I shall not recount this saga, since there are several good chronicles available to the reader (Abbate, 1999; Naughton, 1999). Instead, I will focus on what seem to be the critical lessons we can distill from the processes that led to the formation of the Internet, from the building of the ARPANET in the 1960s to the explosion of the world wide web in the 1990s. Indeed, the historical production of a given technology shapes its content and uses in ways that last beyond its original inception, and the Internet is no exception to this rule. The history of the Internet helps us to understand the paths of its future history-making. However, before embarking on interpretation, to simplify the reader's task, I will summarize the main events that led to the constitution of the Internet in its current form; that is, as a global network of computer networks made user-friendly by the world wide web, an application running on top of the Internet.

The History of the Internet, 1962–1995: An Overview

The origins of the Internet are to be found in ARPANET, a computer network set up by the Advanced Research Projects Agency (ARPA) in September 1969. ARPA was formed in 1958 by the Defense Department of the United States with the task of mobilizing research resources, particularly from the university world, toward building technological military superiority over the Soviet Union in the wake of the launching of the first Sputnik in 1957. ARPANET was only a minor program emerging from one of ARPA's departments, the Information Processing Techniques Office (IPTO), established in 1962 on the basis of a pre-existing unit. The aim of this department, as defined by its first director, Joseph Licklider, a psychologist turned computer scientist at the Massachusetts Institute of Technology (MIT), was to stimulate research in interactive computing. As part of this effort, the building of ARPANET was justified as a way of sharing computing time on-line between various computer centers and research groups working for the agency.

To build an interactive computer network, IPTO relied on a revolutionary telecommunications transmission technology, packet switching, developed independently by Paul Baran at Rand Corporation (a Californian think-tank often working for the Pentagon) and by Donald Davies at the British National Physical Laboratory. Baran's design of a decentralized, flexible communication network was a proposal from the Rand Corporation to the Defense Department to build a military communications system able to survive a nuclear attack, although this was never the goal behind the development of ARPANET. IPTO used this packet-switching technology in the design of ARPANET. The first nodes of the network in 1969 were at the University of California, Los Angeles, SRI (Stanford Research Institute), the University of

California, Santa Barbara, and the University of Utah. In 1971, there were fifteen nodes, most of them university research centers. The design of ARPANET was implemented by Bolt, Beranek and Newman (BBN), a Boston engineering acoustics firm converted into applied computer science, which was founded by MIT professors, and usually staffed by MIT and Harvard scientists and engineers. In 1972, the first successful demonstration of ARPANET took place at an international conference in Washington, DC.

The next step was to make ARPANET's connection with other computer networks possible, starting with the communication networks that ARPA was managing, PRNET and SATNET. This introduced a new concept: a network of networks. In 1973, two computer scientists, Robert Kahn, from ARPA, and Vint Cerf, then at Stanford University, wrote a paper outlining the basic Internet architecture. They built on the efforts of the Network Working Group, a cooperative technical group formed in the 1960s by representatives from the various computer centers linked by ARPANET, including Cerf himself, Steve Crocker, and Jon Postel, among others. For computer networks to talk to each other they needed standardized communication protocols. This was partly accomplished in 1973, at a Stanford seminar, by a group led by Cerf, Gerard Lelann (from the French Cyclades research group), and Robert Metcalfe (then at Xerox PARC), with the design of the transmission control protocol (TCP). In 1978 Cerf, Postel, and Crocker, working at the University of Southern California, split TCP into two parts, adding an inter-network protocol (IP), yielding the TCP/IP protocol, the standard on which the Internet still operates today. However, ARPANET continued for some time to operate on a different protocol, NCP.

In 1975, ARPANET was transferred to the Defense Communication Agency (DCA). In order to make computer communication available to different branches of the armed forces, the DCA decided to create a connection between various networks under its control. It established a Defense Data Network, operating on TCP/IP protocols. In 1983 the Defense Department, concerned about possible security breaches, decided to create a separate MILNET network for specific military uses. ARPANET became ARPA-INTERNET, and was dedicated to research. In 1984, the US National Science Foundation (NSF) set up its own computer communications network, NSFNET, and in 1988 it started using ARPA-INTERNET as its backbone.

In February 1990 ARPANET, technologically obsolete, was decommissioned. Thereafter, having released the Internet from its military environment, the US government charged the National Science Foundation with its management. But NSF's control of the Net was short-lived. With computer networking technology in the public domain, and telecommunications in full deregulation, NSF quickly proceeded with the privatization of the Internet. The Defense Department had decided earlier to commercialize Internet technology, financing US computer manufacturers to include TCP/IP in their protocols in the 1980s. By 1990 most computers in America had networking capabilities, laying the ground for the diffusion of inter-networking. In 1995 NSFNET was shut down, opening the way for the private operation of the Internet.

In the early 1990s a number of Internet service providers built their own networks and set up their own gateways on a commercial basis. Thereafter, the Internet grew rapidly as a global network of computer networks. This was made possible by the original design of ARPANET, based on a multi-layered, decentralized architecture, and open communication protocols. Under these conditions the Net was able to expand by the addition of new nodes and endless reconfiguration of the network to accommodate communication needs.

Nonetheless, ARPANET was not the only source of the Internet as we know it today. The current shape of the Internet is also the outcome of a grassroots tradition of computer networking. One component of this tradition was the bulletin board systems (BBS) movement that sprung from the networking of PCs in the late 1970s. In 1977, two Chicago students, Ward Christensen and Randy Suess, wrote a program, which they called MODEM, enabling the transfer of files between their PCs, and in 1978 another program, the Computer Bulletin Board System, which made it possible for PCs to store and transmit messages. They released both programs into the public domain. In 1983, Tom Jennings, a programmer, then working in California, created his own BBS program, FIDO, and started a network of BBSs, FIDONET. FIDONET is still the cheapest, most accessible computer communication network in the world, relying on PCs and calls over standard telephone lines. In 2000, it comprised over 40,000 nodes and about 3 million users. Although this represented only a tiny fraction of total Internet use, the practice of BBSs and the culture exemplified by FIDONET were influential factors in the configuration of the global Internet.

In 1981, Ira Fuchs, at the City University of New York, and Greydon Freeman, of Yale University, started an experimental network on the basis of IBM RJE protocol, thus building a network for IBM users, mainly university based, which came to be known as BITNET ("Because it's there," referring to the IBM slogan; it also stood for "Because it's time"). When IBM stopped funding in 1986, users' fees supported the network. It still lists 30,000 active nodes.

A decisive trend in computer networking emerged from the community of UNIX users. UNIX is an operating system developed at Bell Laboratories, and released by Bell to the universities in 1974, including its source code and permission to alter the source. UNIX became the *lingua franca* of most computer science departments, and students soon became adept at its manipulation. Then, in 1978 Bell distributed its UUCP program (UNIX-to-UNIX copy) allowing computers to copy files from each other. On the basis of UUCP, in 1979, four students in North Carolina (Truscott, Ellis, Bellavin, and Rockwell) designed a program for communication between UNIX computers. An improved version of this program was distributed freely at a UNIX users' conference in 1980. This allowed the formation of computer communication networks, Usenet News, outside the ARPANET backbone, thus considerably broadening the practice of computer communication.

In the summer of 1980 Usenet News reached the computer science department of the University of California, Berkeley, where there was a brilliant group of graduate students (including Mark Horton and Bill Joy) working on adaptations and applications of UNIX. As Berkeley was an ARPANET node, this group of students developed a program to bridge the two networks. From then on, Usenet became linked to ARPANET, the two traditions gradually merged, and various computer networks became able to communicate with each other, often sharing the same backbone (courtesy of a university). These networks eventually came together as the Internet.

Another major development resulting from the UNIX users' tradition was the "open source movement"—a deliberate attempt to keep access to all information about software systems open. I shall analyze in more detail, in Chapter 2, the open source movement, and the hackers' culture, as essential trends in the social and technical shaping of the Internet. But I need to refer briefly to it in this summary account of the sequence of events that led to the formation of the Internet. In 1984, a programmer at MIT's Artificial Intelligence Laboratory, Richard Stallman, reacting against the decision by ATT to claim proprietary rights to UNIX, launched the Free Software Foundation, proposing to substitute "copyleft" for copyright. By "copyleft" it is understood that anyone using software that had been made freely available should, in return, distribute over the Net the improved code. Stallman created an operating system, GNU, as an alternative to UNIX, and he posted it on the Net under a license that allowed its use on the condition of respecting the copyleft clause.

Putting this principle into practice, in 1991, Linus Torvalds, a 22-year-old student at the University of Helsinki, developed a new UNIX-based operating system, called Linux, and distributed it freely on the Internet, asking users to improve it and to post their improvements back on the Net. The result of this initiative was the development of a robust Linux operating system, constantly upgraded by the work of thousands of hackers and millions of users, to the point that Linux is now widely considered one of the most advanced operating systems in the world, particularly for Internet-based computing. Other groups of cooperative software development based on open source sprung from the UNIX users' culture. Thus, in the year 2001, over 60 percent of world wide web servers in the world were running on Apache, which is an open source server program developed by a cooperative network of UNIX programmers.

What made it possible for the Internet to embrace the world at large was the development of the world wide web. This is an information-sharing application developed in 1990 by an English programmer, Tim Berners-Lee, working at CERN, the Geneva-based, European high-energy physics research center. Although he was not personally aware of it (Berners-Lee, 1999: 5), Berners-Lee's work continued a long tradition of ideas and technical projects that, for the previous half-century, had imagined the possibility of linking up information sources via interactive computing. Vannevar Bush proposed his Memex system in 1945. Douglas Engelbart designed his On-Line System, including graphics interface and the mouse, working from his Augmentation Research Center in the San Francisco Bay area, and he first demonstrated it in 1968. Ted Nelson, a radical, independent thinker, envisioned a hypertext of interlinked information in his 1965 *Computer Lib* manifesto, and worked for many years on the creation of a utopian system, Xanadu: an open, self-evolving hypertext aimed at linking all the planet's information, past, present, and future. Bill Atkinson, the author of the graphics interface of the Macintosh, developed a HyperCard system of interlinking information while working at Apple Computers in the 1980s.

But it was Berners-Lee who brought all these dreams into reality, building on the Enquire program he had written in 1980. Of course, his decisive advantage was that the Internet already existed, and he could find support on the Internet and rely on decentralized computer power via workstations: utopias could now materialize. He defined and implemented the software that made it possible to retrieve and contribute information from and to any computer connected via the Internet: HTTP, HTML, and URI (later called URL). In cooperation with Robert Cailliau, Berners-Lee built a browser/editor program in December 1990, and named this hypertext system the world wide web (www). The www browser software was released by CERN over the Net in August 1991. A number of hackers from around the world set themselves up to develop their own browsers, on the basis of Berners-Lee's work. The first modified version was Erwise, developed at the Helsinki Institute of Technology in April 1992. Soon after, Viola, at the University of California, Berkeley, produced his own adaptation.

The most product-oriented of these modified versions of www was Mosaic, designed by a student, Marc Andreessen, and a staff member, Eric Bina, at the University of Illinois's National Center for Supercomputer Applications. They incorporated into Mosaic an advanced graphics capability, so that images could be retrieved and distributed over the Internet, as well as a number of interface techniques imported from the multimedia world. They publicized their software on the Usenet in January 1993. Thereafter, Andreessen took a programming job in a small firm at Palo Alto. While there, he was contacted by a leading Silicon Valley entrepreneur, Jim Clark, who was leaving the company he had founded, Silicon Graphics, looking for new business adventures. He recruited Andreessen, Bina, and their co-workers to form a new company, Mosaic Communications, which was later compelled to change its name to Netscape Communications. The company posted on the Net the first commercial browser, Netscape Navigator, in October 1994, and shipped the first product on December 15, 1994. In 1995, they released Navigator software over the Net free for educational uses, and at a cost of 39 dollars for business.

After the success of Navigator, Microsoft finally discovered the Internet, and in 1995, together with its Windows 95 software, introduced its own browser, Internet Explorer, based on technology developed by a small company, Spyglass. Other commercial browsers were developed, such as Navipress, used by America On Line for a while. Furthermore, in 1995, Sun Microsystems designed Java, a programming language that allowed applications programs ("applets") to travel between computers over the Internet, so enabling computers to run programs downloaded from the Internet safely. Sun released Java software free on the Internet, expanding the realm of web applications, and Netscape included Java in its Navigator browser. In 1998, to counter Microsoft's competition, Netscape released over the Net the source code for Navigator.

Thus, by the mid-1990s, the Internet was privatized, its technical, open architecture allowed the networking of all computer networks anywhere in the world, the world wide web could function on adequate software, and several user-friendly browsers were available to the public. While the Internet had begun in the minds of computer scientists in the early 1960s, a computer communication network had been established in 1969, and distributed computing, interactive communities of scientists and hackers had sprung up from the late 1970s, for most people, for business, and for society at large, the Internet was born in 1995. But it was born with the marks of a history whose analytically relevant features I shall now emphasize and interpret.

The Unlikely Formula: Big Science, Military Research, and the Culture of Freedom

First of all, the Internet was born at the unlikely intersection of big science, military research, and libertarian culture.[1] Major research universities and defense-related think-tanks were essential meeting points between these three sources of the Internet. ARPANET originated in the US Defense Department, but its military applications were secondary to the project. IPTO's main concern was to fund computer science in the United States, letting scientists do their work, and hoping something interesting would come out of it. Baran's design was indeed a military-oriented proposal. It played an important role in the building of ARPANET because of its packet-switching technology, and because it inspired a communications architecture based on the three principles on which the Internet still operates today: a decentralized network structure; distributed computing power throughout the nodes of the network; and redundancy of functions in the network to minimize the risk of disconnection. These features embodied the key answer to military needs for survivability of the system: flexibility, absence of a command center, and maximum autonomy of each node.

While all this sounds very much like military strategy, the catch here is that Baran's proposal was rejected by the Pentagon, and no one ever tried to implement it. In fact, some sources suggest that ARPA did not know of Baran's 1964 publications on "distributed networks" until Roger Scantlebury, a British researcher who had been working on similar technologies, brought them to the

17

attention of IPTO's director at a symposium in Tennessee in October 1967 (Naughton, 1999: 129–31). Baran's concepts were critical for the building of ARPANET, but this experimental network was built with a non-military purpose by the scientists working at and around ARPA (Abbate, 1999).

What their purpose was is in fact unclear, besides the general aim of developing computer networking. The explicit goal was to optimize the use of expensive computer resources by on-line time-sharing between computer centers. Yet, the cost of computing quickly came down, and time-sharing was no longer a major need. The most popular use of the network was electronic mail, an application first developed by Ray Tomlinson, a programmer at BBN, in July 1970. It is still the most widely used application on today's Internet. What the evidence suggests is that IPTO was used by computer scientists at the cutting edge of a new field (computer networking) to fund computer science throughout the university research system, so that, in the 1960s and 1970s, most funding for computer science research in the United States came from ARPA (it was still the case in 2000).

A network of talented scientists and engineers (among them Joseph Licklider, Ivan Sutherland, Lawrence Roberts, Leonard Kleinrock, Robert Taylor, Alex McKenzie, Frank Heart, and Robert Kahn) was formed over time, then expanded with the help of a generation of outstanding young researchers, particularly Vinton Cerf, Stephen Crocker, and Jon Postel, students of Kleinrock at UCLA. The original nucleus of ARPANET designers came mainly from MIT, including one of MIT's spin-off companies, BBN (initially working on acoustics!), and from the Lincoln National Laboratory, a major military-oriented research facility in the shadow of MIT. Key members of the network (among others Roberts, Kleinrock, Heart, and Kahn) were graduates of MIT. But academics from other research universities also became part of this informal, yet exclusive club of computer scientists, particularly from UCLA, where Kleinrock, one of the leading theoreticians in the field, was teaching, as well as from Stanford, Harvard, the University of Utah, the University of California at Santa Barbara, and the University of California at Berkeley.

These researchers/designers circulated in and out of ARPA, research universities, and quasi-academic think-tanks, such as RAND, SRI, and BBN. They were protected by the visionary directors of IPTO, among whom were Joseph Licklider and Robert Taylor. IPTO enjoyed considerable freedom in managing and funding this network because the Defense Department had entrusted ARPA with autonomous judgment about how to stimulate technological research in key areas without suffocating creativity and independence, a strategy that eventually paid off in terms of superiority in military technology. But ARPANET was not one of these military technologies. It was an arcane, experimental project whose actual content was never fully understood by the overseeing congressional committees. Once ARPANET was set up, and new, younger recruits came to IPTO in the 1970s, there was a more focused, deliberate effort to create what would be the Internet. Kahn and Cerf clearly intended so, and designed an architecture, and the corresponding protocols, to allow the network to evolve as an open system of computer communication, able to reach out to the whole world.

So, ARPANET, the main source of what ultimately became the Internet, was not an unintended consequence of a research program going sideways. It was envisioned, deliberately designed, and subsequently managed by a determined group of computer scientists with a shared mission that had little to do with military strategy. It was rooted in a scientific dream to change the world through computer communication, although some of the participants in the group were content with just fostering good computer science. In accordance with the university research tradition, ARPANET's creators involved graduate students in the core design functions of the network, in an atmosphere of totally relaxed security. This included the use of ARPANET for students' personal chats and, reportedly, discussions about marijuana procurement opportunities. The most popular electronic mailing list in ARPANET was SF-Lovers for the use of science fiction fans. Furthermore, the transition to the civilian Internet, and then to its privatization, was managed by the National Science Foundation, with the cooperation of the academic community of computer scientists that had developed over the years around IPTO. Many of these scientists ended up working for major corporations in the 1990s.

However, to say that ARPANET was not a military-oriented project does not mean that its Defense Department origins were inconsequential for the development of the Internet. For all the vision and all the competence these scientists displayed in their project, they could never have commanded the level of resources that was necessary to build a computer network and to design all the appropriate technologies. The Cold War provided a context in which there was strong public and government support to invest in cutting-edge science and technology, particularly after the challenge of the Soviet space program became a threat to US national security. In this sense, the Internet is not a special case in the history of technological innovation, a process usually associated with war: the scientific and engineering effort around World War II constituted the matrix for the technologies of the micro-electronics revolution, and the arms race during the Cold War facilitated their development.

The lucky part of the ARPANET story was that the Defense Department, in a rare instance of organizational intelligence, set up ARPA as a funding and guidance research agency with considerable autonomy. ARPA went on to become one of the most innovative technology policy institutions in the world, and in fact the key actor in US technology policy, not just around computer networking, but in a number of decisive fields of technological development. ARPA was staffed by academic scientists, their friends and their friends' students, and was successful in building a network of reliable contacts in the university world, as well as in the research organizations that spun off from academia to work for the government. An understanding of how the research process works led ARPA to grant considerable autonomy to researchers contracted or funded by the agency, a necessary condition for truly innovative researchers to accept involvement in a project. ARPA's hope was that, out of massive resources and scientific ingenuity, something good would happen from which the military (but also the US economy) could benefit.

It turned out to be the right strategy, even in military terms. In the 1980s, when it became clear that the US had achieved technological superiority in conventional warfare, particularly in electronics and communications, the Soviet Union's strategy was reduced to the unthinkable option of a massive nuclear exchange. In fact, as I have argued in a joint study of the Soviet Union with Emma Kiselyova (Castells and Kiselyova, 1995), the realization of this technological inferiority was one of the main triggers for Gorbachev's *perestroika*, ultimately leading to the disintegration of an apparently mighty empire. The Soviet Union had also anchored its science and technology system in its military complex. But, unlike the United States, Soviet science was largely trapped in the security apparatus, with its corollary of secrecy and performance-oriented projects, which ultimately undermined technological innovation in spite of the excellence of Soviet science. ARPA's policy of flexibility and academic freedom paid off in terms of military strategy, while unleashing the creativity of US academics, and providing them with the resources to transform ideas into research, and research into workable technologies.

Once ARPANET became operational in 1975, it was transferred to the Defense Communication Agency, which started to use the network for military operations. Paradoxically, the importance of inter-networking for the armed forces favored the early adoption of the Internet protocols that laid the ground for their diffusion. The uneasy coexistence of military planners and academic researchers who were using the network set the stage for the separation of the network into MILNET (military) and ARPA-INTERNET (research) in 1983, and for the creation of NSFNET in 1984. In turn, as soon as a military-funded technology became available for civilian use, the Defense Department had a political interest in commercializing it, distributing it free, and actually subsidizing its adoption by US computer manufacturers. History cannot be re-written, but with our current script, without ARPA there would have been no ARPANET, and without ARPANET, the Internet as we know it today would not exist.

In Europe, packet-switching technology, computer communication, and transmission protocols were developed in public research centers, such as Britain's National Physical Laboratory, or government-sponsored research programs, such as the French Cyclades.

21

And while the design of the world wide web was the result of individual creativity and initiative (Berners-Lee was a staff member supposedly working on improving the documentation system at CERN, and not on inventing software), Berners-Lee's and Cailliau's work was made possible by the understanding, first, and the support, later, of a highly respected international public research institution, which just happened to be working on a completely different field of science (Berners-Lee, 1999; Gillies and Cailliau, 2000).

In sum, all the key technological developments that led to the Internet were built around government institutions, major universities, and research centers. The Internet did not originate in the business world. It was too daring a technology, too expensive a project, and too risky an initiative to be assumed by profit-oriented organizations. This was particularly true in the 1960s, at a time when major corporations were rather conservative in their industrial and financial strategies, and were not ready to risk funding and personnel in visionary technologies. The most blatant illustration of this statement is the fact that in 1972, Larry Roberts, the director of IPTO, sought to privatize ARPANET, once it was up and running. He offered to transfer operational responsibility to ATT. After considering the proposal, with the help of a committee of experts from Bell Laboratories, the company refused. ATT was too dependent on analog telephony to be ready to move to digital switching. And so, to the benefit of the world, a corporate monopoly missed the Internet. Even as late as 1990 when the US Office of Technology Assessment held a hearing on the NREN, no telephone company accepted an invitation to take part in it. One company explicitly said that it had no interest in this development (Steve Cisler, personal communication, 2001).

But if corporate business did not have much vision, neither did public companies. In another significant example, the British National Physical Laboratory (NPL) researchers built two computer networks, Mark I and Mark II, based on Davies's packet-switching technology. Davies (appointed director of a research division of NPL in 1966) tried to convince the General Post Office to set up a national computer communications network. If implemented in the late 1960s it would have preceded ARPANET. Yet the Post Office showed little interest in computer communication, and when it finally ceded to the pressure of the business world to build a data transmission network in 1977, it used a system developed by Telenet, a US-firm based on ARPANET technology. Thus, British packet-switching technology never left NPL's internal networks, and the development of the Internet in the UK had to wait for the global expansion of American computer networks.

What emerges from these accounts is that the Internet developed in a secure environment, provided by public resources and mission-oriented research, but an environment that did not stifle freedom of thinking and innovation. Business could not afford to take the long detour that would be needed to spur profitable applications from such an audacious scheme. On the other hand, when the military puts security above any other consideration, as happened in the Soviet Union, and could have happened in the US, creativity cannot survive. And when government, or public service corporations, follow their basic, bureaucratic instincts, as in the case of the British Post Office, adaptation takes precedence over innovation. It was in the twilight zone of the resource-rich, relatively free spaces created by ARPA, the universities, innovative think-tanks, and major research centers that the seeds of the Internet were sown.

The Internet and the Grassroots

These seeds germinated in a variety of forms. The culture of individual freedom sprouting in the university campuses of the 1960s and 1970s used computer networking to its own ends—in most cases seeking technological innovation for the pure joy of discovery. The universities themselves played a major role in their support of community networks. Examples of this university–grassroots connection were, among many others, Boulder, Colorado; Blacksburg Electronic Village; Cleveland FreeNet; Chetbuco Suite in Halifax, Nova Scotia. Without the cultural and technological contribution of these early, grassrooted computer networks, the Internet would have looked very different, and probably would have not embraced the whole world. At least, not so quickly. After all, Tim Berners-Lee's idealistic approach to technology was not too far removed from the agendas of cultural revolutionaries, such as Nelson or Engelbart. The fast diffusion of computer communication protocols would not have happened without the open, free distribution of software and the cooperative use of resources that became the code of conduct of the early hackers. The advent of the PC considerably helped the spread of computer networking, as show-cased by the global spread of FIDONET. But most networks required a backbone anchored in more powerful machines, and this was only possible because of the contact between science-based networks and student hacker communities in the universities. Universities were the common ground for the circulation of innovation between big science's exclusive networks and the makeshift countercultural networks that emerged in all kinds of formats. The two worlds were different, but with more points of contact than people usually think.

Graduate students played a decisive role in the design of ARPANET. In the late 1960s, the Network Working Group, which did most of the design of ARPANET's protocols, was composed mainly of graduate students, including Cerf, Crocker, and Postel, who studied together in the same secondary school in Southern California, and then were students of Kleinrock at UCLA. Feeling insecure about their decisions, they communicated their work in progress to BBN and other nodes of the IPTO's research network through "request for comment" memos or RFCs, which provided the style, and the name, for informal technical communication in the Internet world up to our day. The openness of this format was—and continues to be—essential for the development of the Internet's infrastructure protocols. Most of these students were not countercultural in the sense of the social movements' activists of the time. Cerf certainly was not. They were too obsessed with their extraordinary technological adventure to see much of the world outside computers. They certainly did not see any problem in having their research funded by the Pentagon or even in joining ARPA (as Cerf did) in the midst of the Vietnam War. And yet they were permeated with the values of individual freedom, of independent thinking, and of sharing and cooperation with their peers, all values that characterized the campus culture of the 1960s. While the young ARPANETers were not part of the counterculture, their ideas, and their software, provided a natural bridge between the world of big science and the broader student culture that sprung up in the BBSs and Usenet News network. This student culture took up computer networking as a tool of free communication, and in the case of its most political manifestations (Nelson, Jennings, Stallman), as a tool of liberation, which, together with the PC, would provide people with the power of information to free themselves both from governments and corporations.

The grassroots of the Internet, with their creation of autonomous networks and conference systems, decisively influenced the development of commercial services in the 1980s, as business imitated the communication systems created by alternative networks. On the one hand, there were e-mail services developed by telecommunications and computer companies (ATT, MCI, DEC and so on), and wide area networks set up by major corporations for their internal use. On the other hand, "on-line" services were offered by companies such as Compuserve, America On Line (AOL), and Prodigy. These services were not networked in their origin, but they provided the ground on which Internet content providers would later develop. These diverse uses of computer networking did not develop from the ARPANET community but from the varicgated universe of alternative networks emerging from the freedom culture.

The impact of autonomous networks was also decisive in the global expansion of computer networking. The control of the US government of ARPA-INTERNET was an obstacle to its connection to the networks of other countries. UUCP-based networks became global much earlier than the Internet, thus setting the stage for the global Internet once networks were able to connect. After NSF opened up NSFNET access to foreign networks, from 1990 to 1995 (when the Internet was privatized), the proportion of non-US networks linked to the Internet doubled, from 20 to 40 percent of all connected networks.

An Architecture of Openness

From these diverse contributions emerged an Internet whose most distinctive feature was its openness, both in its technical architecture and in its social/institutional organization. Technically speaking, the flexibility of communication protocols allowed backbones such as ARPANET to connect to thousands of local area networks. The TCP architecture proposed by Cerf and Kahn in their seminal 1973 paper, "A Protocol for Packet Network Intercommunication," published in 1974, and completed in 1978 with the IP protocol, provided standards compatible for different networking systems.

The openness of ARPANET's architecture allowed the future Internet to survive its most daunting challenge in the process of becoming global: the difficult agreement on a common international standard. Telecommunication carriers and the post and telecommunications offices (PTTs) of major European governments supported a different communication standard, the x.25, which was approved in 1976 as the common international standard by the International Telecommunications Union. The x.25 protocols were not incompatible with TCP/IP, but because they had been designed separately they could not communicate. The debate was not purely technical. Under x.25 virtual circuits, the control and accountability of the network would be mainly in the hands of public network providers at the expense of private computer owners. This is why the European PTTs favored the option. On the other hand, ARPANET's protocols were based on the diversity of networks. Furthermore, telecommunication carriers were reluctant to let private networks link up with their own networks. By the late 1970s, the PTTs were planning to organize computer data transmission in a series of separate, national public networks, connecting at their nation's borders. Computer owners were expected to link up directly to the public network in their country, rather than set up their own private networks. In fact, MINITEL, the French PTT telematic service provider, was based on this principle of a centralized, government-controlled, computer network. At the international level, CCITT (the relevant committee of the International Telecommunications Union) went on to assign network addresses to each country. The assumption was that computers would usually be connected to the public network, so the committee decided that most countries would not require more than ten network addresses, exceptionally two hundred for the United States. This logic was perfectly understandable in a world in which a few years earlier an IBM study had predicted that the world market for computers in the year 2000 would stabilize at about five computers, and in which, in 1977 (after the development of the personal computer), the chairman of DEC had declared that "there is no reason anyone would want a computer in their home."

In the end, x.25 protocols were adopted by public telecommunication networks and some commercial networks, while ARPANET and most US private networks went on using TCP/IP. The International Organization for Standardization (ISO) intervened in the matter, and when it failed to conciliate different interests between various governments, and between computer manufacturers and telecommunications operators, it approved the principle of layering of protocols. The Open Systems Interconnection (OSI) protocol became the official international standard. However, unable to impose this standard, ISO continued to approve a multiplicity of protocols, including TCP and IP. Because ARPANET's protocols had the flexibility to integrate different networking systems, while the other protocols could not do so, TCP/IP standards were able to accommodate x.25-based protocols, and ultimately prevailed as the common standards for the global Internet.

Self-evolution of the Internet: Shaping the Network by Using it

The openness of the Internet's architecture was the source of its main strength: its self-evolving development, as users became producers of the technology, and shapers of the whole network. Since nodes could be easily added, the cost remained low (provided that a backone was available), and the software was open and available; by the mid-1980s (after UUCP allowed the connection between

ARPANET and Usenet) everybody with technical knowledge could join the Internet. A flurry of never-planned applications resulted from this multiple contribution, from e-mail to bulletin boards and chat rooms, the MODEM, and, ultimately, the hypertext. No one told Tim Berners-Lee to design the world wide web, and in fact he had to conceal his true intent for a while since he was using the time of his research center for purposes other than his assigned job. But he could do it because he could rely on widespread support from the Internet community, as he posted his work, and was helped and stimulated by numerous hackers from around the world. True, some of these hackers went on to commercialize his ideas, and made a fortune, while Berners-Lee, by his own choice, continued to work in the public interest, lately as chairperson of the World Wide Web Consortium (W3C). But by behaving as a true hacker he earned the respect of his community of reference, and his place in history; as was the case with Ted Nelson, Douglas Engelbart, Richard Stallman, Linus Torvalds, and so many other, less famous, hackers and anonymous users.

It is a proven lesson from the history of technology that users are key producers of the technology, by adapting it to their uses and values, and ultimately transforming the technology itself, as Claude Fischer (1992) demonstrated in his history of the telephone. But there is something special in the case of the Internet. New uses of the technology, as well as the actual modifications introduced in the technology, are communicated back to the whole world, in real time. Thus, the timespan between the processes of learning by using and producing by using is extraordinarily shortened, with the result that we engage in a process of learning by producing, in a virtuous feedback between the diffusion of technology and its enhancement. This is why the Internet grew, and keeps growing, at unprecedented speed, not only in the number of its networks, but in the range of its applications. For this sequence to take place, three conditions are necessary: first, the networking architecture must be open-ended, decentralized, distributed, and multi-directional in its interactivity; secondly, all communication protocols and their implementations must be open, distributed, and susceptible of modification (although network manufacturers keep some of their software proprietary); thirdly, the institutions of governance of the network must be built in accordance with the principles of openness and cooperation that are embedded in the Internet. Having analyzed the historical production of the first two conditions, let me now turn to the third one. It is, in fact, a remarkable story.

Governance of the Internet

I am not addressing here the relationship between governments and the Internet, which I shall examine with care later in the book (Chapters 5 and 6). In this chapter I focus on the procedures to ensure communication and coordination functions in the network. This refers, essentially, to shared protocol development, agreements on standards, and assignments of Internet names and addresses. Once these matters are settled, the decentralized structure of the Internet takes care of the rest, as each host and each network establishes its own rules. But how coordination functions are assured was critical for the development of the network, and remains crucial for its expansion beyond any central control.

In the early stages, in the 1960s, ARPA assumed benevolent authority over the network, and the Network Working Group (NWG) produced the technical standards by consensus, on the basis of request for comment (RFC) documents. It set the tone for future coordination tasks in the Internet: membership based on technical expertise, consultation with the Internet community, consensus-based decision-making. NWG was disbanded in the 1970s, once ARPANET began operation. Its role was assumed, within ARPA, by an Internet program, run by Cerf and Kahn, which took responsibility for protocol development. They established an advisory group made up of networking experts: the Internet Configuration Control Board (ICCB) which encouraged the participation of the overall Internet community in improving the protocols. In 1984, Barry Leiner, ARPA's network program manager, decided to broaden this coordinating group, and set up an Internet Activities Board (IAB), chaired by another MIT computer scientist, Dave Clark. This new board included the leading experts from the institutions that had created ARPANET, but reached out to other networking experts from anywhere in the world. Indeed, membership of the IAB was open, at least in principle, to anyone with the interest and technical knowledge, although I suspect that experts from the Soviet Academy of Sciences would not have been welcome at the time. In 1989, with membership of the IAB then in the hundreds, the board was split into two organizations, both built on the basis of open working groups: the Internet Engineering Task Force (IETF), focusing on protocol development and other technical matters, and the Internet Research Task Force (IRTF), specializing in long-range planning for the Internet. Working groups communicated by e-mail but also met several times a year. Agreements reached by the working groups were published as RFCs and became the Internet's unofficial standards, in a cumulative, open process of cooperation. Later on, relevant US government agencies, such as the NSF, NASA, and the Department of Energy, followed the IETF in adopting the use of the Internet's protocols. Through this channel, Internet protocols became the networking standards for the US government at large.

By 1992, however, the Internet was expanding on a global scale, and the NSF was planning its privatization. On both grounds it was necessary to move beyond the direct control of the US government. So, in January 1992, the Internet Society was formed, a non-profit organization which was given oversight of both the IAB and the IETF. Cerf and Kahn, widely trusted by the Internet community for their technical knowledge and their record of commitment to openness and consensus-building, took charge of the Internet Society. Under their impulse, international participation in the coordination functions increased substantially during the 1990s. However, with the internationalization of the Internet, the ambiguous status of its institutions (ultimately under the supervision of the US government, yet exercising their autonomy on the basis of the fairness and prestige of the Internet's founders) came under attack from other governments, particularly in Europe. Furthermore, the process of privatization unbalanced the delicate equilibrium that had for years characterized the assignment of domain names.

In one of the most stunning stories in the development of the Internet, the US government had delegated authority for Internet addresses to an organization, the Internet Assigned Numbers Authority (IANA), set up and managed singlehandedly by one of the original designers of the Internet, Jon Postel, from the University of Southern California. Postel, a computer scientist of impeccable integrity, was probably the most respected member of the Internet's scientific community. His management was widely recognized as fair, sensible, and neutral, so that for many years he acted as a global arbiter for the assignment of Internet domains, with remarkable results in terms of the relative stability and compatibility of the system. Yet Postel died in 1998 at the age of 55. The trust in one man could not be replaced by global trust in a US government institution.

In fact, the Clinton administration had proposed the privatization of IANA and of other over-seeing institutions of the Internet since 1997. The last legacy of Jon Postel was his design for the privatized institution that he offered to the US government in September 1998, one month before his death. His proposed organization, the Internet Corporation for Assigned Names and Numbers (ICANN), was approved by the US government in late 1998, and completed its formative phase in 2000. Although its actual practice and organizational structure are still unfolding, its by-laws embody the spirit of openness of the Internet community, decentralization, consensus-building, and autonomy that characterized the *ad hoc* governance of the Internet over thirty years, while adding a global orientation to its membership, although its administration is headquartered in Marina del Rey, California. It is a non-profit, private corporation that assumes the management of IP address space allocation, protocol parameter assignment, domain name system management, and root server system management, all functions previously performed by IANA under contract from the US government.

ICANN has four components: one at-large membership, and three supporting organizations, which deal with the substantive issues of Internet coordination (address supporting organization, domain name supporting organization, and protocol supporting organization). Each one of these organizations is decentralized in a diversity of working groups linked electronically and by regular meetings. ICANN's governing body is a board of eighteen directors, three appointed by each of the supporting organizations, and nine elected by the at-large membership in a worldwide electronic voting process. Any individual with technical knowledge can apply for membership. By 2000, there were 158,000 at-large members and the first at-large election was held. The election was organized by nominations issued both by advisory committees and by support from local constituencies. Each of the five posts elected in 2000 was assigned to a different area of the world to ensure some kind of global representation.

The romantic vision of a global Internet community self-representing itself by electronic voting has to be tempered with the reality of lobbying, powerful support networks, and name recognition in favor of certain candidates. And there is no scarcity of articulate critics of ICANN's lack of true democracy. Indeed, in the 2000 election, only 35,000 of the 158,000 members part-icipated in the vote. Among the directors elected there was a hacker, former member of the notorious German Computer Chaos Club, to the alarm of government representatives. Furthermore, the links between ICANN and the US Commerce Department have not really been severed. Governments around the world, and par-ticularly European governments, are extremely critical of what they see as American dominance of ICANN. For instance, ICANN refused recognition of the ".eu" domain address, applicable to all companies and institutions from the European Union. For Euro-pean Union representatives this was a most important trademark to denote European companies working within the institutional rules established in the European Union, for instance in the protection of privacy on the Internet. Thus, the contradiction between the historical roots of the Internet in America, and its increasingly global character, seems to point toward the eventual transformation of ICANN into a culturally broader institution.

Yet, in spite of all these conflicts and shortcomings, it is revealing that the emerging institutions of the Internet in the twenty-first century had to be established, in order to be legitimate, on the tradition of meritocratic consensus-building that characterized the origins of the Internet. A similar, consensus-based, non-mandatory, open (albeit, often for a signicant fee), international organization presides over the protocols and development of the world wide web: the World Wide Web Consortium, anchored in the US by MIT, in Europe by the French Institute INRIA, and directed, most naturally, by Tim Berners-Lee, now the holder of an MIT chair.

Without prejudging the effectiveness of these new institutions, the truly surprising accomplishment is that the Internet reached this relative stability in its governance without succumbing either to the bureaucracy of the US government or to the chaos of a decentralized structure. That it did not was mainly the accomplishment of these gentlemen of technological innovation: Cerf, Kahn, Postel, Berners-Lee, and many others, who truly sought to maintain the openness of the network for their peers, as a way to learn and share. In this communitarian approach to technology, the meritocratic gentry met the utopian counterculture in the invention of the Internet, and in the preservation of the spirit of freedom that is at its source. The Internet is, above all else, a cultural creation.

Note

1. "Libertarian" has a different meaning in the European and in the American context. In Europe, it refers to a culture or ideology based on the uncompromising defense of individual freedom as the supreme value—often against the government, but sometimes with the help of governments, as in the protection of privacy. In the US context, "libertarian" is a political ideology that primarily means a systematic distrust of government, on the understanding that the market takes care of everything by itself, and that individuals take care of themselves. I use it in the European sense, as a culture of liberty, in the tradition of John Stuart Mill, without prejudging the tools by which liberty is achieved.

Reading Links

Abbate, Jane (1999) *Inventing the Internet*. Cambridge, MA: MIT Press.

Berners-Lee, Tim, with Mark Frischetti (1999) *Weaving the Web*. San Francisco: HarperCollins.

Botkin, J., Dimanescu, D., and Stata, R. (1984) *The Innovators*. New York: Harper and Row.

Castells, Manuel and Kiselyova, Emma (1995) *The Collapse of Soviet Communism: The View from the Information Society*. Berkeley, CA: University of California International Area Studies Book Series.

Conseil d'Etat (1998) *The Internet and Digital Networks*. Paris: La Documentation Française.

Fischer, Claude (1992) *America Calling*. Berkeley, CA: University of Calfornia Press.

Gillies, James and Cailliau, Robert (2000) *How the Web was Born: The Story of the World Wide Web*. Oxford: Oxford University Press.

Hafner, Katie and Lyon, Matthew (1996) *Where Wizards Stay up Late: The Origins of the Internet*. New York: Touchstone.

Hughes, Thomas O. (1998/2000) *Rescuing Prometheus*. New York: Random House.

Naughton, John (1999) *A Brief History of the Future: The Origins of the Internet*. London: Weidenfeld and Nicolson.

Stefik, Mark (ed.) (1996) *Internet Dreams: Archetypes, Myths, and Metaphors*. Cambridge, MA: MIT Press.

—— (1999) *The Internet Edge: Social, Technical, and Legal Challenges for a Networked World*. Cambridge, MA: MIT Press.

Tuomi, Ilkka (2002) *Participatory Innovation: Change and Meaning in the Age of the Internet* (forthcoming).

e-Links

Leiner, B. M., Cerf, V. G., Clark, D. D., Kahn, R. E., Kleinrock, L., Lynch, D. C., Postel, J., Roberts, L. G., and Wolff, S. (2000) *A Brief History of the Internet* at http://www.isoc.org/internet-history/brief.html

www.icann.com

www.election.com/us/icann

www.ispo.cec.be./eif/InternetPoliciesSite/DotEUMay2000/ENhtml
Various sites concerning ICANN and the Internet governance debate.

www.isoc.org/
The site of the Internet Society, overseeing the development of the Internet.

Chapter 2

The Culture of the Internet

Technological systems are socially produced. Social production is culturally informed. The Internet is no exception. The culture of the producers of the Internet shaped the medium. These producers were, at the same time, its early users. However, in the present stage of global diffusion of the Internet, it makes sense to differentiate between the producers/users and the consumers/users of the Internet. By producers/users I refer to those whose practice of the Internet feeds directly back into the technological system; while consumers/users are those recipients of applications and systems who do not interact directly with the development of the Internet, although their uses certainly have an aggregate effect on the evolution of the system. In this chapter I deal with the culture of the producers/users at the source of the Internet's creation and configuration.

The Internet culture is the culture of the creators of the Internet. By culture I understand a set of values and beliefs informing behavior. Repetitive patterns of behavior generate customs that are enforced by institutions, as well as by informal social organizations.

Culture is different from ideology, psychology, or individual representations. While culture is explicit, it is a collective construction that transcends individual preferences, while influencing the practices of people in the culture, in this case the Internet producers/users.

The Internet culture is characterized by a four-layer structure: the techno-meritocratic culture, the hacker culture, the virtual communitarian culture, and the entrepreneurial culture. Together they contribute to an ideology of freedom that is widespread in the Internet world. However, this ideology is not the founding culture because it does not interact directly with the development of the technological system: freedom has many uses. These cultural layers are hierarchically disposed: the techno-meritocratic culture becomes specified as a hacker culture by building rules and customs into networks of cooperation aimed at technological projects. The virtual communitarian culture adds a social dimension to technological sharing, by making the Internet a medium of selective social interaction and symbolic belonging. The entrepreneurial culture works on top of the hacker culture, and on the communitarian culture, to diffuse Internet practices in all domains of society by way of money-making. Without the techno-meritocratic culture, hackers would simply be a specific countercultural community of geeks and nerds. Without the hacker culture, communitarian networks in the Internet would be no different from many other alternative communes. Similarly, without the hacker culture, and communitarian values, the entrepreneurial culture cannot be characterized as specific to the Internet.

An example: it can hardly be denied that Bill Gates, and Microsoft, epitomize entrepreneurial culture, at least in the early stages of the company. But they were not producers of the Internet in technological terms. In fact, they missed it. Gates, although he hacked in his youth, was not part of the hacker culture—indeed, he denounced hackers as thieves in his notorious "Open Letter to Hobbyists" (Levy, 2001: 229). By asserting the primacy of proprietary rights (Gates: "Who can afford to do professional work for nothing?"), Gates put money-making before technological innovation. So, Microsoft represented the entrepreneurial current that developed by commercializing the process of technological innovation in computing, without sharing its founding values.

On the other hand, the hacker culture (in the sociological meaning of the term) is too restrictive a characterization of the Internet culture. Not only is the Internet dependent on entrepreneurialism to diffuse into society at large, but it is also tributary from its origins in the academic and scientific community, where the criteria of excellence, peer review, and open communication of research work originated.

I will elaborate on the origins and characteristics of each one of these four layers, then I will show how their articulation constitutes the Internet culture. But before proceeding along these lines, I want to emphasize the direct link between these cultural expressions and the technological development of the Internet. The key connection is the openness and free modification of Internet software, and particularly of the source code of software. Open distribution of the source codes allows anyone to modify the code and to develop new programs and applications, in an upward spiral of technological innovation, based on cooperation and the free circulation of technical knowledge. As I indicated in Chapter 1, the TCP/IP protocols on which ARPA-INTERNET was built were open and free. So was, in the 1970s, the UNIX operating system, and the UUCP protocols that made Usenet News possible. So were the modem protocols used in the development of PC networks. So were the world wide web server and browser, the Mosaic browser, and the first commercial browser, Netscape Navigator. With certain restrictions, so are Java and Jini languages developed by Sun Microsystems. So is the server program, Apache, used, in 2001, by the majority of web servers in the world. And so is the operating system GNU/Linux, and its derivatives. Thus, open source software is the key technological feature in the development of the Internet. And this openness is culturally determined.

Techno-elites

First, openness is determined by a techno-meritocratic culture rooted in academia and science. This is a culture of belief in the inherent good of scientific and technological development as a key component in the progress of humankind. So, it is in direct continuation with the Enlightenment and with modernity, as Tuomi has pointed out (2000). But its specificity is in the definition of a community of technologically competent members, who are acknowledged as peers by the community. Within this culture, merit results from contribution to the advancement of a technological system that provides a common good for the community of discoverers. This technological system is computer networking, which is the essence of the Internet. Standard academic values became specified in a mission-oriented project: the construction and development of a global (even universal, in the future) electronic communication system that brings computers and humans together in a symbiotic relationship that grows exponentially by interactive communication. The key features of this techno-meritocracy are as follows:

- Technological discovery (always specific to computer programming in a networked environment) is the supreme value.
- The relevance and relative ranking of the discovery depends on the contribution to the field as a whole, in a context of problem-solving objectives defined by the community of scientists/technologists. In other words, it is not knowledge *per se* that matters, regardless of the importance of the theoretical contribution, but specific knowledge applied to a given objective that will improve the overall technological artefact (that is, computer communication networks or an operating system).
- Relevance of the discovery is determined by peer review among the members of the community. Who becomes a member of the community is established by individual performance as measured, and published, in the historical process of development of the Internet. Reputation is central both to membership and to seniority in the community ranking.
- Coordination of tasks and projects is assigned by authoritative figures who, at the same time, control resources (essentially

machines) and enjoy the technological respect and ethical trust of their peers. Thus, Cerf and Kahn were at the same time given control of ARPANET by the Defense Department and relied upon by most of their peers in the Internet designers' community.

- To be respected as a member of the community, and, even more so, as an authoritative figure, technologists must abide by the formal and informal rules of the community and not use common resources (knowledge) or delegated resources (institutional positions) for their own exclusive benefit, beyond the shared good of advancing technological skills by learning from the network. Personal advantage is not shunned unless it is to the detriment of other members of the community.

- The cornerstone of the whole process is the open communication of software, as well as all of the improvements resulting from networked collaboration. Without this openness, members of the community would pursue their individual, competitive strategies, and the process of communication would stall, hampering the intellectual productivity of the cooperative effort. This is not too different from the basic rule of scholarly research under which all findings must be open, and communicated in a form that allows peer review, criticism, and eventual replication. Only members of the academic organizations that submit themselves to this scrutiny are acknowledged as scholars by their peers. This is precisely why there is no direct equivalence between being a scholar and having a university job.

Thus, the culture of the Internet is rooted in the scholarly tradition of the shared pursuit of science, of reputation by academic excellence, of peer review, and of openness in all research findings, with due credit to the authors of each discovery. Historically, the Internet was produced in academic circles, and in their ancillary research units, both in the heights of professorial ranks and in the trenches of graduate student work, from where the values, the habits, and the knowledge diffused into the hacker culture.

Hackers

Pekka Himanen (2001) considers the hacker ethic to be the cultural characteristic of informationalism. I concur with him in general terms, but I will specify this analysis in the case of the Internet. The hacker culture plays a pivotal role in the construction of the Internet for two reasons: it is arguably the nurturing milieu of breakthrough technological innovations through cooperation and free communication; and it bridges the knowledge originated in the techno-meritocratic culture with the entrepreneurial spin-offs that diffuse the Internet in society at large. But, first, we need to clarify what we mean by the hacker culture since the ambiguity of the term is a source of misunderstanding (Himanen, 2001; Levy, 2001).

Hackers are not what the media say they are. They are not reckless computer geeks aiming to crack codes, illegally penetrate systems, or bring havoc to computer traffic. Those who behave in such a way are called "crackers," and they are usually rejected by the hacker culture, although I personally consider that, in analytical terms, crackers and other cyber types (such as the "warez d00dz," many of them belonging to the category of "script kiddies") are subcultures of a much broader, and usually not disruptive, hacker universe. One of the leading analysts/participant observers of the hacker culture, and an icon of the culture, Eric Raymond, defines a "hacker" somewhat tautologically: hackers are those whom the hacker culture recognizes as such. As for the hacker culture: "There is a community, a shared culture, of expert programmers and networking wizards that traces its history back through decades to the first time-sharing minicomputers and the earliest Arpanet experiments" (Raymond, 1999: 231). He chronicles the first use of the term "hacker" at MIT's Tech Model Rail Road Club and the Artificial Intelligence Laboratory. This is, however, too broad a definition, under which all expert computer programmers connected to the building of ARPANET and the development of the Internet would be hackers. We need a more specific concept of hacker to identify the actors in the transition from an academically and institutionally constructed milieu of innovation to the emergence of self-organizing networks transcending organizational control.

In this restricted sense, the hacker culture, in my view, refers to the set of values and beliefs that emerged from the networks of computer programmers interacting on-line around their collaboration in self-defined projects of creative programming (Levy, 2001). Two critical features must be emphasized: on the one hand, the autonomy of projects *vis-à-vis* institutional or corporate assignments; on the other hand, the use of computer networking constitutes the material, technological basis for institutional autonomy. In this sense, the Internet was originally the creation of the techno-meritocratic culture; it then became the basis for its own technological upgrading through the input provided by the hacker culture, interacting on the Internet.

The specific values and social organization of the hacker culture can be better understood by considering the process of development of the open source movement, as an extension of the original free software movement. In a sense, open source was a structural feature in the development of the Internet, as I stated earlier, since all its key technical developments were communicated to universities, and then shared over the Net. But the free software movement, as a deliberate practice, at the roots of the open source movement, stems from the struggles to defend the openness of the UNIX source code.

UNIX was a powerful, innovative operating system created in 1969 by Ken Thompson, at ATT's Bell Laboratories, on the basis of a time-sharing operating system, MULTICS. Another Bell's hacker (and Berkeley graduate, as Thompson was), Dennis Ritchie, invented a new language, called C, for use on Thompson's UNIX. They both worked on these developments without specific instructions from Bell Labs. UNIX became a software environment for all kinds of systems, so liberating programmers from the need to invent specific languages for each machine: software became portable, thus allowing communication between computers and cumulative computer programming.

When in 1974 ATT was compelled by the US government to diffuse the results of Bell Labs' research, it distributed UNIX, including its source code, to universities for a nominal fee. In 1977, in cooperation with Ken Thompson and Bell Labs, a group of Berkeley computer science students, led by Bill Joy and Chuck Halley, created the Berkeley Software Distribution (BSD), an improved version of UNIX. Graduate students in computer science, in the US and in other countries, made UNIX their preferred language, using PDP-11 and VAX computers. As described in Chapter 1, the Berkeley UNIX team (Computer System Research Group) designed UNIX support for ARPANET protocols, solving the networking problems of UUCP, and enabling the communication between ARPANET and Usenet, thus expanding the Internet.

In the early 1980s there were three computer cultures, clustered at the intersection between types of machines and preferred language programs: the ARPANET culture based on DEC's PDP-10 machines, with a preference for LISP language; the UNIX culture, using C language; and the PC culture, using microcomputers and working on BASIC, at a much lower technological level than the other two cultures. Then, in a few years, the three cultures underwent a major technological/institutional shock and subsequent transformation. ARPA decided to support the development of an operating system that could be common to the research community, and most of the universities involved in contracts with ARPA did not want to be dependent on DEC and its machines. The result of these discussions was ARPA's decision to support the development of UNIX as a reliable, common operating system that could run on different machines. BSD, the Berkeley variant of UNIX running on VAX, and using C language, became the most advanced operating system. ATT's UNIX and Berkeley's UNIX fought endless legal battles, as ATT tried to impose proprietary rights on the system, but ultimately they learned from each other to the point that, by the early 1990s, their programs were very similar. In 1994, they reached a legal settlement, enabling the free diffusion of UNIX, coexisting with UNIX-based proprietary systems. In the process, however, the Berkeley group exhausted its resources and lost the funding. Several versions of BSD (Net BSD, Free BSD, Open BSD) emerged from the process, as different hacker groups developed their own software in line with the UNIX tradition.

Advances in micro-electronics also transformed the computing world. In 1983, Motorola's 68000 microchip allowed the development of microcomputers with unprecedented power. A group of young computer scientists from Stanford, with additions from Berkeley, including Bill Joy, founded Sun Microsystems (for Stanford University Networks), with UNIX running on 68000 microchips, enabling affordable workstations. Later, their machines ran on Solaris, a proprietary version of the UNIX operating system.

As for the PC culture, constituted by the MS-DOS and Mac programmers, according to Raymond (1999), they were much more numerous than the "network nation" culture of UNIX users. But DOS/Mac people never became a self-aware culture themselves. The absence of a really pervasive network comparable to UUCP or the Internet prevented them from doing so. Collaborative hacking was limited by the absence of networking. And Raymond (1999: 21) concludes: "The mainstream of hackerdom, (dis)organized around the Internet, and by now largely identified with the UNIX technical culture, didn't care about the commercial services. They wanted better tools and more Internet, and cheap 32-bit PCs promised to put both in everyone's reach."

The key requirement for the expansion of the new computing frontier was new, powerful software able to run on all kinds of machines and link up Internet servers. UNIX provided a shared environment for advanced researchers to communicate in the development of programs for networks and servers. Yet, the divestiture of ATT in 1984 allowed Bell Laboratories to legally claim its proprietary rights on UNIX. As reported in Chapter 1, Richard Stallman, a programmer at MIT's Artificial Intelligence Laboratory took upon himself and a close group of collaborators the gigantic task of writing a new system, inspired by UNIX but not submitted to UNIX copyright: GNU (standing for "GNU is not UNIX"). Stallman turned his effort into a political crusade for free speech in the computer age, establishing the Free Software Foundation (FSF) and proclaiming the principle of free communication and use of software as a fundamental right. He single-handedly created the free software movement, and became one of the icons of the hacker culture. But his political commitment was not sufficient to solve the huge technical obstacles he had to deal with in the creation of a new operating system, equivalent to UNIX, yet different from it. While the release of his, and his team's, efforts over the Net paved the way for the future of open source software, his system (HURD) did not really work until 1996. By all accounts, this was not the result of his technical limitations, as he was (and is) a giant of software programming, as was proved by his outstanding emacs editor program. But he did not fully realize the power of the network. Only a network of hundreds, thousands of brains working cooperatively, with spontaneous division of labor, and loose, but effective coordination, could accomplish the extraordinary task of creating an operating system able to handle the complexity of increasingly powerful computers interacting via the Internet.

In the meantime, UNIX proprietary systems were blocking the open communication of software development. The Berkeley UNIX group was disbanded in 1994. In this context, Microsoft corraled the operating system software market, in spite of its inferior technology, because it had no real competition. The alternative emerged from the GNU/Linux operating system that developed on the basis of Stallman's work, but with a fundamentally different methodology, serendipitously promoted by Linus Torvalds. In Raymond's (1999) terms, the "bazaar" approach to software succeeded where the "cathedral-building" design principles (whether commercial or hacker-driven) had failed.

As described in Chapter 1, Linus Torvalds, a student at Helsinki University, obtained his first Intel 386 PC in 1991, and wanted a UNIX operating system for it. Lacking resources, he devoted several months to designing his own UNIX kernel for 386 machines, using the GCC compiler (for C language) for its implementation. He called it Freix, but the server's administrator called it Linux. Needing help, and wanting others to join in the development, Linus released the source code on the Internet, and asked for cooperation. He continued to release frequent improvements. So did hundreds of hackers who picked up on the project. Quick releases, widespread cooperation, and total openness of the information allowed for extensive testing and de-bugging of the code, so that, by 1993, Linux was a better operating system than UNIX proprietary systems. Over time, the most competitive commercial UNIX systems became those that package Linux while respecting its open source code rules.

Linux is widely recognized as one of the most reliable operating systems, particularly for computers working on the Internet. In 2001, there were about 30 million Linux users in the world, and counting. In 2001, a number of governments (including Brazil, Mexico, India, China, and France) were adopting Linux and promoting its use. True, the overwhelming majority of Linux operating systems are used in web servers, and in big computers, serving large networks. So, for most individual users, Linux is too complicated to use and does not provide a simple user interface. Yet, nothing in its kernel or derivative software excludes the development of user-friendly applications that could take on the Microsoft core market. In fact, it seems that the main obstacle to Linux development into low-end consumer users is the lack of interest of sophisticated computer programmers for this kind of application. This is why the user-oriented commercialization of Linux, always respecting its open source rules, appears to be the next frontier of open source development.

What are the features of the hacker culture, and how do they relate to Internet development? First of all, it is based on what I called the techno-meritocratic culture, which, if I may use a software metaphor, is the kernel code of the hacker culture. So, all the features presented above are applicable to the hacker culture. Particularly important is the overarching goal of performance and technological excellence because this is what determines the common need for sharing and for keeping the source code open. As Raymond (1999: 170) puts it, "The open source peer review is the only scalable method for achieving high reliability and quality." Although many experts seem to concur with him on this point, the accuracy of the statement is less important than its effects on the hacker culture: if hackers believe this to be so, they will build a community around open source in order to perform better. But better performance, when it is disembedded from institutions of reward, requires adherence to a set of values that combine the joy of creativity with a reputation among peers.

Paramount in this set of values is freedom. Freedom to create, freedom to appropriate whatever knowledge is available, and freedom to redistribute this knowledge under any form and channel chosen by the hacker. In fact, Richard Stallman built his Free Software Foundation on this principle of freedom, regardless of the quality of the software produced as a result of freedom and cooperation. For most other hackers, freedom is not the only value (technological innovation is the key goal, and the personal enjoyment of creativity is even more important than freedom), but it is certainly an essential component of their worldview and of their practice as hackers. Paradoxically, it is because of this principle of freedom that many hackers also claim the right to choose commercial development of their innovations. On the condition of not betraying what is the most fundamental principle of all: open access to all the program's information, with the freedom to modify the program.

Freedom combines with cooperation through the practice of the gift culture, eventually leading to a gift economy. A hacker will post his or her contribution to software development on the Net in the expectation of reciprocity. The gift culture in the hacker world is specific *vis-à-vis* other gift cultures. Prestige, reputation, and social esteem are linked to the relevance of the gift to the community. So, it is not only the expected return for generosity, but the immediate gratification of displaying to everybody the hacker's ingenuity. In addition, there is also gratification involved in the object of the gift. It not only has exchange value, but also use value. The recognition comes not only from giving but from producing a valuable object (innovative software).

Beyond the satisfaction of achieving status in the community, the inner joy of creation has often been identified as an attribute of the hacker culture. It brings it close to the world of art, and to the psychological drive for creativity, identified by Csikszentmihalyi (1997). Being a hacker starts with the individual surge for creation, independent of the organizational setting of this creation. This is why there are hackers in academia, in high schools, in corporate business, and in the margins of society. They do not depend on institutions for their intellectual existence, but they do depend on their self-defined community, built around computer networks.

There is a communal feeling in the hacker culture, based on active membership in a community, which is structured around customs and principles of informal social organization. Cultures are not made of free-floating values. They are rooted in institutions and organizations. There is such an organization in the hacker culture, but it is informal; that is, not enforced by the institutions of society. In the Linux community, for instance, there are "tribal elders" (most of them under 30 years old), with Linus Torvalds as the supreme authority. They are owners/maintainers of each project; for example, Linus owns and maintains the Linux kernel because he created its beginning. In other instances, there is a collective authority, with rotating maintainers, such as in the Apache servers' community. Co-maintainers help to maintain subsystems around projects derived from the original project.

The modular structure of Linux software allows a great diversity of projects to branch out without losing compatibility. Co-developers assume new projects on their own initiative, while ordinary contributors are members of the community helping to test and debug new programs, and to discuss problems arising from their own programming practice. The key for the community is to avoid "forking" as much as possible; that is, the division of the community's energy into many different lines of work. But it is acceptable when all other forms of conflict resolution fail.

Naturally, money, formal proprietary rights, or institutional power are excluded as sources of authority and reputation. Authority based on technological excellence, or on an early contribution to the code, is respected only if it is not seen as predominantly self-serving. In other words, the community accepts the hierarchy of excellence and seniority only as long as this authority is exercised for the well-being of the community as a whole, which means that, often, new tribes emerge and face each other. But the fundamental cleavages are not personal or ideological: they are technological. This does not mean that the conflicts are less acute. Technological subcultures may use all the resources at their disposal to undermine the position of their rival techno-communities. Thus, the main divide in the open software world is between the BSD tradition and the GNU/Linux tradition. These social rules and customs are practiced and enforced collectively over the Net. Sanctions for transgression take the form of open "flaming," public blame, and, if sins are grave, exclusion from the community, thus from the network of collective creation of innovative software.

The Internet is the organizational foundation of this culture. The hacker community, by and large, is global and is virtual. While there are moments of physical encounter—parties, conferences, and fairs—most interaction is electronic. Most hackers know each other only by their Internet name. Not because they hide their identity. Rather, their identity as hackers is the name posted on the Net. Although the highest degree of recognition is usually associated with identification by real names, in general terms, informality and virtuality are key features of the hacker culture—features that sharply differentiate this culture from the academic culture and from other manifestations of the meritocratic culture. This is why ARPA researchers practiced hacking (creative, open source programming), and were creators of the Internet, but they were not hackers in the cultural sense.

There are some myths surrounding the hacker culture that it is worth while to dispel. One is its psychological marginality. It is true that there is a pervasive feeling of superiority over the rest of the computer-illiterate world, and a tendency to communicate with the computer, or with other humans via computers, focusing essentially on software issues, incomprehensible for the rest of humankind. A closeness to the world of music, art, or literature can also be seen in this: hackers' permanent temptation to cut their ties of communication with society, and fly into the formal structures of computing. Yet, it is fair to say that most hackers live normal lives, at least as normal as most people, which does not necessarily mean that hackers (or anybody else) fit into the ideal type of normalcy, conforming to the dominant ideology in our societies. Linus Torvalds, among many others, is a dedicated family man, living a regular life with his wife and children in a Silicon Valley suburb. Yes, if you go to a hackers' conference, you can see many people dressed in black, some wearing beards (if they are old enough to grow them), and most displaying provocative T-shirts (e.g. "BURN Venture Capital BURN"). Often you may find references to their emblematic, favorite movies, depending on their age cohort: "Star Wars," "The Matrix," "Enemy of the State." But this folklore is not exclusive to hackers: it is one of many expressions of youth culture in the times and places where hackers live. Indeed, serious hackers primarily exist as hackers on-line. If postmodern anthropologists landed in a hacker meeting and tried to identify tribal clans on the basis of these symbols, they would miss the essence of the culture. Because, as Wayner (2000) emphasizes, the hacker culture, and its internal distinctions, are all about mental constructions and technological divides.

Another powerful myth, often put forward by hacker icon themselves, is that cooperation, freedom, and the gift culture are able to develop only under the conditions of the new, immaterial production system that takes place in a post-scarcity society. According to this view, only when people have their basic needs covered can they afford to dedicate their lives to intellectual creativity, and only then they can practice the gift culture. In fact, this belies the experience of hackers in poor countries, such as Russia or Latin America. It is precisely in situations of extreme poverty, when creative individuals have no access to resources, that they are bound to invent their own solutions, and they do. The social avenues of innovation are highly diverse, and cannot be reduced to the material conditions of living. But what is common to the hacker culture, in all social contexts, is the urge to re-invent ways to communicate with and by computers, building a symbiotic system of people and computers interacting over the Internet. The hacker culture is, in its essence, a culture of convergence between humans and their machines in a process of unfettered interaction. It is a culture of technological creativity based on freedom, cooperation, reciprocity, and informality.

There are, however, hacker subcultures built on political principles, as well as on personal revolt. Richard Stallman considers the achievement of technological excellence to be secondary to the fundamental principle of free software, which, for him, is an essential component of free speech in the Information Age. Indeed, he was an active participant in the free speech movement during his student years at Berkeley. His Free Software Foundation is about protecting programmers' rights to the products of their work, and about mobilizing the community of hackers to join together in an effort to keep their collective creation out of the reach of governments and corporations. Other hacker groupings are constructed around libertarian political principles, such as the defense of freedom of expression and privacy on the Internet. A case in point is the Electronic Frontier Foundation created in 1990 by John Perry Barlow and Mitch Kapor to fight government control of the Internet. They played an important role in the widespread mobilization leading to the defeat in the US courts of the 1995 Communications Decency Act (see Chapter 6). Both Barlow and Kapor symbolize an interesting connection between some of the social subcultures of the post-1960s period and the hacker culture. People remember Barlow as a lyricist of the Grateful Dead rock band, but he is also a third generation Montana rancher, and he currently spends much of his time criss-crossing the planet preaching freedom and the Internet. As for Kapor, besides being a brilliant programmer (he invented Lotus), and making a lot of money, he was a meditation instructor, immersed in spiritualism.

Other hackers recognize themselves in the "cyberpunk" characters of science fiction literature. They build their social autonomy on the Internet, fighting to preserve their freedom against the intrusion of the powers that be, including corporate media takeover of their Internet service providers. On the margins of this rebel hacker subculture emerge the crackers. Most of them are individuals, often very young, trying to prove themselves, usually with limited technical knowledge. Others, such as Kevin Mitnik, blend technological savvy with a strategy of political sabotage in their efforts to watch the world that watches them. This behavior must be differentiated from cybercrime—committing robberies over the Internet for personal profit—the old habit of "white-collar crime" performed by new technological means. The most political crackers build networks of cooperation and information, with all due precautions, often diffusing the code of encryption technology that would allow the formation of these networks beyond the reach of surveillance agencies. The battle lines are shifting from people's right to encrypt (against the government) to people's right to decrypt (against corporations) (Levy, 2001; Patrice Riemens, personal communication, 2001).

The mainstream hacker culture feels very nervous about crackers, as they taint the whole community with a stigma of irresponsibility, amplified by the media. But, from an analytical perspective, we must acknowledge the diversity of the hackers' world, while emphasizing what unifies all its members beyond ideological cleavages and personal behavior: a shared belief in the power of computer networking, and a determination to keep this technological power as a common good—at least for the community of hackers.

Virtual Communitarians

The cultural sources of the Internet cannot be reduced, however, to the values of technological innovators. Early users of computer networks created virtual communities, using the term popularized by Howard Rheingold (1993/2000), and these communities were sources of values that patterned behavior and social organization. People involved in the Usenet News networks, in FIDONET, and in the bulletin board systems, developed and diffused forms and uses of the net: messaging, mailing lists, chat rooms, multi-user games (expanding the early multi-user dungeons or MUDs), conferences, and conference systems.

Some of the users involved in this social interaction were technologically sophisticated, such as the ARPANET researchers who created one of the first thematic mailing lists, SF-Lovers (for science fiction fans), with the tolerance of the Defense Department. Many early UUCP users were also participants in the hacker culture. But most users of most networks from the 1980s onwards were not necessarily skilled in programming. And when the world wide web exploded in the 1990s, millions of users brought into the Net their social innovations with the help of limited technical knowledge. Yet, their contribution to the shape and evolution of the Internet, including many of its commercial manifestations, was decisive. For instance, one of the earliest BBSs in the San Francisco Bay area was a sex-oriented system Kinky Komputer: it spearheaded a blossoming form of on-line practice, both private and commercial, for years to come. Or else, the Institute for Global Communication (IGC), also founded in San Francisco, articulated some of the first computer networks dedicated to the advancement of socially responsible causes, such as the defense of the environment and the preservation of world peace. The IGC was instrumental in setting up the women's computer network (La Neta) used by the Mexican *Zapatistas* to build international solidarity with their struggle on behalf of exploited Indian minorities. Community networks, such as the one created in Seattle by Douglas Schuler, or the Digital City in Amsterdam, renewed and enhanced citizen participation (see Chapter 5). In the final years of the Soviet Union, early computer networks, independently organized by academics, such as RELCOM, were very important in the struggle for democracy and freedom of expression during the critical moments of *perestroika*.

Thus, while the hacker culture provided the technological foundations of the Internet, the communitarian culture shaped its social forms, processes, and uses. But what is this culture? I will deal in detail later in this book with the social uses of the Internet, and the habits and social patterns emerging from the practice of virtual communities (see Chapter 4). I am focusing here on the specificity of cultural values and social rules emerging from these practices as they relate to the structuration of the Internet (Hiltz and Turoff, 1995; Rheingold, 1993/2000).

The origins of on-line communities were very close to the countercultural movements and alternative ways of life emerging in the aftermath of the 1960s. The San Francisco Bay area was home in the 1970s to the development of several on-line communities that experimented with computer communication, among which were the legendary Homebrew Computer Club and the Community Memory projects. In 1985, one of the most innovative, early conference systems, WELL, was started in the San Francisco Bay area by Stewart Brand (a biologist, artist, and computer hobbyist, creator of the Whole Earth Catalog, the rallying publication of the 1970s' counterculture) and Larry Brilliant (a member of the prankster-associated Hog Farm commune, who was one of the organizers of Woodstock). Among the WELL's early managers, hosts, and supporters were people who had tried life in rural communes, PC hackers, and a large contingent of the Deadheads, the followers of the Grateful Dead rock band. As mentioned in Chapter 1, FIDONET was started in 1983 by Tom Jennings, with a vague anarchist agenda. Amsterdam's Digital City developed in the aftermath of the squatters movement of the 1970s, and at least one of its founders had been closely associated with the squatters. Many of the early on-line conferences and BBSs seem to have grown out of the need to build some kind of communal feeling after the failure of counter-cultural experiments in the physical world.

Nonetheless, as virtual communities expanded in size and reach, their original connection to the counterculture weakened. Values and interests of all kinds sprung from computer networks. Empirically speaking, there is no such thing as a unified Internet communal culture. Most observers, from Howard Rheingold to Steve Jones, emphasize the extreme diversity of virtual communities. Moreover, their social characteristics tend to specify their virtual culture. Thus, MUDs are the privileged domain for role-playing and fake identities, to the delight of postmodern theorists. But, as far as we can tell, most MUD players were/are teenagers or college students, enacting on-line much of the typical role-playing behavior of the period of their life when they often experiment with their personality. Users have a tendency to twist new technology to fulfill their interests or desires. In France, the very bureaucratic, official Minitel became popular on the basis of one of its systems, the sex-oriented Messageries Roses. Social movements of all kind, from environmental movements to right-wing extremist ideologies (e.g. Nazism, racism) took advantage of the flexiblity of the Net to voice their views, and to link up across the country and across the globe. The social world of the Internet is as diverse, and contradictory, as society is. So, the cacophony of virtual communities does not represent a system of relatively coherent values and social rules, as in the case of the hacker culture.

Yet, these communities work on the basis of two major, common cultural features. The first one is the value of horizontal, free communication. The practice of virtual communities epitomizes the practice of global free speech, in an era dominated by media conglomerates and censoring government bureaucracies. As John Gilmore put it "The Net interprets censorship as damage and routes around it" (cited by Rheingold, 1993: 7). This freedom of expression from many to many was cherished by Net users from the very early stages of on-line communication, and became one of the overarching values of the Internet. The second shared value emerging from virtual communities is what I would label self-directed networking. That is, the capacity for anyone to find his or her own destination on the Net, and, if not found, to create and post his or her own information, thus inducing a network. From the primitive 1980s' BBSs to the most sophisticated interactive systems of the turn of the century, self-publishing, self-organizing, and self-networking constitute a pattern of behavior that permeates the Internet, and diffuses from the Internet into the entire social realm. Thus, while the communitarian source of the Internet culture is highly diverse in its content, it does specify the Internet as a technological medium for horizontal communication, and as a new form of free speech. It also lays the foundation for self-directed networking as a tool for organization, collective action, and the construction of meaning.

Entrepreneurs

The diffusion of the Internet from the inner circles of technologists and communal living to society at large was enacted by business entrepreneurs. It happened only in the 1990s, with lightning speed. Because business firms were the driving force in its expansion, the Internet has been largely shaped around its commercial uses. But since these commercial uses were built on forms and processes invented by the communal culture, the hackers, and the technological elites, the actual outcome is that the Internet is not more business determined than other domains of life in our societies. Not less, but not more either. In fact, more significant than the business domination of the Internet around the turn of the century is the kind of business that the Internet helped to develop. It would not be fanciful to say that the Internet transformed business as much, if not more, than business transformed the Internet.

The Culture of the Internet

The Internet was the indispensable medium and the driving force in the formation of the new economy, built around new rules and procedures of production, management, and economic calculation. I shall analyze in detail the relationship between the Internet and the new economy in Chapter 3. Here I want to focus on the cultural dimension of Internet entrepreneurs, since culture is the source of meaning. Without meaning people do not act, and without the action of these entrepreneurs, oriented by a specific set of values, there would be no new economy, and the Internet would have diffused at a much slower pace and with a different range of applications.

If we reflect on the formation of Internet companies in Silicon Valley, the seedbed of the new industry, a number of cultural features stand out from the practice of the entrepreneurs who created these firms around technological and business projects. The key point is that they made money out of ideas, while the lack of new ideas led to money losses for established corporations. So, entrepreneurial innovation rather than capital was the driving force of the Internet economy. More often than not, they did not invest their own money. They did not risk much, maybe just their dreams, or the seed money they obtained from their dreams—save a few mortgage foreclosures. When they failed, they could always go back to their garages, to their schools, or to their well-paid corporate jobs—and to a new dream. So, they were not the risk-taking entrepreneurs of Sombart's historical account. Nor were they the technological innovators of the Schumpeterian version of entrepreneurship. Some were, some were not. Some were excellent salesmen rather than great engineers. But they were all able to transform their capacity to imagine new processes and new products into business projects adapted to the Internet world—a world they had not imagined, let alone invented.

The realization of the potential of transforming mind power into money-making became the cornerstone of the entrepreneurial culture in Silicon Valley and of the Internet industry at large. Ideas were sold to venture capitalists, so enabling investment that transformed these ideas into business. And these ideas, embodied as companies (with or without products, with or without profits), were sold to investors via public offerings on the stock market. While this mechanism has extraordinary consequences for the new economic logic, it also determines the kind of culture at the source of entrepreneurial innovation. It is a culture where the amount of money to be made, and the speed at which the money is made, are the supreme values. This goes beyond usual human greed. Money-making becomes the benchmark for success and, as importantly, for freedom *vis-à-vis* the traditional, corporate world. The only way for entrepreneurs to be freed from capital is to be able to attract capital by themselves, and to do so in ways in which they can control a large enough share of the future wealth that would come from investors. This is why stock options are the fundamental mechanism connecting individual freedom to entrepreneurship.

Furthermore, in a world of ebullient innovation, the only way to measure competition and to earn the respect of peers, as well as the fear of the corporate establishment, is money. But the way money is made in the Internet business specifies its entrepreneurial culture *vis-à-vis* other money-seeking cultures, let's say Wall Street. While financial investors try to make money predicting future market behavior, or simply betting on it, Internet entrepreneurs sell the future because they believe they can make it. They rely on their technological know-how to create products and processes that they are convinced will conquer the market. Then the critical point is first to convince the financial markets that the future is there, then to try to sell the technology to the users—by all means—making the prediction work. The strategy is to change the world through technology, and then to be rewarded with money and power, via the workings of financial markets. The foundation of this entrepreneurial culture is the ability to transform technological know-how and business vision into financial value, then to cash some of this value to make the vision a reality somehow.

In its actual incarnation, the Internet entrepreneur is a two-headed creature. Techno-business entrepreneurs could not achieve any of their dreams without venture capitalists. Venture capitalists need the creators to be successful capitalists, so that they can cut a deal in the broader financial world, as gatekeepers to the sources of new wealth creation. Often they hate each other. But they cannot escape their symbiotic relationship, so that the Internet entrepreneur, in social terms, is not a person, in spite of the mythology often surrounding the heroes of the Net-economy. It is a composite of persons and organizations, made up of inventors, technologists, and venture capitalists. They come together in a process of production and innovation that ultimately creates companies, makes money, and, as a byproduct, delivers technology, goods, and services. In this process, the relationship between capital and innovation is internalized. The venture capitalist is very much a part of the actual process of innovation that he or she has identified as promising. He or she nurtures the innovation, shapes it, gears it toward market image. On the other hand, technological innovators/producers internalize capital in their workings, through stock options, and their business plan is targeted on its impact on market capitalization. Quality of production and innovative design are still crucial in this economy, as I will argue in the next chapter, but research excellence and manufacturing pride coexist with the conscious orientation to the financial market as the giver of the last judgment on the company's performance.

This entrepreneurial culture is, above all else, a culture of money. Of money in such staggering amounts (so goes the entrepreneurial myth) that it is worth all the effort. But it is also a culture of work, of workaholism. In this sense, it links up with the work ethic of traditional, industrial entrepreneurs. Yet the fact that the reward is external (money) rather than internal (puritan ethic of self-improvement by honest work) has considerable consequences for the culture. Personal savings are less important than investment in stocks, so that ideas, work, and the personal accumulation of wealth tend to be associated in the same movement. It is making the future, rather than surrendering it to cautious savings, that provides security for life. Under these conditions, consumption is organized around an immediate gratification pattern, rather than the deferred gratification pattern of bourgeois entrepreneurial culture ("Study, my son, keep working, my son, and life will reward you in your old age"). This immediate gratification pattern materializes in goods and services inaccessible to most mortals. Rather than conspicuous consumption, we observe a pattern of superfluous consumption; that is the acquisition of consumer items that have little use to their owner, but provide satisfaction in the few moments left by working life. Mansions, a variety of transportation vehicles, as exotic as possible, extravagant vacations, outlandish parties (albeit infrequent), sophisticated spas, and personal meditation trainers. This superfluous consumption goes together with the joy of informality at work, and in life, including individualistic dressing habits and hairstyle, breaking codes associated with the traditional corporate world. Thus, Internet entrepreneurs seem to be at the same time personal iconoclasts and adorers of the golden calf—in which they see the sign of their personal triumph.

This kind of entrepreneurial culture cuts across ethnic lines, since, precisely, it is more multi-ethnic and global than any entrepreneurial culture in history. It often goes hand in hand with an impoverished personal life, as families and spouses are necessarily sacrificed to this extraordinary drive for technology, money, and power. It is predominantly a world of single persons, with no time to find real soul mates, just accessible bodies occasionally. Unlike the wives of nineteenth-century bourgeois entrepreneurs, most women follow their own path, either being entrepreneurs themselves, or, when they are partners of entrepreneurs, adapting to the norms by pursuing their own professional careers with a similarly frantic way of life. Personal partnerships are instrumental rather than expressive. Civic involvement is at a significantly lower level than in America as a whole. Socialization with co-workers in the US at large is 22 percent higher than in Silicon Valley. The main reason given for both low socialization and low civic involvement is the lack of free time, given that work takes up all available time and energy (Koch and Miller, 2001). Individualism is the rule; so, left alone to themselves, entrepreneurs use their extra dose of adrenalin to speed up their drive of creative destruction that ultimately leads to destructive creation. That is, to a creation of wealth in money and technology that thrives on the ruins of the social and personal lives consumed in the process.

Entrepreneurialism, as an essential dimension of the Internet culture, comes in with a new historical twist: it creates money out of ideas, and merchandise out of money, making both capital and material production dependent on the power of the mind. Internet entrepreneurs are creators rather than businessmen, closer to the artists' culture than to the traditional corporate culture. Their art, however, is unidimensional: they escape from society, as they thrive in technology, and worship money, with a decreasing feedback from the world as it is. After all, why pay attention to the world if they are re-making it in their own image? The Internet entrepreneurs are, at the same time, artists and prophets and greedy, as they hide their social autism behind their technological prowess. By themselves, from their specific culture, they could never have created a medium based on networking and communication. But their contribution was/is indispensable to the multi-layered cultural dynamics that induced the Internet world.

The Internet Culture

I will now turn to specifying the articulation of the four layers of the culture that, together, produced and shaped the Internet. At the top of the cultural construct that led to the creation of Internet is the techno-meritocratic culture of scientific and technological excellence, emerging essentially from big science and the academic world. This techno-meritocracy was enlisted on a mission of world domination (or counter-domination) by the power of knowledge, but kept its autonomy, and relied on a community of peers as the source of its self-defined legitimacy.

The hacker culture specified meritocracy by strengthening the inner boundaries of the community of the technologically initiated, and making it independent of the powers that be. Only hackers can judge hackers. Only the capacity to create technology (coming from any context), and to share it with the community, are respected values. For hackers, freedom is a fundamental value, particularly freedom to access their technology, and use it as they see fit.

The appropriation of networking capacity by social networks of all sorts led to the formation of on-line communes that reinvented society and, in the process, dramatically expanded computer networking, in its reach and in its uses. They assumed the technological values of the meritocracy, and they espoused the hackers' belief in the value of freedom, horizontal communication, and interactive networking, but they used it for their social life, rather than practicing technology for the sake of technology.

Finally, the Internet entrepreneurs discovered a new planet, populated by extraordinary technological innovation, new forms of social life, and self-determined individuals, whose technological capacity gave them substantial bargaining power *vis-à-vis* dominant social rules and institutions. They went one step further. Rather than retrenching in the communes built around the Internet technology, they would take over the world by using the power that came with this technology. In our kind of world, this means, essentially, to have money, more money than anyone else. Thus, the money-oriented entrepreneurial culture went on to conquer the world, and, in the process, they made the Internet into the backbone of our lives.

The culture of the Internet is a culture made up of a technocratic belief in the progress of humans through technology, enacted by communities of hackers thriving on free and open technological creativity, embedded in virtual networks aimed at reinventing society, and materialized by money-driven entrepreneurs into the workings of the new economy.

Reading Links

Csikszentmihalyi, Mihaly (1997) *Creativity: Flow and the Psychology of Discovery and Invention.* New York: HarperCollins.

DiBona, Chris, Ockman, Sam, and Stone, Mark (eds) (1999) *Open Sources: Voices from the Open Source Revolution.* Sebastopol, CA: O'Reilly.

Hafner, Katie and Markoff, John (1995) *Cyberpunks: Outlaws and Hackers in the Computer Frontier.* New York: Touchstone.

Hiltz, S. R. and Turoff, M. (1995) *Network Nation,* rev. edn. Cambridge, MA: MIT Press.

Himanen, Pekka (2001) *The Hacker Ethic and the Spirit of the Information Age.* New York: Random House.

Kiselyova, Emma and Castells, Manuel (2000) "Russia in the Information Age," in Victoria Bonnell and George Breslauer (eds), *Russia in the New Century*, pp. 126–57. Boulder, CO: Westview Press.

Koch, James and Miller, Ross (2001) "Building community: social connections and civic involvement in Silicon Valley," Santa Clara University California, Center for Science, Technology, and Society, research report.

Levy, Steve (2001) *Hackers: Heroes of the Computer Revolution*, rev. edn (orig. pub. 1984). New York: Penguin-USA.

Lewis, Michael (2000) *The New New Thing: A Silicon Valley Story*. New York: W.W. Norton.

Moineau, Laurent and Papatheodorou, Aris (2000) "Coopération et production immatérielle dans le logiciel libre," *Multitudes*, 1 (March): 144–60.

Raymond, Eric (1999) *The Cathedral and the Bazaar: Musings on Linux and Open Source by an Accidental Revolutionary*. Sebastopol, CA: O'Reilly.

Reid, Robert H. (1997) *Architects of the Web: 1,000 Days that Built the Future of Business*. New York: John Wiley.

Rheingold, Howard (1993/2000) *The Virtual Community: Homesteading on the Electronic Frontier*. Cambridge, MA: MIT Press.

Saxenian, Anna L. (1999) *Immigrant Entrepreneurs in Silicon Valley*. San Francisco: Public Policy Institute of California.

Schuler, Douglas (1996) *New Community Networks*. Reading, MA: Addison Wesley.

Southwick, Karen (1999) *High Noon: The Inside Story of Scott McNealy and the Rise of Sun Microsystems*. New York: John Wiley.

Tuomi, Ilkka (2000) "Internet, innovation, and open source: actors in the network," paper delivered at the First Conference of the Association of Internet Researchers, Lawrence, University of Kansas, September 14–17.

Wayner, Peter (2000) *Free for All: How Linux and the Free Software Movement Undercut the High Tech Titans*. New York: HarperBusiness.

e-Links

www.SiliconValley.com
Silicon Valley cultures website.

www.hackerethic.org
Sources on the hacker culture, built on Pekka Himanen's book, *The Hacker Ethic and the Spirit of the Information Age* (New York: Random House, 2001).

www.nettime
Amsterdam-based network of the alternative cultures of the Internet.

e-Business and the New Economy

In a society where private firms are the main source of wealth creation it should come as no surprise that, once the technology of the Internet became available in the 1990s, the fastest, most comprehensive diffusion of its uses took place in the realm of business. The Internet is transforming business practice in its relation to suppliers and customers, in its management, in its production process, in its cooperation with other firms, in its financing, and in the valuation of stocks in financial markets. The proper uses of the Internet have become a key source of productivity and competitiveness for all kinds of business. For all the hype surrounding the dot.com firms, they only represent a small, entrepreneurial vanguard of the new economic world. And, as with all daring enterprises, the business landscape is littered with the wreckage of unwarranted fantasies. Yet, there are also phoenix-like business projects, many of which emerge from their own ashes again and again, learning from their mistakes to try anew, in a productive spiral of creative destruction. In the year 2000, in the United States, business traded about 400 billion dollars over the web. Projections published in March 2001 by the Gartner Group, a market research company, put the 2003 figure at about 3.7 trillion. Furthermore, rapid growth of e-commerce in the world could mean that by 2004, according to International Data Corporation projections, US-based e-commerce could represent less than 50 percent of the total value traded on the Net, in contrast to the US share of 74 percent in 1999—an indication of the projected faster growth of e-commerce in Europe than in the United States in the first years of the twenty-first century. The Gartner Group estimated that even taking into consideration the slowdown of the Internet economy, global business-to-business (B2B) transactions in 2003 could reach about 6 trillion dollars. Forrester Research's projection estimated a global e-commerce figure of 6.8 trillion dollars in 2004, of which 90 percent would be B2B (*Business Week*, 2001: 128).

Yet, the importance of e-business goes well beyond its quantitative value. Because, as of 2001, about 80 percent of the transactions over the web are B2B, and this implies a profound reorganization of the way in which business operates. Internal networks, by which employees communicate among themselves and with their management, are critical for the performance of the firm. The entire business organization needs to conform to the Internet-based technology through which it relates to customers and suppliers. Furthermore, as individual entrepreneurs blossom in this kind of economy, linkages between consultants, subcontractors, and firms over the web become as significant as the firm's own operations. What is emerging is not a dot.com economy, but a networked economy with an electronic nervous system.

This is not to say that purely on-line firms are a passing anecdote of the early moments of the Information Age. AOL, Yahoo!, Amazon, e-Bay, e*Trade, e-Toy and so many other daring start-ups did invent a new business model, making use of the opportunities offered by the Internet, and learning by doing. Indeed, financial markets believed their claims of inventing the future, rewarding their audacity with a staggering market capitalization value—for a while. And venture capitalists became attracted by their prospects, providing enough investment to pump-prime an entirely new economic sector, and beyond that, a new economy, before the dust settled.

e-Business and the New Economy

From the whirlwind of the dot.com firms emerged a new economic landscape, with e-business at its core. By e-business I understand any business activity whose performance of the key operations of management, financing, innovation, production, distribution, sales, employee relations, and customer relations takes place predominantly by/on the Internet or other networks of computer networks, regardless of the kind of connection between the virtual and the physical dimensions of the firm. By using the Internet as a fundamental medium of communication and information-processing, business adopts the network as its organizational form. This socio-technical transformation permeates throughout the entire economic system, and affects all processes of value creation, value exchange, and value distribution. Thus, capital and labor, the key components of all business processes, are modified in their characteristics, as well as in the way in which they operate. To be sure, the laws of the market economy continue to work in this networked economy, but they do so in a specific manner, whose understanding is crucial in order to live, survive, and prosper in this brave, new economic world.

Therefore, I will analyze in sequential order: the transformation of the practice of the firm; the relationship between the Internet and capital markets; the role of work and flexible employment practices in the networking business model; and the specificity of innovation in the e-conomy, at the source of labor productivity growth. These analytical threads will be reunited in a synthetic characterization of the actual meaning of what has come to be known as the new economy. The new economy is not the fantasy land of unlimited high economic growth, able to supersede business cycles and be immune to crises. If there is a new economy, there also are and will be new forms of business cycle, and, eventually, economic crises—shaped by the specific processes that characterize the new economy. Thus, in the conclusion to this chapter I will suggest some hypotheses concerning the characteristics of the new business cycle and of potential crises, prompted by a sharp downturn in the value of technology stocks in financial markets, on the basis of observation of the period from March 2000 to March 2001.

e-Business as an Organizational Model: The Network Enterprise

As happened with the adoption of other technologies by companies in the past, the Internet diffused rapidly in the business world during the 1990s because it was the appropriate tool for the business model that had emerged in the practice of the most productive, competitive firms since, at least, the 1980s. This model, on the basis of observation, I conceptualized some years ago as the network enterprise (Castells, 1996/2000). By such, I understand the organizational form built around business projects resulting from the cooperation between different components of different firms, networking among themselves for the duration of a given business project, and reconfiguring their networks for the implementation of each project. The network enterprise evolved from the combination of various networking strategies. First, the internal decentralization of large corporations, which adopted lean, horizontal structures of cooperation and competition, coordinated around strategic goals for the firm as a whole. Secondly, the cooperation between small and medium businesses, pulling together their resources to reach a critical mass. Thirdly, the linkage between these small and medium businesses networks, and the diversified components of large corporations. And, finally, the strategic alliances and partnerships between large corporations and their ancillary networks. Taken together, these trends transformed business management into a variable geometry of cooperation and competition depending on time, place, process, and product.

Thus, the network enterprise is neither a network of enterprises nor an intra-firm, networked organization. Rather, it is a lean agency of economic activity, built around specific business projects, which are enacted by networks of various composition and origin: *the network is the enterprise*. While the firm continues to be the unit of accumulation of capital, property rights (usually), and strategic management, business practice is performed by *ad hoc* networks. These networks have the flexibility and adaptability required by a global economy subjected to relentless technological innovation and stimulated by rapidly changing demand.

The complexity of this networking structure beyond a certain size could not have been managed without micro-electronics-based information and communication networks. This is why, since the mid-1980s, communication networks, such as electronic data interchange (EDI), and more primitive networks made up of faxes and telephone hook-ups, were critical in the organizational restructuring that swept the business world. The need for chosen-time, high-capacity, high-speed, interactive communication, via data transmission, was met by computer communication networks, including the Internet. On-line companies, as well as the most innovative computer and telecommunications equipment companies, aware of the potential of the Internet, were the first to seize the opportunity to set themselves up entirely on the basis of computer networks that would open up the company's information and operations to both customers and suppliers. They also set up intranets to create channels of electronic communication between their employees, and between management and employees. At this point in the analysis, some examples from business practice could help to convey the importance, and the originality, of the organizational transformation enacted with the help of the Internet and other computer networks.

Cisco Systems might well be the pioneer of the business model characterizing the Internet economy. In spite of my reluctance to highlight any particular firm, I think a summary account of Cisco's "networked business model" may provide a concrete image of the transformation under way, with most data referring to mid-2000, except for figures on Cisco's decline in revenues and stock valuation which date to April 2001.

Cisco Systems, headquartered in San Jose in Silicon Valley, is the largest maker of Internet backbone equipment, with a market share of about 85 percent of the global market of routers, the computers that organize and direct traffic on the Internet. Originally started in 1984 as a spin-off from a love affair between a computer scientist man and a business school woman at Stanford University, at the peak ot its valuation, in March 2000, it reached a market capitalization value of 555 billion dollars, the largest in the world. The sharp decline of technology stocks in 2000–2001 cut drastically into the value of Cisco's shares. After averaging 100 percent annual returns during the period 1996–2000 (March), between March 2000 and April 2001 the value of Cisco's share declined by 78 percent. And after seeing its revenue drop by 30 percent in three months, in April 2001 Cisco laid off 8,500 of its 44,000 workers, although most of them were temporary workers, and others were part of the company's usual 5 percent annual attrition rate. I will analyze Cisco's sudden reversal of fortune in the last section of this chapter since it has to be placed in the framework of the overall crisis of the new economy.

However, its 2001 woes do not cancel out its extraordinary performance during the 1990s. In the second half of the 1990s, Cisco's sales increased between 50 percent and 70 percent per year, and its revenues for the fiscal year 2000, at 18.9 billion dollars, were more than four times the level of four years earlier. So, do not count Cisco out (particularly if it succeeds in updating its software architecture and improves its technology in optical networks). Unless we plunge into an "Internet Depression," Cisco appears to be positioned to remain as the dominant company in the design and manufacturing of Internet networks—an obviously expanding trade in a global outlook. Therefore, it is still relevant to analyze the business model of one of the leading technology companies in the world to understand the relationship between the production of the Internet and the uses of the Internet in production.

Although much of the performance of Cisco was due to good engineering, as well as good timing (being ready to provide the plumbing systems for the Internet at the precise moment of the Internet explosion), other companies, as mighty as Lucent Technologies, were also in the same market. Yet revenues per employee at Cisco in 2000 were three times the level of Lucent Technologies, and its market share increased over time.

There is widespread consensus in business circles that much of the competitiveness and productivity achieved by Cisco derives from its business model. Cisco is organized around a network open to both suppliers and customers: Cisco's Connection Online (CCO) had in 2000 about 150,000 registered users, and was accessed monthly 1.5 million times. Entering the system through Cisco's website, customers specify their needs and are helped by pricing and configuration agents which allow thousands of authorized representatives of customers and partners to define and price Cisco products on-line. When the interactive process between customers and suppliers reaches an agreement, Cisco's suppliers manufacture most of the products, and ship them directly to the customer. Customer service and technical help are largely automated, with most technical information posted on-line. Cisco also provides free consulting and training on the installation, maintenance, and repair of computer communication networks. Using this system, in the first half of the year 2000, Cisco sold 40 million dollars a day on-line, accounting for 90 percent of its orders. Of these orders about 60 percent are fully automated, without requiring any action from Cisco personnel. About 80 percent of customer service requests were also handled over the web.

In addition, Cisco also organizes its production on-line, a networked manufacturing environment built as an extranet, Manufacturing Connection Online (MCO), first established in June 1999, and accessed by suppliers, Cisco's employees, and logistics partners. One of the most valuable manufacturing companies in the world manufactures very little by itself, having outsourced over 90 percent of its production to a network of certified suppliers. But Cisco controls its supply chain closely, integrating key suppliers into its production systems, automating routing data transfer through EDIs, automating the gathering of product data information from suppliers, and decentralizing testing procedures at the production point, under standards and methods tightly controlled by Cisco engineers. So, Cisco is indeed a manufacturer, but based on a global, virtual factory, of which it has final responsibility in terms of R&D, prototype engineering, quality control, and brand name. Cisco has also automated its inventory system, with a dynamic information system that has prevented major supply problems in several instances. Furthermore, the Cisco Employee Connection is an intranet that provides instant communication to thousands of employees, across the building or across the globe. From joint engineering to marketing and training, information flows directly in chosen time around the network, according to the needs of each department and employee. Accounting procedures are streamlined, and conducted by an intranet, thus allowing, for instance, the company to close its accounting books at the end of the quarter in two days.

The cornerstone of this networked business model is the real-time feedback between customers and production. John Chambers, Cisco's CEO and innovator, was, primarily, a salesman, and it shows. By recording, and personalizing, customer requests, via the Internet, and reporting back to the production chain in real time, Cisco is able to correct major production flaws in record time and with precision.

Finally, the networking structure also allows Cisco to develop an effective model of technological innovation, the ultimate source of competitiveness. As many other Silicon Valley companies, Cisco invests heavily in R&D, about 13 percent of its revenues in 1999–2000. But its main strategy to keep its leading edge was an active acquisitions policy, buying companies with technology and talent in the areas that Cisco needed and did not have. Using its valuable stock at the time is was highly valued, Cisco bought seventy companies between 1993 and 2000. Thus, in August 1999, Cisco paid 6.9 billion dollars for a promising start-up, Cerent, a California company with only 10 million dollars in annual sales, but holding critical technology in optical networks. However, this and many other acquisitions could have been a wasteful initiative if, in the process of integration between Cisco and these companies, the chemistry of innovation were disrupted. Here is where the networking model allows Cisco to let companies continue to do what they were doing before being bought, and yet to link up their efforts, research, and business strategies with Cisco's overall business plan. By internalizing resources in a flexible manner, Cisco constitutes itself as the node and the brand of a vast network of network enterprises that projects into the financial markets the image of its performance.

To be sure, Cisco is a ruthless competitor, and while employee satisfaction seems to be high (as indicated by low personnel turnover), not everything is rosy in Cisco's business practice. Talk to the Latino cleaners who keep Cisco's offices in good order (naturally hired through subcontractors), and they see nothing grandiose about being paid 8 dollars an hour, and living in miserable quarters in the midst of Silicon Valley's affluence. And yet, the entrepreneurial adventure epitomized by the Cisco business model during the 1990s innovated on the conditions of wealth creation in our world, by bringing together networking and the Internet in a virtuous circle of distributed innovation and positive feedbacks between management, producers, and consumers.

Cisco is not a special case. Rather, it is just one of several trend-setters. In fact, some analysts consider that the true pioneer in the on-line networked business model is the leading laptop computer-maker in the world, Dell. Dell also works on the basis of a well-designed website, updated in real time, that customers use to self-design the computer they want, by using a variety of options. In 2000, 90 percent of Dell's orders were processed on-line. As Cisco, Dell also outsources most of its production, in a global network of manufacturers that are connected by the Internet.

The network business model is rapidly becoming the predominant form of organization in the electronics industry, with Nokia, Hewlett Packard, IBM, Sun Microsystems, and Oracle being among the most advanced firms in reorganizing themselves around the Internet, both in product and process.

Nokia, in particular, restructured itself as a network enterprise in the 1990s, building a layered network of hundreds of manufacturers in Finland and around the world, with whom the company keeps in close working interaction, jointly developing products, and improving the production process. It also has close partnerships with major companies, including its direct competitors, in R&D and the development of new technologies, such as the promising "Blue tooth" short-range communication technology, and the IPv6 communication protocol, developed by the Internet Engineering Task Force (Ali-Yrkko, 2001).

In 2000, the company embarked on what its leaders, Jorma Ollila and Pekka Ala-Pietila, define as a process of transformation of Nokia into a global e-business powered by a process of corporate-wide e-enablement, moving from "a static value chain towards a value-net." In their words: "we are not just creating a duplicate electronic organization alongside the old, we are re-inventing and re-skilling ourselves in preparation for a totally new way." This process, under way in 2000–2001, was expected by 2003 to reach a level of penetration of the entire Nokia network such that "substantially all the company's revenues would be generated by e-mode" (Nokia/Insight, 2001: 4). By using a networking model, Nokia, a company that was on the verge of extinction in 1991, has become the dominant company of mobile communications, and in 2001 increased its global market share of mobile phone handsets to 35 percent, way ahead of Motorola (14 percent) and Ericsson (9 percent). In 2000 Nokia's revenues were over 30 billion euros (up 54 percent from 1999), and its operating profits were almost 6 billion euros (up 48 percent from 2000). In the first quarter of 2001, in spite of the general technology slump, Nokia's sales increased by 22 percent over the same period in 2000, and its profit went up by 9.4 percent. We can expect to see Nokia's competitors engage in similar e-networking strategies in the coming years.

The network enterprise model, powered by the Internet, is not confined to the technology industry. It is expanding fast in all sectors of activity. I could describe similar forms of management, production, and distribution by reporting on Valeo, a French automobile parts manufacturer, which serves 50 percent of its orders on-line; or on Webcor, a San Mateo, California, construction company that has become a leader in the building industry by posting on its website all relevant information for each project, so that architects, workers, suppliers, and clients can interact and adjust throughout the construction process; or, else, on Weyerhauser, a Wisconsin manufacturer of metal doors, which has automated its entire business in an interactive network, reducing delivery and distribution costs, reducing errors, and doubling its earnings; or on the scheme of collaboration between General Motors, Ford Motor Company, and Daimler Chrysler to set up jointly an on-line exchange for auto-part suppliers, in what could well become the largest e-business, with projected revenues of 6.9 billion dollars in 2002; or on John Deere, the multinational agricultural machinery company, also building networking connections with its suppliers and customers; or on Merita Nordbanken, a

Finnish–Swedish banking conglomerate that managed the world's largest on-line banking system in the year 2000, with 1.2 million customers, able to bank via their mobile phones, and pay electronically with smart cards and phones, entirely virtualizing money. Or, on ABB, the largest engineering company in the world, which in early 2001 reorganized itself completely to set up an Internet-based model of "collaborative commerce" between suppliers, manufacturers, and customers, in what its new CEO called a "highly flexible mass customisation" production system.

Yet probably a more telling illustration of the emergence of the network enterprise model in the whole spectrum of business comes from one of the most traditional sectors of activity: clothing. Zara is a family-owned Spanish company, based in A Coruña (Galicia), designing, producing, and selling in its licensed chain of stores moderately priced, fashionable, ready-to-wear garments. In a few years, in the late 1990s, Zara came from nowhere to compete with other major clothing chains, like Gap: by the end of 2000, Zara had hundreds of stores in thirty-four countries, including several stores in New York, London, and Paris, and was moving toward selling on-line in the United States. Its parent company had reached a market capitalization value of 2 billion dollars. Not impressive in Silicon Valley, but certainly respectable in the clothing retail industry. The secret of its success, besides some good-quality design from the great Galician fashion tradition, lies in its computerized networking structure. At the sales point, store employees record all transactions in a handheld device programmed with a profiling model. Data are processed, on a daily basis, by the store manager, and sent to the design center in A Coruña, where two hundred designers work on market responses, and redesign their products in real time. The new patterns are transmitted to computerized laser cutting machines in the main plant in Galicia, then the fabric is assembled according to the patterns, mostly in nearby factories. Using this networked system, Zara produces 12,000 designs a year, and re-supplies its stores around the world twice a week. The flexibility of this network-based production system allows the company to bring a new design from pattern to store in two weeks. In the 1980s, the pioneer of the networking model in the clothing industry, Benetton, had a design/production/distribution cycle of six months. It was overtaken by Gap when the American firm cut the cycle to two months. Now, Zara does it in two weeks: this is Internet speed.

The purely on-line companies, such as portals, Internet content providers in general, and exclusively on-line commerce, rely even more, as one would expect, on the ability to organize management, production, and distribution on the Internet (Vlamis and Smith, 2001). Indeed, there is a shift in the value chain of the e-commerce industry toward the information distribution systems at the expense of the value of information itself. But it would be misleading to confine their business purely to the virtual domain. Amazon, the on-line seller, first of books and records, then of a growing range of goods and services, is also at the center of a large system of warehousing and transportation, most of it outsourced to other companies, such as UPS. Furthermore, a new sector is developing, the so-called "click and mortar" companies, traditional firms moving on-line to ensure their direct relationship to their customers, both to receive their orders and to improve their customer services. Examples are decoratetoday.com, an on-line spin-off of American Blind and Wallpaper; or performancebike.com, a subsidiary of Performance Technologies, a major American bicycle parts supplier; or the Internet retail exchange, set up jointly by Sears Roebuck and Carrefour, to handle 80 billion dollars a year in supplies. Electronic market places, in fact virtual malls, are growing at such a speed that, according to a survey conducted by Forrester Research in 2000, two-thirds of on-line buyers and sellers were planning to use e-market places, that is specialized electronic exchanges, by 2002. Another Forrester Research survey in early 2001 reported that 35 percent of 1,000 large North American companies were selling products on-line, either to consumers or other business, and an additional 46 percent were planning to do so.

The essence of e-business is in the Internet-based, interactive, networked connection between producers, consumers, and service providers. Here again, the network is the message. It is the capacity to interact, retrieve, and distribute globally, in a customized form, that lies at the source of cost reduction, quality, efficiency, and customer satisfaction—unless the management of complexity collapses the system, as is too often the case, outraging consumers with the realization that they may well be the guinea-pigs of this new business model.

However, if the network enterprise preceded the diffusion of the Internet, what is the specific contribution of this technological medium to the new business model? The answer is: *it enables scalability, interactivity, management of flexibility, branding, and customization in a networked business world*.

Scalability: the network can include as many or as few components, locally or globally, as required for each operation and for each transaction. For the network, to be local or global is not a technical obstacle, and it can evolve, expand, or retrench with the variable geometry of business strategy, without major costs in unutilized production capacity, since the production system can be reprogrammed or redirected with a simple procedure.

Interactivity, in real or chosen time, with suppliers, customers, subcontractors, and employees, in a multi-directional system of information and decision-making that bypasses the vertical channels of communication without losing track of the transaction. The result is better-quality information, and better adjustment between partners in the business process.

Management of flexibility allows the possibility of keeping control of the business project while extending its reach, and diversifying composition, according to the needs of each project. This ability to combine strategic guidance with decentralized, multiple interaction with the partners is critical in order to achieve the goals set by the firm for itself. The Internet provides the technology necessary for integrating other firms in an economy in which the successful management of acquisitions and mergers determines the life or death of the conglomerates resulting from these fusion strategies.

Branding is essential as a recognized sign of value in a business world where customers have multiple choices, and where investors need a symbol of acknowledged capacity for value creation. But how to exercise branding in the practice of an economy in which every business project is the result of a broad, multilateral effort? The firm nominally in charge of each project collects success or failure, and accumulates symbolic value in its brand name. But to be able to use branding without major risk of losing reputation, the firm needs to ensure that quality control is performed all along the value chain. So, "Intel inside" was a genius marketing strategy to obtain product recognition and quality branding. Yet it was easy to accomplish this in an oligopolistic market, such as the one represented by Intel-based PCs. But in a world of complex production and distribution networks, branding can be exercised primarily on the basis of control of innovation and tight control on the final result of the product. Internet-based information systems allow positive feedback from all components of the network into the production and sales processes, as well as error detection and correction, under the responsibility of the coordinator of the entire sequence, the holder of the brand name.

Customization: this is the key to the new form of conducting business. Cultural change, and the diversity of global demand, make it increasingly difficult to resort to standardized, mass production to satisfy the market. On the other hand, economies of scale still count, prompting the need for high-volume production as a way to lower marginal costs per unit. The right mix between volume and customized production can be achieved by operating a large-scale network of production, yet customizing the final product (be it good or service) to the individual consumer. This is accomplished by personalized, iterative, on-line interaction. But it is also helped by automated profiling incorporated into the model of on-line transactions, which allows business to target specific consumer preferences. As I will analyze in Chapter 6, such profiling raises major questions about privacy and consumer rights. But it is an efficient method to target advertising and sales, building a dynamic database for the constant adaptation of production to market demand. If customization is the key to competitiveness in the new global economy, the Internet is the essential tool to ensure customization in a context of high-volume production and distribution.

Thus, what the Internet adds to the network enterprise model of business is its capacity to evolve organically with innovation, production systems, and market demand, while keeping its focus on the ultimate goal of any business: money-making. The problem is, however, that the way of making money in the Internet economy is not as straightforward as it used to be in the industrial era. Because computer networks have also transformed financial markets, the place in which the value of all business is ultimately set.

e-Capital and Market Valuation in the Age of the Internet

The transformation of capital markets is at the source of the development of Internet firms, and, for that matter, of the entire new economy. Without the financing of innovative start-ups by venture capital firms there would have been no Internet-led economic growth. And venture capitalists were able to go on a risky financing spree, in spite of the high mortality rate of their ventures (about one-third of projects in the US), only because of the high rewards provided by unprecedented market capitalization valuation granted by the financial markets to many of these innovative business projects. The sharp fall in the value of technology stocks that began on March 10, 2000 could not erase the extraordinary growth in value of technology firms, including the surviving dot.com companies, over the past decade. In spite of the liquidation of numerous Internet start-ups around the world, which were too fragile in their business plans to survive the change of mood in the market, the amount of capital attracted by high yields in the technology sector during the 1990s and beyond has been the fuel of the new economy. In a five-year perspective, between 1996 and early 2001, in the midst of a volatile financial market, and even after entering bear territory in 2000–2001, all major technology firms, as well as a sizeable number of Internet start-ups, increased their market value substantially. Indeed, after its dramatic decline in 2000–2001, the Nasdaq index, in February 2001, stood at over three times its level in 1996. It may well go down further, for reasons that I will analyze below, but the long period of high growth in the 1990s has already transformed the US economy and the core of the global economy.

78

I will argue that this growth, for the most part, was not speculative or exuberant, and that the high valuation of technology stocks was not a financial bubble, in spite of the obvious over-valuation of many individual firms. But I also reject the notion that we are in an economy that defies the laws of gravity. The historical record and economic theory show that values that go up ultimately come down, as they did in 2000–2001—and they may go up again. The questions—the real questions—are when, how much, and why. To answer these questions we need to consider the transformation of financial markets in the past decade, due to deregulation, liberalization, technology, and business restructuring.

What we are witnessing is the gradual development of a global, interdependent financial market, operated by computer networks, with a new set of rules for capital investment and valuation of stocks, and of securities in general. As information technology becomes more powerful and flexible, and as national regulations are bent by capital flows and electronic trading, financial markets are becoming integrated, eventually working as a unit in real time throughout the globe. Thus, the computer networking capacity of trading systems is transforming financial markets, and the new rules of financial markets are providing the necessary capital for the financing of the Internet economy. Let us follow, step by step, this fundamental, yet complex argument.

I will first describe the mechanism through which capital markets finance e-business innovation. A typical Silicon Valley sequence in the late 1990s started with a daring business plan, and with some knowledge of how Internet technology could contribute to it, yet focusing more on business innovation than on technological innovation. After all, most technology these days is open source or "off the shelf": the real issue is to know what to do with it, and for this the essential item is talent. Talent can be obtained with money, lots of money—or, as is most often the case, with the promise of it. The business plan is then sold to a venture capital firm. Silicon Valley's venture capitalists are located next door. In fact, one-third of all venture capital in the United States is invested in the San Francisco Bay area. In most cases, these are not purely financial firms. Often they are firms grown from the high-technology industry.

HIGHLINE COLLEGE LIBRARY

Sometimes rich, high-tech entrepreneurs (angels) invest individually in promising business projects. In most instances, investors
with a knowledge of the industry create a venture capital firm and
link up with outsider investment firms eager to enter a promising
market. Venture capital firms work closely with their start-ups,
guiding their business projects, nurturing their activity as long as
they are considered a promising investment.

Nevertheless, many projects fail. They do not reach the operational stage, or they lose out in the market. But the pay-off
from successful ventures is such that venture capitalists come, on
average, way ahead in their returns, far above the yield of alternative financial investments (Gupta, 2000; Zook, 2001). This is
exactly why they keep doing it, albeit tightening their controls
when the market goes down. Because, ultimately, the success of a
project depends on the judgment of the financial market. With the
seed money obtained from venture capitalists, entrepreneurs set up
a firm, hire talent, and pay the talent mainly with stock options;
that is, with deferred income (or the expectation of it), and do
enough work to make it possible to go public with an initial public
offering (IPO). How the IPO works—that is, how investors judge
the project in the financial market—determines the life or death of
the project. If it is successful enough, then the firm uses market
capitalization value to obtain more capital, and then goes into
serious business: not expecting to make profits soon, but expecting
to generate enough expectations so that either it becomes a viable
company, or, in the process, is acquired by a richer company,
which usually pays with its stock. Thus, rather than becoming real
billionaires, the entrepreneurs who sell out become richer on
paper, partners of a bigger dream, with greater opportunities to
impress the financial market in the long term. In principle, the
market will ultimately react according to the bottom-line rules of
the economy; that is, the company's ability to generate revenues
and to make profits. But the timing of this judgment is highly variable. Expectations for high returns may extend the patience of
investors, giving a chance for innovation to yield results.

This model of high growth combines technological innovation,
business creativity, and financing by the market on the basis of

expectations. It is not limited to Internet start-ups or to purely on-line companies, such as AOL, Yahoo!, e-Bay and Amazon. It also underlies the success of new, major technology companies (Intel, Cisco, Sun Microsystems, Dell, Oracle, EMC, and even Hewlett Packard and Microsoft in their pioneer days). The fate of traditional companies that reinvent themselves in the new economy (such as Nokia or IBM) is also dependent on their ability to attract investors in the financial market on the basis of their valuation. And this valuation is a function of technological innovation, business innovation, and image-making in the financial world. For instance, the successful, global expansion of Nokia relied on technological innovation (cell phone in sequential generations, with a variety of applications, including mobile Internet access, and new technology in networks infrastructure), an effective management model (integration at the core, networking at the periphery, flat corporate structure), and high performance in the stock markets (until the value of its shares followed the general stumbling of technology stocks) (Ali-Yrkko *et al.*, 2000). The new financial market is the key to the new economy. I shall characterize its main features.

First of all, there is a process of increasing globalization and interdependency between financial markets. While national regulations still matter (indeed, differences in regulatory environments provide opportunities for speculation), the ability of capital to flow in and out of securities and currencies across markets, and the hybrid nature of financial derivatives, often composed of securities from various origins, are intertwining the markets at an accelerated pace. This financial interdependence is technologically powered by a network of computer networks that ensures the capacity to trade and decide globally in real time. Strictly speaking, these networks are not the Internet because they are not based on Internet protocols. But they are computer networks, and they are connected to the Internet. The global integration of financial markets is making their regulation by national, or even international, bodies increasingly difficult. With currency markets exchanging, on average in 2000, well over 2 trillion dollars daily, it is easy to understand why the joint intervention of the central banks of the European Union, the United States, and Japan in support of the euro in September

2000 could not reverse its decline until the markets decided otherwise. It follows that financial movements that originate in any market, anywhere in the world, have the potential to spread to other markets, regardless of differences between national economies and market values. This contagion effect characterized the crisis in emerging financial markets in 1997–9, as the Asian, Russian, and Brazilian crises fed into each other in spite of the dissimilarity of the economies in these three areas of the world. In spite of some fears, these crises did not spread to the US and Western European markets, for the simple reason that, for all the talk of emerging markets, these markets only accounted, at that time, for 7 percent of global financial value, and their integration with core capital markets was still limited. As emergent markets grow in importance, and as electronic networks link them more closely to global financial markets, the extent and speed of the diffusion of financial movements is likely to increase, resulting in further interdependence of markets and multiplying the sources of volatility.

Secondly, electronic trading is transforming financial markets. Electronic communication networks (ECNs) grew on the basis of Nasdaq transactions. Nasdaq, created in 1971, and merged with the American stock exchange in 1998, is, like the New York stock exchange, a non-profit association that organizes stocks trading. But it does not have a central trading place; it is an electronic market place, based on computer networks. Nasdaq has been essential to the development of the new economy, as innovative companies issued their public offerings on Nasdaq, taking advantage of its greater flexibility. ECNs, set up by brokerage firms, such as US-based Instinet (a subsidiary of the Reuters Group plc), provide individual investors with the ability to retrieve information and invest on-line. Brokerage companies such as Charles Schwabb and e*Trade have substantially increased their market share by setting up an Internet-based network of individual accounts. Traditional brokerage and financial firms, such as Merrill Lynch, after vowing to resist the trend, finally opened their own electronic investment networks, as the action, and the money, were clearly heading toward Internet-based access to information and trading.

Individual day traders, using their own tools of information and communication, populated the American financial stage in the late 1990s, then made some inroads into Europe, before being shaken and ultimately decimated by the increasing volatility of the market—to which they had contributed. ECNs had a slower growth in Europe due to national fragmentation and tighter regulation. Yet, with the coming of the euro, technological change, and deregulation, electronic trading expanded in the second half of the 1990s. Easdaq, Tradepoint, and Jiway, among others, became major trading systems in European markets. In March 2000, e-Crossnet was created in London, a matching system supported by global fund-management firms.

Exchange markets themselves are becoming electronic. In the futures market, the German–Swiss electronic exchange, Eurex, overtook the Chicago Board of Trade in 1999 as the largest futures market in the world. Then, in 2001, the Chicago Board of Trade finally jumped on the bandwagon and entered into an alliance with Eurex. MATIF and LIFFE, the French and British futures exchanges, moved to an electronic system as well in 1998–2000. In New York, Cantor Fitzgerald Broker, the largest bond broker in the world, began an electronic exchange in 1998 to trade future contracts on US treasury bonds. The threat of electronic trading led to projects of merger between European stock exchanges. In 2000, the London stock exchange and the Frankfurt stock exchange tentatively agreed to a merger, with one market based in London for established values, and another market in Frankfurt, in a joint venture with Nasdaq, for growth values. The agreement fell apart, largely as a result of the Swedish OM exchange attempt to take over the London stock exchange, but the writing is on the wall for the financial markets. The French, Dutch, and Belgian stock exchanges decided to unite as Euronext, and the Spanish and Italian stock markets were expected to gravitate toward one of the two or three mega-markets being formed in Europe. In a significant move, in the projected joint venture between Nasdaq and the London and Frankfurt stock exchanges, the scheme included the Tokyo stock exchange, on the basis of an electronic trading system, thus setting the stage for the development of a global

Nasdaq. The New York stock exchange is also planning a mixed system of electronic trading and floor trading. Furthermore, under competitive pressure, New York, Nasdaq, London, Stockholm, and other stock exchanges are moving toward a shareholding status, adding flexibility, increasing their competitiveness, and downplaying regulation. Overall, the trend points toward an essential role for electronic trading as the core of the financial market place, and toward the consolidation of stock exchanges around the world in a few nodes able to attract investors because of their critical mass and their trading flexibility. This will mean greater interdependence of global financial markets, higher volume, and faster speed of transactions.

Why does the technology of transactions matter? It reduces transaction costs, at least by 50 percent, thus attracting more investors, and generating more transactions. It opens up opportunities to invest on-line, with four consequences. First, it increases market volume to unprecedented amounts because the market becomes able to mobilize savings from anywhere to be invested anywhere, while accelerating the turnover of investment. For instance, the US Depository of Trust and Clearance Corporation (DTCC), the main clearer of US equities and bonds, processed 70 trillion dollars' worth of securities in 1999, while in the first semester of 2000 the volume of transaction increased by 66 percent in comparison with the same period in 1999 (representing, on an annualized basis of trading volume, over ten times the value of US GDP at that time). Secondly, on-line information becomes a critical factor in investors' decisions. Thirdly, there is a greater possibility of disintermediation, as individual investors and on-line brokers bypass traditional brokers and investments firms. Finally, investors react instantly to changing market trends, as they must be alert to the movements of a complex market moving at high speed, and they are equipped with the technological capacity for executing financial decisions in real time.

Thus, electronic trading increases the number of investors, with highly diversified strategies, operating through a decentralized network of investment sources in a global, interdependent market operating at high velocity. The overall result leads to an exponential increase in market volatility—as complexity, size, and speed induce a quick reaction pattern of behavior among Internet-powered investors, leading to chaotic dynamics and attempts to out-guess the market in real time. So, both the transformation of finance and the transformation of trading technology converge toward market volatility as a systemic trend.

It is in this new financial/technological context that markets value firms and, for that matter, any other object of valuation, since the new financial calculus, equipped with powerful computer models, has led to a process of securitization of almost everything: from entire countries (the "sovereign ceiling" doctrine of financial appraisal) to church-issued bonds, environmental programs, cultural and educational institutions, local governments, regional governments, or financial derivatives (synthetic securities combining the present and future value of stocks, bonds, commodities, and currencies).

Valuation in the financial market is the decisive process of our economy. To be sure, from a structural point of view, what counts for economic growth is productivity. From the point of view of the firm, the bottom line is to generate revenue, and profits. But the process of economic growth starts with investment. And for investors what really matters is the return on their money. This is determined by the valuation of the stocks representing their investment in the financial market. That is, investment is led by the growth of value of stocks, not by earnings and profits. It may well be that there is a direct relationship between profits and growth of value, and, in this case, valuation criteria in the financial market should be straightforward, entirely depending on the measurable performance of the firm in terms of revenues and profits.

But this is not what we observe empirically at the outset of the twenty-first century: for a period of almost a decade the gap between the value of stocks and earnings per share has grown steadily. Empirical evidence shows that the stock market valuation of firms has increasingly diverged from their measured book value. Valuation in the financial markets certainly includes profits and earnings in assessing value to stocks. But these are not the only criteria by any means. Intangibles count: according to some studies, each dollar of installed computer capital in a firm is associated with at least five dollars of market value, after controlling for other assets. The valuation of the firm is even more favorable when investment in information technology is combined with organizational change (Brynjolfsson, Hitt, and Yang, 2000). Other important intangibles for market valuation are branding, corporate image, management efficiency, and sector of activity. This is why, once the markets decided that the Internet was the technology of the future, any stock related to the Internet had an instant premium, regardless of its high risk and, too frequently, of its unrealistic business prospects. And when the markets reacted negatively to what was perceived to be an over-valuation of technology stocks from March 2000, devaluation of many of these stocks proceeded largely without correspondence to the actual performance of specific firms.

But markets also react to macro-economic conditions, and to policy decisions—or to their anticipation. Or to the disparity between the anticipation and the actual event. Markets react as well on the basis of non-economic criteria. They are influenced by what I call *information turbulences* from various sources, such as political uncertainty, legal/judicial developments (for example, the anti-trust law suit against Microsoft), technological anticipations (the demise of the PC or the rise of the mobile Internet), or even personal moods and statements from key decision-makers (Greenspan, Duisenberg). As Paul Volcker (2000: 78) has written, analyzing the transformation of global financial markets, "Flows of funds and their valuation in free financial markets are influenced as much by perceptions as by objective reality—or perhaps, more precisely, perception is the reality."

This is not really new. But, as with other information processes, there is a qualitative change in the age of the Internet. First, there is a proliferation of gossip and news easily available to everybody. Financial gurus of various sorts publish on-line the letters of privileged information that they used to address to their corporate clients. Specialized firms, such as Whisper.com, post on the Internet rumors and leaks that, in the past, did not diffuse beyond initiated circles. Financial manipulations and image-making announcements, some serious, some not, but most in-between (and who knows?), create an environment of uncertain information. In this environment investors have to react in real time, before the speed of the market makes them pay for their hesitation. Individual investors, by their numbers, increase the sources of volatility. But major institutional investors, also reacting at Internet speed, with colossal funds, may twist and bend market trends in an unpredictable pattern of interaction between individual decisions and systemic trends.

Financial markets, by and large, are outside anyone's control. They have become a sort of automaton, with sudden movements that do not follow a strict economic logic, but a logic of chaotic complexity, resulting from the interaction of millions of decisions reacting in real time, in a global span, to information turbulences from various origins—including economic news concerning profits and earnings. Or their anticipation. Or the reversal of what was expected.

This reality check on the actual functioning of financial markets in the age of the Internet helps to put into perspective the famed debate on the over-valuation of Internet firms and, for that matter, of the new economy as a whole. To be sure, there have been, and still are, even in the downturn, substantial over-valuations concerning the prospects of many firms to become profitable businesses. However, the anticipation of yields from technological breakthroughs or business innovation does not seem to be a proof of irrational exuberance, as Shiller (1999) put it in a popular critique of the financial valuation of the new economy. Indeed, some of the famous financial "bubbles" in history (so often referred to by conservative economic minds these days) in retrospect do not seem to have been as speculative as generally thought (Garber, 2000). To consider that the Internet or genetic engineering are the driving technological engines of the twenty-first century economy, and to invest in firms that are producers or early users of these major technological innovations, regardless of their short-term profitability, does not seem entirely irrational. It would seem to be less exuberant than betting on the continuation of business as usual in the midst of a technological revolution centered on information-processing in an economy where well over half of the workers process information.

So, maybe some stocks have been, or are, excessively valued. But how much is too much? The obvious answer ("the market will decide") is purely tautological because it is the market that assigned high value in the first place, above what traditional standards would have warranted. So, the implicit notion is that the market will ultimately set the "right value." But, when, at what point in time? Over the long term? But long terms are not the result of fate: they are made up of a succession of short terms. They are not pre-scripted, they are locked in by *ad hoc* trajectories following *ad hoc* events. Furthermore, if we look at the behavior of financial markets in early 2001 they appeared to have rung the bell for new economy values. Yet, over-valuation went hand in hand with under-valuation, using traditional criteria of sound business per-formance. Yes, many Internet start-ups were not viable, and the test of financial markets may have been necessary for a Darwinian correction to muscle up the Internet economy. But, at the same time, major technology companies, on the cutting edge of innova-tion, efficiently managed, generating revenues, and posting profits, were chastised by financial markets out of proportion to the appar-ent causes of their downturns. Thus, Nokia stock suffered a major loss, in August 2000, in spite of good business results, because of the delay announced in receiving on time the next model of mobile phones, and because of its warning that earnings in the next quarter would grow at a slower pace than in the previous one. Dell, the leading laptop maker, and Intel, the acknowledged leader in the micro-electronics industry, lost 50 percent of their value because earnings were not as high as anticipated. Yahoo! consoli-dated its position as the world's leading portal, continued to increase revenue, posted profits, and yet its stock lost 80 percent of its value—forcing the resignation of its CEO in March 2001. Microsoft, threatened with a split, and holding on to the monopoly of a vanishing market (the PC) also lost, but less than other com-panies that were not facing the same critical juncture, and its value went up in the first quarter of 2001. Amazon stock went down by 60 percent in the summer of 2000, in spite of a dramatic increase in sales of 84 percent in the second quarter of 2000, reaching total sales of almost 3 billion dollars for the year. Granted, Amazon had still not turned out any profit. But, in spite of this, from its creation, Amazon had attracted investors by its conviction that the early winner in the business of selling books and records on-line would build a substantial base for future profits as part of a learning curve. It did not seem unreasonable. Yet, the mood turned sour by contagion from disappointment with more adventurous Internet start-ups—forcing Amazon into thousands of lay-offs and the closing of two facilities in early 2001.

In short: the 2000–2001 shake-up did not concern only, or even mainly, the infant Internet companies. It affected virtually all technology companies, and even more the stock market in general, across the board. Sound companies, with all their credentials in terms of traditional valuation, went down together with the crowd of unruly start-ups. Only a few companies escaped devaluation in the stock market, particularly utility companies, well known to Californians for their impeccable business practices. On the other hand, better spinning ability, or business image-making, were helpful in slowing down the decline in the value of stocks. A telling case is Nokia. Having learned the lesson of untimely announcements the hard way when its stock declined in the summer of 2000, on October 19, 2000 the company announced promising earnings for the end of the quarter: its stock value increased by 27 percent in one day, lifting the Nasdaq index (in spite of the fact that Nokia is not traded on Nasdaq!).

So, rather than a return to the traditional valuation criteria, what the severe downturn of the technology market in 2000–2001 showed was the extent of volatility in financial markets, and particularly in high-growth markets, where investors move at Internet speed. The lesson does not seem to be one of irrational exuberance followed by sudden temperance, but, on the contrary, of jittery behavior structurally determined by globalization, deregulation, and electronic trading. What the record shows is not the return of the traditional business cycle, but the emergence of a new kind of business cycle, indeed of a new business pattern, marked by volatility and by an alternating sharp rise and fall of market valuation, as a result of information turbulences that combine economic criteria with other sources of valuation (Mandel, 2000). In the Internet Age, characterized by systematically volatile, information-driven financial markets, the ability to live dangerously becomes a part of the business way of life.

Work in the e-conomy

If valuation in the financial market provides the bottom line for the performance of the company, it is labor that remains the source of productivity, innovation, and competitiveness. Furthermore, labor is more important than ever in an economy dependent on the ability to retrieve, process, and apply information, increasingly on-line. Indeed, we are in the midst of an information explosion. According to a University of California, Berkeley study (Lyman and Varian, 2000), there are about 550 billion documents on the web (95 percent publicly accessible), and on-line information is growing at the rate of 7.3 million web pages per day. Production of e-mail per year is five hundred times greater than web-page production. The world's annual production of information in different forms amounts to 1.5 billion gigabytes, of which, in 1999, 93 percent were produced in digital form. Therefore, on the one hand, business firms have access to an extraordinary array of information that, with the help of magnetic storage, digital processing, and the Internet, can be recombined and applied to all purposes in all contexts. On the other hand, this puts extraordinary pressure on labor. The e-conomy cannot function without workers able to navigate, both technically and in terms of content, this deep sea of information, organizing it, focusing it, and transforming it into specific knowledge, appropriate for the task and purpose of the work process.

This kind of labor must be highly educated and able to take initiatives. Companies, large or small, depend on the quality and the autonomy of labor. Quality is not simply measured in years of education, but in type of education. Labor in the e-conomy must be able to reprogram itself, in skills, knowledge, and thinking according to changing tasks in an evolving business environment. Self-programmable labor requires a certain type of education, in which the stock of knowledge and information accumulated in the worker's mind can be expanded and modified throughout his or her working life. This has extraordinary consequences for the demands placed on the education system, both during the formative years, and during the constant re-training and re-learning processes that continue throughout adult life. Among other consequences, an e-conomy requires the development of e-learning as a durable companion of professional life. The most important features of this learning process are, first, learning how to learn, since most specific information is likely to become obsolete in a few years, as we operate in an economy changing at Internet speed; secondly, having the ability to transform the information obtained from the learning process into specific knowledge.

However, self-programmable labor cannot deploy its capacity in a traditional, rigid, business environment. Bresnahan, Brynjolffson, and Hitt (2000) have empirically shown the positive feedback loops between information technology, organizational flexibility, and highly skilled labor at the level of the firm. The e-firm, on-line or off-line, is based on a flat hierarchy, a teamwork system, and open, easy interaction between workers and managers, across departments and between levels of the firm. The network enterprise is enacted by net-workers, using Internet capability, and equipped with their own intellectual capital.

Talent is the key factor of production for e-business. Literally everything is based on the capacity to attract, retain, and efficiently use talented workers. In such a competitive, tight labor market for self-programmable labor, firms resort to a number of incentives to retain their best employees. Besides anecdotal gimmicks (perks, gifts, bonuses), the most important strategy to attach employees to the firm is partial payment in stock options, to share the results of the firm. This links the fate of the employee to the success of the firm—at least for some time, until the employee makes enough money to be independent. Examples of extraordinary market capitalization valuation act as magnets to attract the best and brightest to the next promising venture: in 1999, there were about sixty-five new "paper millionnaires" a day in Silicon Valley. Even the sobering downturn of the market in 2000 did not eliminate the motivation, just induced greater caution in mixing life options with stock options.

The stock options form of payment is, in fact, extremely beneficial for firms, not only because it helps to retain labor, but because firms are less burdened with wages. Besides, in the US, companies can deduct the value of stock options from their taxes: in some instances major companies did not pay any corporate taxes as a result of this tax loophole, a remnant from a time when stock options were an exceptional occurrence reserved for a few top executives. As for the employees, the payment in stock options revives, somewhat ironically, the old anarchist ideology of self-management of the company, as they are co-owners, co-producers, and co-managers of the firm.

Autonomy, involvement, and a watered down form of cooperative ownership come at a price: total commitment to the business project, well beyond what contractual arrangements stipulate. For professionals working in, or around, Silicon Valley companies, working time in excess of 65 hours per week is the norm. And there are no rest nights on the brink of a major project delivery. Similar working schedules seem to be pervasive in the Internet industry in Barcelona, Paris, and Helsinki.

The historical revival of work autonomy, after the bureaucratization of the industrial era, is even more evident in the development of small businesses, very often made up of individuals working as consultants and subcontractors. These business entrepreneurs own their means of production (a computer, a telephone line, a mobile phone, a place somewhere, often at home, their education, their experience, and, the main asset, their minds). They accumulate their own capital, which they often invest in the stocks of companies for whom they work. This double movement of aggregation of capital and disaggregation of labor seems to be one of the historical surprises of the e-conomy.

The essential role played by self-programmable labor in e-business has led to a shortage of this kind of labor in the most dynamic industries and areas of the world. From Silicon Valley to Stockholm, and from England to Finland, the most important problem for leading companies has become where to find engineers, computer programmers, e-business professionals, financial analysts, or, for that matter, anyone with the capacity to develop new skills as required by a changing market. However, the growing number of women graduating from college, and the massive entry of women into the paid labor force, are providing a major supply of skilled, flexible, and autonomous labor, as required by the e-conomy. In spite of the persistence of gender discrimination in the corporate world, women have made substantial in-roads at all levels of the occupational structure and, under pressure from women, the wage gap with their male counterparts was reduced during the 1990s. The structural incorporation of women into the labor market has been the indispensable basis for the development of the new economy, with lasting consequences for family life, and for the overall social structure.

The other major source of supply of talent, particularly in the United States, has been immigration. In 2000–2001, the United States was absorbing over 200,000 highly skilled workers a year, on special visas, besides employing additional tens of thousands on line, working from their countries of origin or in "development centers" off-shore, particularly in the Caribbean. Many of these immigrants set up their own companies after obtaining permanent residence. According to a study by Saxenian (1999), in the 1990s of all new companies created in Silicon Valley, about 30 percent had an immigrant CEO from China or India. And this is without counting the numerous cases of immigrant entrepreneurs from other nationalities, particularly from Russia, Israel, and Mexico. Europe, in spite of growing xenophobia, woke up to the reality of the need for professional immigrant labor, as projections for 2004 indicated that over 25 percent of the demand for workers in information technology could not be supplied by European labor markets. In 2000, the UK approved legislation for 100,000 special immigrant visas a year, and Germany did the same, in the midst of public protest, for 20,000 visas. In Finland, Nokia lobbied the government to obtain a reduction of the very high income tax to a 30 percent maximum taxation ceiling for employees working in Finland for a limited period: a necessary condition for Nokia to be able to attract the kind of professional labor that it needs to keep up with the new round of technological innovation.

Interestingly enough, studies by Saxenian and others indicate that immigrants coming to Silicon Valley are not necessarily a loss to their countries of origin (Saxenian, 1999; Balaji, 2000). Many of them, as soon as they are established in a leading technology/business center, create companies in their own countries, and set up a bridge between California and India, Taiwan, Israel, Mexico, and the like. The newly founded companies extend their own networks into the country, so that new entrepreneurs migrate to Silicon Valley, and reproduce the process. So, overall, rather than a case of brain drain, we see the emergence of a system of brain circulation.

To be sure, not all labor either in the e-conomy or in e-business is self-programmable labor. I proposed in my earlier writings the distinction between self-programmable labor and generic labor. Generic labor is embodied in workers who do not have special skills, or special ability to acquire skills in the production process, other than those necessary to execute instructions from management. Generic labor can be replaced by machines, or by generic labor anywhere else in the world, and the precise mix between machines, on-site labor, and distant labor depends on *ad hoc* business calculations. Of course, generic labor does not depend on the qualities of the person. It is the result of the lack of social and personal investment of intellectual capital in a given human being. Also, the tasks performed by generic labor are necessary to the overall economy, and they are not necessarily unskilled in nature. It is the judgment of social organization that makes these tasks unskilled. For instance, one of the fastest-growing, low-skill, service occupations in all countries is private security guards. In itself the activity should be highly skilled. To carry a gun, with a license to use it, should require appropriate training, not only in marksmanship and martial arts, but in legal knowledge, in psychological assessment, in the ability to behave in high-stress situations. All these qualities should require a college-level training, as well as a general capacity to self-program the skills depending on contexts and technological evolution. Yet, social institutions assign low priority to these jobs, in terms of pay, training, and recruitment procedures, so they are filled by generic labor, often with low-quality performance. As knowledge and information diffuse throughout society and throughout the world, the entire labor force could and should become self-programmable. But as long as social institutions, business priorities, and patterns of inequality proceed differently, generic labor is a necessary quantity rather than a specific quality in the decisive contribution of labor to productivity and innovation in the e-conomy.

One fundamental transformation of labor relations is common to both self-programmable and generic labor: flexibility. The networking form of business, the fast pace of the global economy, and the technological ability to work on-line, for individuals and for firms, leads to the emergence of a flexible pattern of employment. The notion of a predictable career pattern, working full-time in a firm or in the public sector, over a long period of time, and under precise, contractual definition of rights and obligations common to much of the workforce, is vanishing from business practice—in spite of its persistence in highly regulated labor markets and in the shrinking public sector. Martin Carnoy (2000) has documented, in his path-breaking book on the transformation of labor in the new economy, how self-employment, part-time work, temporary work, subcontracting, and consulting are expanding in all advanced economies. In less-developed economies, informal activities, entirely unregulated and based on *ad hoc* patterns of employment, account for the majority of the urban labor force in most countries. As a general trend, the "organization man" is out, the "flexible woman" is in. Thus, research by Chris Benner (2001) demonstrated how flexible employment practices, enacted by labor intermediaries and flexible hiring policies, are the distinctive feature of the Silicon Valley economy. A UCSF/Field Institute (1999) survey of a representative sample of the Californian labor force in 1999 provided empirical evidence of the dwindling proportion of traditional employment patterns. Defining a traditional job as a single, full-time, day-shift job, year round, as a permanent employee, paid by the firm for which the work is done and not working from home or as an independent contractor, the study found that only 33 percent of Californian workers fit this pattern. If we add to this

95

"traditional" status the requirement of having three or more years of tenure in the same company, the proportion of working-age Californians fulfilling these criteria drops to 22 percent.

While European labor markets display less flexibility, the overall trend points in the same direction, as documented by Carnoy (2000). What varies between countries, depending on labor legislation and tax laws, is the form of this flexibility. Thus, Italy and the UK have the highest proportion of self-employed workers in the OECD, while The Netherlands went from a considerable unemployment problem in the 1980s to the lowest rate of unemployment in Europe in 2000 by creating numerous part-time jobs (mainly held by women) under the coverage of full social benefits provided by the government.

Work flexibility, variable employment patterns, diversity of working conditions, and individualization of labor relations are systemic features of e-business. From this core of the new economy, flexible labor practices tend to diffuse into the entire labor market, contributing to a new form of social structure that I have characterized under the concept of the network society.

Productivity, Innovation, and the New Economy

If there is a new economy it is because there is a substantial surge in productivity growth. Without a sharp upturn of productivity growth we could still claim that there is a technological revolution, but not necessarily a new economy. Consequently, debate has raged for years among economists on the actual evolution of the rate of productivity, as well as on its sources. Productivity measurement is always tricky, and is particularly complicated in our economy for three major reasons: most people work in services, where labor productivity is most difficult to measure; statistical categories, produced during the industrial era, are woefully inadequate to measure the information economy (for example, the US Labor Department practice, until 1998, of measuring spending in software as consumption, rather than as investment); business works in global networks of production and distribution, so that productivity accounting should, in fact, take into account the contribution to productivity along the entire value chain, which is out of the reach of current accounting methods. Add to these factors the time lag observed by economic historians between technological revolutions and the moment of their impact at the level of the firm, and we can better understand the "productivity paradox" that has baffled economists for years.

However, recent changes in statistical categories in the US and better accounting procedures seem to indicate substantial productivity growth as a result of massive investment in information technology, coupled with network-based organizational change. After all, in terms of economic theory, only an increase in productivity can explain an economy able to grow at a sustained high rate, with quasi-full employment, increase in earnings, and low inflation, for a long period of time, as was the case for the United States between 1993 and the end of 2000. While during 1985–95 US labor productivity grew at an average annual rate of 1.4 percent, from 1996 to 2000 the rate of growth doubled, to 2.8 percent. In the twelve months between the second quarter of 1999 and the second quarter of 2000, labor productivity grew at a staggering rate of 5.2 percent. Various estimates put projected productivity growth for the decade 2000–2010 somewhere between 2.3 and 4 percent per year, although the decline of stock prices in 2000–2001 and beyond could significantly alter the prediction by slowing down investment, and therefore innovation, productivity growth, and economic growth. Yet, in the last quarter of 2000, in the midst of a significant slowdown of the US economy, labor productivity grew at an annual rate of 2.4 percent, lower than in the previous quarter, but still enough to bring the annual productivity growth for the whole of 2000 to 4.3 percent. Thus, even using the lower threshold of the estimates for future productivity growth, at around 2.3 percent per year, this would substantially improve on the performance of US productivity in the two preceding decades, providing the basis for the rise of a new economy, whose shape and logic are still unfolding.

Studies by Stephen Oliner and Daniel Sichel at the Federal Reserve Bank in Washington, and by Harvard's Dale Jongerson and New York Federal's Kevin Stiroh, among others, concluded that investment in information technology, and high productivity in the computer industry, have been decisive factors in spurring productivity growth (Oliner and Sichel, 1994; Sichel, 1997; Jorgenson and Stiroh, 2000; Jorgenson and Yip, 2000). Indeed, the information-technology sector increased its productivity by an annual rate of 24 percent during the 1990s. According to the historical record, the innovators and producers of new techno-logies are the first to adopt their use, as well as the first to train their labor and change their organization accordingly. Thus, early users benefit first from productivity growth. But as their business model diffuses, together with new technology, to other sectors, productivity growth increases as well. This was observed by Brynjolffson and Hitt (2000) in their study of six hundred American firms between 1987 and 1994: they demonstrated that the internal decentralization of the firm and adoption of network-ing forms of organization were the necessary conditions for infor-mation technology to increase productivity. Lucas (1999) has also shown, on the basis of a series of case studies, that the benefits of information-technology investment for the firm, while generally positive, are of different kinds. They are not all measurable in terms of return per investment, but technology is usually an essential factor in positioning the firm in product, process, and market.

In sum, in the US in the second half of the 1990s, there was a substantial increase of investment in information-technology equipment and software, which, in 2000, accounted for 50 percent of total business investment. This investment, together with organ-izational restructuring, and particularly with the diffusion of Internet-based networking as a pervasive business practice, seem to be critical factors in explaining labor productivity growth— which is the ultimate source of value creation, and the foundation of the new economy.

In other areas of the world, both investment in information tech-nology and the diffusion of networking are also proceeding rapidly, particularly in Scandinavia, Western Europe, and in the industrial-ized countries of Asia. Yet, the effects of these changes on labor productivity, measured at the level of national economies, are not observed as yet, except in Finland and Sweden. This can be explained by a combination of factors: the inadequacy of statistical categories, which are even more out of date than in the United States; a smaller proportion of information technology in total capital stock, about 3 percent in Germany and Japan, compared to 7 percent in the US; and the fact that European firms have substantially lagged behind in organizational change and labor flexibility. However, case studies of e-business, as well as productivity statistics and revenue/employee ratios in information-technology sectors, seem to point in the same direction as in the United States. Indeed, as the new economy is a global economy, if e-business were to be confined within the borders of the United States its expansion would ultimately come to a halt, since its productivity growth would outpace the growth of global markets, leading to a crisis of overproduction. The emergence of Do-Co-Mo in Japan, the new entrepreneurial networks in high-technology industries in Taiwan and South Korea, the fast growth of mobile telecommunication industries and services in Scandinavia, the restructuring of the French and German automobile industries around the networking business model, the retooling of the Dutch and German micro-electronic industries, and the emergence of competitive, on-line financial services in London and Frankfurt are illustrations of a deep transformation of the global economy, along the lines of technology-led productivity growth that was first observed in the United States. If these trends, as I believe, are actually rooted in a transformation of the business model, and the diffusion of information technology, they should overcome the downturn of late 2000–2001. But this would require the management of the new kind of business cycle, as I will analyze in the last section of this chapter.

The new economy, spearheaded by e-business, is not an on-line economy, but an economy powered by information technology, dependent on self-programmable labor, and organized around computer networks. These seem to be the sources of labor productivity growth, and thus of wealth creation, in the Information Age. Yet, if labor is the source of productivity, the creative power of labor and the efficiency of business organization ultimately depend on innovation. Innovation is a function of highly skilled labor, and of the existence of knowledge-creation organizations. And the process of innovation is also transformed in the e-conomy, as the uses of the Internet play a fundamental role in how innovation is achieved.

Innovation in the e-conomy

In an e-conomy based on knowledge, information, and intangibles (such as image and connections), innovation is the primordial function. Innovation depends on knowledge generation facilitated by open access to information. And information is on-line. My analysis of the open source movement in the previous chapter shows the essential role of cooperation and open access in the process of innovation. The relationship between cooperation and innovation can be analyzed, following Brian Arthur's (1994) formal economic theory, as a result of network effects, path dependency, and increasing returns in the information economy.

Network effects: the more nodes there are in the network, the greater the benefits of the network to each individual node.

Path dependency: once a given innovation is achieved, technological trajectories will tend to follow the path marked by this innovation, giving a decisive edge to the discoverers and early adopters of the innovation: it is the winner-takes-all system that characterizes business competition in the new economy.

Increasing returns: in an innovation-based economy, the higher investment cost is in the early stages of the process, while marginal costs go down rapidly as innovation becomes embodied in products. For instance, in the production of a new software program, or of a new drug, the R&D costs are usually very high. So, the first disk or the first pill may cost billions. The cost of the second disk, or the first pack of pills, may be negligible.

Let us now apply these mechanisms to a process of innovation taking place in an open-source system, and facilitated by on-line interaction. A product of superior quality (for example, a software program) is generated by the collective effort of a network, an effort in which each participant finds a reward from the freely contributed effort of others. So, innovation is still the product of intelligent labor, but of a collective intellect. No R&D department can match the power of a global, cooperative network—indeed, this is how basic science develops, with extraordinary yields. Once the innovation is generated, the path dependency characteristic of the application of this innovation gives an advantage to those who participated in the networked process of innovation: they are first adopters, first users, first learners, and know better which kinds of products and processes can be developed from this innovation path. So, the process of innovation in the e-conomy is gradually migrating to open-source networks of cooperation, formed not only by freelance individuals, but by entrepreneurs and company employees as well, as it is in the interest of firms to contribute to innovation and to be early beneficiaries of the results of the cooperative effort. How can business make profits out of this co-operatively produced innovation? By designing applications, by selling services, by packaging and customizing, as Red Hat does with Linux, as IBM does with Apache. Or else, by selling equipment that works well on open-source technology, as Sun Microsystems does with Java and Jini.

The logic of cooperation and open source as the crucible of innovation is not limited to software. It is the logic permeating the entire on-line service industry, as portals give access to information and services, as a way to sell advertising, and obtain information that can be re-used for marketing purposes. In this logic, customers are producers, as they provide critical information by their behavior, and their demands, helping e-companies constantly to modify their products and services. In customer-oriented business practice, the ability to interact with consumers as sources of critical information becomes an essential component of the business model. Thus, cooperation in innovation, and competition in applications and services, seem to be the division of labor in the new economy. This logic is also present in the internal workings of e-business. On-line engineering, and open-access management systems within a company, allow workers to organize *ad hoc* cooperation systems as their tasks dictate. When information and interaction are organized in extranets, customers and suppliers (even competitors) enter the network. I have discussed above the economic benefits of this networking model. But there is something else: by ensuring real-time feedback of all those involved in a production/management process, innovation is tested at the outset: product and process constantly innovate themselves, in the common interest of increasing returns for all those participating in the network.

These developments are inducing a new model of relationship between property relations and production relations in the generation and appropriation of wealth. There are areas of cooperation, and common appropriation, linked to areas of competition and private appropriation. While these trends are still embryonic, they may herald a profound transformation of the social logic of innovation, productivity, and economic growth

The New Economy and its Crisis

e-Business is not the business that is exclusively conducted on-line but a new form of conducting business, all kinds of business, by, with, and on the Internet, and other computer networks—with various forms of linkage with on-site production processes and physical transactions. e-Business is at the heart of the emergence of a new economy that is characterized by the critical role of self-programmable labor, technological innovation, and financial market valuation as drivers of the economy. As in all economies, labor productivity growth is the engine of development, and innovation is at the source of productivity. Each one of these processes is enacted and transformed by the use of the Internet as the indispensable medium of networking organization, information-processing, and knowledge generation. The e-conomy gradually transforms the old economy into a new economy, which reaches the entire planet, albeit in an extremely uneven pattern. We now have the threads that, together, constitute the new economy. Exploring the configuration of their structure, and the dynamics of their interaction, may also lead to the understanding of mechanisms of recession and crisis in the new economy, as the expression of new forms of the business cycle.

In its historical debut, the new economy appears to be characterized by a long span of technology-led high growth, with quasi-full employment and low inflation, followed by a sharp downturn that, under certain conditions, could lead to recession, and even to a widespread economic crisis (Mandel, 2000). The new economy emerged in the US in the mid-1990s, inducing the longest, uninterrupted growth period of the past half-century. In the late 1990s it started to spread to the dynamic sectors of other economies around the world, particularly in Europe. On March 10, 2000, technology stocks fell sharply in value, and kept sliding thereafter, inducing a slowdown of economic growth that continued one year later.

The existence of a new economy can be asserted on the basis of enhanced labor productivity and increased competitiveness of firms, as a result of innovation. This innovation refers to technology, process, and product. New information and communication technologies, and particularly the Internet and computer networking in general, are critical in economies essentially based on information-processing and communication. Process is transformed by networking as an efficient, flexible form of management and organization. Networking is highly dependent on communication technology. As in previous technological revolutions, this socio-technical transformation opens the way for a flurry of new products—with varying degrees of fit between these products and market demand and social needs. For instance, the mobile phone, which appeared to be a minor product innovation, became the hottest communication device on the planet, while the much-hyped interactive TV is still waiting for transmission capacity and enticing content to become a profitable business.

Innovation is itself a function of three main factors. The first one is the creation of new knowledge, in science, technology, and management. This refers to the existence of a well-developed R&D system (both public and private) able to supply the fundamentals of innovation. The second is the availability of highly educated, self-programmable labor, able to use new knowledge to increase productivity. In general, this kind of labor is a direct result of the quality and quantity of graduates from the education system. In the case of the United States, immigration of technical professionals has been an equally important element in the development of the new economy. The third factor is the existence of entrepreneurs, able and willing to take the risks to transform innovative business projects into business performance. This partly relates to the existence of an entrepreneurial culture, but also to the openness of the institutions of society toward entrepreneurialism. Thus, in the case of the United States, the openness of its institutions to immigration, and the ease with which new companies can be created, made the US, and particularly some regions, such as California and New York, a point of attraction to any willing entrepreneur from anywhere in the world. But the notion of entrepreneurship cannot be limited to young start-ups or dream-pursuing immigrants. When Jorma Ollila and his team restructured the Nokia Group in 1992, the company was on the edge of being sold, hampered by its diverse investments in multiple, mature, low-profit markets. The decision to sell most of the assets of the company, and focus its entire business on mobile phones and networks infrastructure, was, at that time, a risky one. It was an act of entrepreneurship.

Yet, even the most daring entrepreneurs, counting on the best technology, and conceiving a sound business plan, cannot do much without money. This is why the financing of the new economy is the cornerstone of its existence. And this finance essentially relies on the stock market, and venture capital, according to the mechanisms analyzed above in this chapter. Therefore, while productivity and competitiveness are the factors underlying high economic growth without inflation, and innovation is the driver of the new economy, finance is the source of everything. High valuation of potential innovation on the stock market, and its anticipation by venture capital, were the mechanisms that mobilized capital from all sources (and particularly from large, institutional investors, such as pension funds) and channeled it into innovation.

The key question is, then, why valuation of stocks reached such unprecedented high levels. I have explained earlier in this chapter the mechanisms of financial valuation, largely dependent on information turbulences that include traditional economic criteria, but also many other sources combining with each other to affect investors' behavior. But I want to emphasize what appears to be an essential factor in the valuation process: expectations, anticipation of higher value in the long run. In fact, investors were betting on the technological revolution. It was not a foolish idea. The notion that early producers and adopters of new technologies and business models would be among the winners in the future market is not speculation. It is risk-taking investment, linked to the development of innovation in the economy, to the potential network effects in the growth of new forms of business, and to the anticipation of increasing returns on investment. In fact, higher productivity growth, and sustained, low-inflation economic growth, vindicated this claim. But for the new economy to keep growing, innovation and productivity had to continue to grow at a fast pace, and this required a steady flow of investment, dependent on the continuity of expectations of high rewards for new investors. Because these expectations did not discriminate between risky, but sound, business projects and unreasonable ventures, they were prone to sharp reversal as soon as cases of obvious failure became apparent. Yet, it is still unclear why the market nose-dived in 2000–2001 without much differentiation between a variety of technology stocks with different business prospects. Dot.com stocks (obviously the riskier projects) went down first, but all technology stocks followed over the ensuing year, and this had an impact on stock values in most other industries. From their peak in early 2000, by March 2001 the Nasdaq index was down by 60 percent, the Standard & Poor 500 by 23 percent, and the Dow Jones by 12 percent. In the US stock market, about 4.6 trillion dollars in nominal wealth vanished, equivalent to about 50 percent of the US GDP, or four times the amount of losses sustained in the October 1987 market crash. In the UK and Germany, average stock value in 2000–2001 declined by 10 percent (*Business Week*, 2001).

For some analysts, this "market adjustment" was the overdue bursting of a speculative financial bubble. I think the "bubble" metaphor is misleading because it refers to an implicit notion of natural market equilibrium, which seems to be superseded in the world of interdependent global financial markets operating at high speed, and processing complex information turbulences in real time. What we observed empirically in the period 1996–2000 was that the market rewarded without much discrimination all kinds of technology stocks, and the same market in 2000–2001 punished all technology stocks with the same equal-opportunity approach to devaluation. This was regardless of the performance of companies, as I illustrated with some examples of technology companies above. So, what happened? Trying to open the black box of information turbulences that hit the market in 2000, reversing expectations, we find a disparate collection.

Most dot.com companies failed their business model. Business-to-consumer (B2C) e-commerce underestimated the cost and complexity of physical delivery to customers. Virtual commerce discovered the reality of click-and-mortar business—requiring much greater investment, logistics, and management skills than anticipated. For all the assurances about credit-card security, customers were nervous about giving away their information on-line, and with good reason. Advertising as the predominant form of financing free content provision on the web was a monumental fiasco: it was the result of misunderstanding the specificity of the Internet *vis-à-vis* television. Targeted advertising (disregarding consumer privacy) also received a partial rebuttal from people unwilling to tolerate their profiling. To some extent the fast commercialization of the Internet betrayed the promise of free access, so that many potential customers decided to bypass fee-paying websites, except for those directly fitting their needs. The once booming on-line market for pet supplies was quickly saturated.

Technological restructuring in the information-technology industry added to the level of uncertainty. The anticipated end of the PC era, and the actual decline in PC orders, hit Intel, Hewlett Packard, and Microsoft. The trial against Microsoft, while hailed by many in Silicon Valley, threw a cloud of suspicion on the future of mighty technology companies. The high expectations of the "mobile Internet," while justified in the long term in my opinion, turned into a short-term disappointment in the face of the technical and business difficulties to deliver the promise on time, particularly in the US market. In Europe, the staggering sums paid by companies to governments for UMTS licenses of mobile telephony sent jitters throughout the markets, concerned about the financial standing of major telecommunication companies.

There was also, in 2000, a significant decline in the rate of growth of information-technology spending by companies, particularly in the United States. This may have been the only real casualty from the bogus year 2000 (Y2K) crisis. Faced with the need (or the belief in the need) to update their aging systems before Y2K, many companies and public services decided to leapfrog into new networking technology and cutting-edge software. This led to a boom of investment in ICT in 1998 and 1999, which included replacement levels usually scheduled for a later date, lessening the need for new equipment in 2000–2001. In the midst of a tense market, any announcement by major technology companies (such as Cisco) of lower earnings than expected because of a slowdown in capital equipment spending added to the negative mood of investors.

There is also the fact that many of these investors, particularly institutional investors and banks, had been buying stocks in the boom period way beyond what their prudence should normally dictate regarding the protection of their creditors. They did it because they were confident that their information systems would send warning signals in advance to pull out of the risk market before losses would offset their substantial gains. Thus, when the market pointed downwards, many of the largest investors could not afford to wait: they pulled back their investment strategies to a more conservative approach, contributing to the devaluation of the technology stocks they were holding.

Political instability also contributed a great deal to market uncertainty, particularly in two cases. Japan, in 2000–2001, seemed to be heading for another political crisis, as mismanagement and government corruption were exposed, and the Japanese economy, the second largest in the world, appeared unable to pull itself out of stagnation. In the United States the soap opera of the contested presidential election added uncertainty and held back investors at a critical moment of market transition.

Finally, in a financial market working at high speed on the basis of expectations and information, investors' perception is influenced by the values and opinions of the business establishment and of academic economists. It is a well-known fact that some prominent academic economists never believed in the existence of a new economy, rejected the importance of information technology, disregarded or downplayed the evidence of productivity growth and business innovation, and kept pounding away at the inevitability of the bursting of the bubble, until they were gratified with the realization of their self-fulfilling prophecy many years after their earlier predictions. Echoed by traditional leaders of traditional companies, a number of academic economists played a substantial role in diminishing expectations of the harvest of innovation in the information economy. In retrospect, it is a miracle that investors could fuel the new economy with their expectations for so long, in the face of so many expert opinions forecasting doom. It is probably to the credit of Alan Greenspan that markets still believed in what they were seeing through the screen of mainstream economic analysis. Greenspan kept defending the reality of the new economy, based on information-technology investment and productivity growth, partly because he was surrounded, in the Federal Reserve, by some of the best economic minds in productivity analysis in the United States (such as Oliner and Sichel, among others), and partly because he instinctively perceived that only an underlying productivity surge could explain, in strict economic theory, the behavior of an economy whose pulse he was feeling in real time. As soon as signs of a downturn appeared in the stock market, many conventional economists and veterans of the old economy, with a sigh of relief, seized the opportunity to push for a return to business as usual. And, yet, business can probably never be as it was, after its transformation by almost a decade of development of the new economy.

Under these circumstances, processed in a complex system of information turbulences, expectations for stock valuation in the technology sector were reversed, drying out risk capital investment, and therefore slowing down the pace of innovation, in a process analyzed, and in fact predicted, by Michael Mandel in the summer of 2000, although his gloomy prospect of a full-scale Internet depression is unlikely to materialize for reasons that Mandel himself explains.

Since I never dare to predict the future, I concentrate here on the analytical implications of the new economy's slowdown in 2000–2001. In the scheme of analysis presented above, the main driver of the new economy is the financial market. Without IPOs, without stock options, and without the expectation of high growth of stock value, there is no risk capital investment, and entrepreneurialism and technological discovery do not translate into business innovation. Without innovation, productivity growth slows down, and competition is limited, thus potentially allowing traditional firms to raise prices and trigger inflation, as Mandel (2000) suggests. The combination of lower growth and employment with higher inflation leads to lower consumption, thus increasing the severity of the downturn. Since both companies and households borrowed massively during the boom, often using their equity as collateral, and much of their wealth evaporated with the fall of the stock market, the prospects of a recession increase. However, if the stock market bounces back before the damage from disinvestment becomes extensive, the growth engine of the new economy could be quickly re-started. By the time you read this you will know the continuation of the story. But not the end—because this is not the end of the new economy, but the beginning of its second stage, in its different versions, in its upswings followed by its downturns.

So there is indeed a business cycle in the new economy. But what is different from the industrial economy—and I concur again in this with Michael Mandel's (2000) remarkable analysis—is that the fluctuations of the stock market are synchronized with the business cycle, for the simple reason that they drive the investment and innovation cycles. The convergence of financial cycles, innovation cycles, and business cycles reinforces each other in the dynamics of their upturns and downturns. This results in both an acceleration of growth and an accentuation of the severity of recession.

The crisis of one of the icons of the new economy, Cisco Systems, is a good illustration of the link between financial cycle and business cycle. Faced with uncertainties in the economy, with sliding stock-market values, and having stockpiled Internet equipment in 1999, in the second half of 2000, companies in the US, and around the world, put the brakes on their capital spending—particularly on Internet networking equipment. Cisco did not read the market signals correctly. Having previously lost sales because of its underestimation of rapid market expansion in the previous quarters, and having experienced a quarterly increase of revenue of over 50 percent during 1999–2000, Cisco kept building up capacity and inventory in the fall of 2000. Its forecasting models could not seize the extreme volatility of the market. In the first quarter of 2001, faced with declining demand, Cisco's revenues dropped 5 percent from a year earlier, for the first time in a decade of high-flying expansion, and further decline was expected for the following quarter. It proceeded with lay-offs of thousands of workers, and took a 2.5 billion dollar charge to write down inventory. Its stock plummeted to 18 dollars a share, down 78 percent from its high-water mark in March 2000. Devaluation of its stock deprived Cisco of the financial ability to continue its acquisitions policy, a key element of its strategy to enhance technology in the company by buying know-how and expertise embodied in innovative firms. Thus, devaluation of stock, decline in revenue and profits, and diminishing technological capacity fed into each other. This weakened Cisco's position *vis-à-vis* some of its competitors, particularly in the high-end router market, in which Juniper Networks cut into Cisco's share of the market, which dropped from 78 percent in 1999 to 65 percent in 2000. Cisco still expected 30 percent revenue growth for 2002–2005, counting on a new wave of global expansion of the Internet. It may be right, and in any case, the company will remain among the top manufacturers of networking equipment, a clearly expanding market in the coming decade.

But this is beyond my point. The analytical meaning of Cisco's crisis is two-fold. First, electronic networking cannot substitute for a flawed strategy: the volatility of the new economy is systemic, and, therefore, business projections cannot rely on the data of the past, including the recent past. What flexible networking allows is the ability of companies to practice "just-in-time reaction" to market signals. In this sense, Cisco's networked business model still has a long way to go because the technology seems to be better than the economics implicit in the model of management. Secondly, the connection between financing, innovation, and market demand opens the possibility of sharp downturns for any given business, following prolonged periods of high growth. For instance, the reliance on stock-based acquisitions to spur technological innovation makes the company excessively dependent on its stock valuation. With limited capacity to raise capital and without autonomous sources of innovation, a new economy company is in serious difficulty. It is therefore essential to maintain endogenous R&D capacity in the company to grow technological innovation organically from within, since it is this innovation that can help the company to regain competitiveness, and thus upgrade the value of its stock. The relative crisis of Cisco (a highly innovative and productive manufacturer of essential networking equipment) shows that the downturn of the new economy in 2000–2001 was not simply the bursting of the financial bubble of dot.com companies. It was the expression of new forms of business cycle that affect industries across the board, with particularly serious consequences for those companies that are based on a high-growth strategy, which can suddenly reverse into a fast deacceleration of its activity.

Let me recapitulate the analytical lessons. The new economy is driven by a highly sensitive stock market that finances high-risk innovation at the source of high productivity growth. This is a high-stakes economy: high growth and extraordinary wealth creation go hand in hand with potential sharp downturns and wealth destruction. Once market-valuation mechanisms spiral downwards, the slump cannot be halted simply by price mechanisms: it requires a reversal of expectations. Otherwise, by the time stock prices become a bargain, there may be too little money to buy them, and too much fear to abandon the safe havens for savings that appear in times of retrenchment. Even new waves of technological innovation (in biotechnology, in the mobile Internet, in nanotechnology) cannot reactivate the economy unless there is trust in their future business prospects.

At its core, the new economy is based on culture: on the culture of innovation, on the culture of risk, on the culture of expectations, and, ultimately, on the culture of hope in the future. Only if this culture survives the nay-sayers of the old economy of the industrial era may the new economy prosper again. However, the knowledge and the experience of the fragility of this process of wealth creation may induce a new personal philosophy in the way we will live the second stage of the new economy.

Reading Links

Ali-Yrkko, Jyrki (2001) *Nokia's Network: Gaining Competitiveness from Cooperation*. Helsinki: Toulestieto Oy.

—— Paija, Laura, Reilly, Catherine, and Yla-Anttila, Pekka (2000) *Nokia: A Big Company in a Small Country*. Helsinki: Toulestieto Oy, The Research Institute of the Finnish Economy.

Arthur, Brian (1994) *Increasing Returns and Path Dependence in the Economy*. Ann Arbor: University of Michigan Press.

Balaji, P. (1999) "The transformation and structure of the high technology industrial complex in Bangalore," unpublished PhD dissertation, University of California, Department of City and Regional Planning, Berkeley, California.

Benner, Chris (2001) *Flexible Work in the Information Economy: Labor Markets in Silicon Valley*. Oxford: Blackwell.

Bresnahan, Timothy, Brynjolffson, Erik, and Hitt, Lorin M. (2000) "Information technology, workplace organization, and the demand for skilled labor: firm-level evidence," Cambridge, MA: MIT–Sloan School Center for E-business, working paper.

Brynjolfsson, Erik and Hitt, Lorin M. (2000) *Computing Productivity: Firm-level Evidence*. Cambridge, MA: MIT–Sloan School Center for E-business, working paper.

—— —— and Yang, Shinkyu (2000) "Intangible assets: how the interaction of computers and organization structure affects stock market valuations," Cambridge, MA: MIT–Sloan School Center for E-business, working paper.

Bunnell, David (2000) *Making the Cisco Connection: The Story Behind the Real Internet Superpower*. New York: John Wiley.

Burton-Jones, Alan (1999) *Knowledge Capitalism: Business, Work, and Learning in the New Economy*. Oxford: Oxford University Press.

Business Week (2001) "Rethinking the Internet: Special Report," March 26: p. 116 ff.

Carnoy, Martin (2000) *Sustaining the New Economy: Work, Family and Community in the Information Age*. Cambridge, MA: Harvard University Press.

Castells, Manuel (1996/2000) *The Rise of the Network Society*. Oxford: Blackwell.

Chandler, Alfred D. and Cortada, James W. (eds) (2000) *A Nation Transformed by Information: How Information has Shaped the United States from Colonial Times to the Present*. New York: Oxford University Press.

Garber, Peter (2000) *Famous First Bubbles: The Fundamentals of Early Mania*. Cambridge, MA: MIT Press.

Gupta, Udayan (ed.) (2000) *Done deals: Venture Capitalists Tell their Stories*. Boston, MA: Harvard Business School Press.

Hartman, Amir and Sifonis, John, with John Kador (2000) *Net Ready: Strategies for Success in the E-conomy*. New York: McGraw-Hill.

Jorgenson, Dale and Stiroh, Kevin (2000) *Raising the Speed Limit: US Economic Growth in the Information Age*, Brooking Papers on Economic Activity, volume 2. Washington, DC: The Brookings Institution.

—— and Yip, Eric (2000) "Whatever happened to productivity? Investment and growth in the G-7," in E. R. Dean *et al.* (2000) *New Developments in Productivity Analysis*. Chicago, IL: University of Chicago Press.

Kelly, Kevin (1998) *New Rules for the New Economy*. New York: Viking Press.

Lucas, Henry C. (1999) *Information Technology and the Productivity Paradox*. New York: Oxford University Press.

Mandel, Michael (2000) *The Coming Internet Depression*. New York: Basic Books.

Nokia/Insight (2001) *Business Review 2000*.

Oliner, Stephen and Sichel, Daniel (1994) *Computers and Output Growth Revisited: How Big is the Puzzle?*, Brooking Papers on Economic Activity. Washington, DC: The Brookings Institution.

Saxenian, Anna L. (1999) *Immigrant Entrepreneurs in Silicon Valley*. San Francisco: Public Policy Institute of California.

Schiller, Dan (1999) *Digital Capitalism: Networking the Global Market System*. Cambridge, MA: MIT Press.

Shapiro, Carl and Varian, Hal R. (1999) *Information Rules. A Strategic Guide to the Network Economy*. Boston, MA: Harvard Business School Press.

Shiller, Robert (1999) *Irrational Exhuberance*. New Haven, CT: Yale University Press.

Sichel, Daniel (1997) *The Computer Revolution: An Economic Perspective*. Washington, DC: The Brookings Institution.

UCSF/Field Institute (1999) *The 1999 California Work and Health Survey*. San Francisco: University of California at San Francisco, Institute for Health Policy Studies.

Vlamis, Anthony and Smith, Bob (2001) *Do You? Business the Yahoo! Way*. Milford, CT: Capstone.

Volcker, Paul (2000) "A sea of global fianance," in Will Hutton and Anthony Giddens (eds), *On the Edge: Living in Global Capitalism*. London: Jonathan Cape.

Zook, Matthew (2001) "The geography of the Internet industry: venture capital, Internet start-ups, and regional development," unpublished PhD dissertation, University of California, Department of City and Regional Planning, Berkeley, California.

e-Links

www.forrester.com
An authoritative source of estimates and projections on the evolution of e-business.

www.internetindicators.com
University of Texas study of e-commerce.

www.neweconomyindex.org
Collection and analysis of data on the impact of the new economy on cities, states, and the country in the United States.

www.industrystandard.com
A useful website of one of the leading publications on high-technology industries.

www.business2.com
The website of a well-informed publication on e-commerce.

www.redherring.com/
Website of *Red Herring*, one of the leading journals on venture capital and e-commerce.

www.dotcom.com/
Network solutions database on businesses using the web.

www.ventureeconomics.com/
Information on private equity investing.

www.pwcmoneytree.com/
PriceWaterhouseCoopers quarterly study of venture capital investments.

http://ebusiness.mit.edu/erik
Website posting a series of research papers by Erik Brynjolffson and his collaborators, leading analysts of the relationship between information technology, business organization, and productivity.

www.sims.berkeley.edu/people/hal/articles.html
Lyman, Peter and Varian, Hal (2000) "How much information?," Berkeley, CA: University of California, SIMS, Research Report, October 19. Two respected scholars' estimate of the amount of information in the world in its various formats.

Chapter 4

Virtual Communities or Network Society?

The emergence of the Internet as a new communication medium has been associated with conflicting claims about the rise of new patterns of social interaction. On the one hand, the formation of virtual communities, primarily based on on-line communication, was interpreted as the culmination of an historical process of separation between locality and sociability in the formation of community: new, selective patterns of social relations substitute for territorially bound forms of human interaction. On the other hand, critics of the Internet, and media reports, sometimes relying on studies by academic researchers, argue that the spread of the Internet is leading to social isolation, to a breakdown of social communication and family life, as faceless individuals practice random sociability, while abandoning face-to-face interaction in real settings. Moreover, a great deal of attention has been focused on social exchanges based on fake identities and role-playing. Thus, the Internet has been accused of gradually enticing people to live their own fantasies on-line, escaping the real world, in a culture increasingly dominated by virtual reality.

Much of this rather sterile debate has been flawed by three limitations. First, it largely preceded the widespread diffusion of the Internet, building its statements on the observation of a few experiences among early users of the Internet—thus maximizing the social distance between the users of the Internet and society at large. Secondly, it proceeded in the absence of a substantial body of reliable empirical research on the actual uses of the Internet. And, thirdly, it was built around rather simplistic, and ultimately misleading, questions, such as the ideological opposition between the harmonious local community of an idealized past and the alienated existence of the lonely netizen, too often associated in the public image with the stereotype of a computer nerd.

At present, these limitations are fading away, and we should be able to assess the patterns of sociability arising from the use of the Internet, at least in developed societies, where there is already mass diffusion of the Internet. While scholarly research in this field still does not match the importance of the topic, we do now have enough evidence and analysis to base our interpretation on grounds less shaky than those of futurology and pop journalism. However, the kind of questions dominating the public debate are still couched in simplistic, ideological dichotomies that make an understanding of the new patterns of social interaction difficult. Thus, I shall proceed with caution in building the argument presented in this chapter, first dispelling some common errors concerning social behavior associated with communication on the Internet, then trying to sort out what we know about the matter, and finally trying to make sense of this knowledge in order to propose a few hypotheses on the patterns of sociability emerging in our societies.

In so doing, I will be relying on the efforts of several scholars to synthesize and interpret available evidence on the relationship between the Internet and society. Particularly valuable for the elaboration of my reflections have been the studies of Barry Wellman and his colleagues, the overview of studies on virtual communities by Steve Jones, and the remarkable review of Internet-related social studies written by Di Maggio, Hargittai, Neuman, and Robinson. Other sources used and commented on in this chapter are indicated as Reading Links at the end of the chapter.

The Social Reality of the Internet's Virtuality

First of all, the uses of the Internet are, overwhelmingly, instrumental, and closely connected to the work, family, and everyday life of Internet users. e-Mail represents over 85 percent of Internet usage, and most of this e-mail volume is related to work purposes, to specific tasks, and to keep in touch with family and friends in real life (Anderson and Tracey, 2001; Howard, Rainie, and Jones, 2001; Tracey and Anderson, 2001). While chat rooms, news groups, and multi-purpose Internet conferences were meaningful for early Internet users, their quantitative and qualitative importance has dwindled with the spread of the Internet.

The Internet has been appropriated by social practice, in all its diversity, although this appropriation does have specific effects on social practice itself, as I will discuss below. Role-playing and identity-building as the basis of on-line interaction are a tiny proportion of Internet-based sociability, and this kind of practice seems to be heavily concentrated among teenagers. Indeed, teenagers are the people who are in the process of discovering their identity, of experimenting with it, of finding out who they really are or would like to be, thus offering a fascinating field of research for the understanding of identity construction and experimentation. Yet, the proliferation of studies on this matter distorted the public perception of the social practice of the Internet as the privileged terrain for personal fantasies. Most often, it is not. It is an extension of life as it is, in all its dimensions, and with all its modalities. Moreover, even in role-playing and informal chat rooms, real lives (including real lives on-line) seem to shape the interaction on-line. Thus, Sherry Turkle, the pioneer of the studies of identity-building on the Internet, concludes her classic study by observing that "the notion of the real fights back. People who live parallel lives on the screen are nevertheless bound by the desires, pain, and mortality of their physical selves. Virtual communities offer a dramatic new context in which to think about human identity in the age of the Internet" (Turkle, 1995: 267). Similarly, Nancy Baym, studying the behavior of on-line communities on the basis of her ethnographic study of r.a.t.s. (a news group discussing soap operas), states that the "reality seems to be that many, probably most social users of computer mediated communication, create on-line selves consistent with their off-line identities" (Baym, 1998: 55). In short, role-playing is a telling social experience, but one that does not represent a significant proportion of social interaction on the Internet nowadays.

The early stages of Internet use, in the 1980s, were heralded as the coming of a new age of free communication and personal fulfillment in the virtual communities built around computer-mediated communication. Statements such as that by John Perry Barlow, co-founder of the libertarian Electronic Frontier Foundation, are representative of this prophetic vein: "We are now creating a space in which people of the planet can have [a new] kind of communication relationship: I want to be able to completely interact with the consciousness that's trying to communicate with me" (Barlow, 1995: 40). The influential book by Howard Rheingold, *The Virtual Community* (1993) set the tone of the debate by forcefully arguing for the birth of a new form of community, bringing people together on-line around shared values and interests, and creating ties of support and friendship that could also extend into face-to-face interaction. Unbounded sociability was the promise. And the experience of the WELL, a virtual community that emerged in the San Francisco Bay area in the mid-1980s, with the participation of key figures of the early Internet culture, such as Stuart Brand, Larry Brilliant, and Howard Rheingold, seemed fo fit the model. Yet, as the Internet diffused into the mainstream of society, its effects on sociability became considerably less dramatic. Even the WELL experienced a considerable transformation over the years, as pressures of commercialization, and subsequent changes of ownership, transformed its character, and its membership, as documented in a study by Zhou (2000).

In contrast to claims purporting the Internet to be either a source of renewed community or a cause of alienation from the real world, social interaction on the Internet does not seem to have a direct effect on the patterning of everyday life, generally speaking, except for adding on-line interaction to existing social relationships. Thus, Karina Tracey, reporting on a major longitudinal study of household uses of the Internet in the UK, conducted for British Telecom, observes not much difference between Internet users and non-users in their social behavior and everyday life, after the proper controls for social and demographic variables are introduced (Tracey, 2000). Anderson *et al.* (1999), analyzing the data of the same BT study, find that computer-mediated communication and telephone comunication reinforce each other, particularly in contacts with friends. While computer users are less likely to have regular person-to-person contact with relatives than non-computer users, the researchers assign these differences to social class differences: people of higher social status tend to have more friends, who are more diverse and live at a greater distance, so e-mail is a good instrument to keep in touch with this wider network of personal contacts. On the other hand, people from lower social classes tend to have more casual contacts with family and friends, so they have less need to reach out at a distance.

Summarizing the findings of their study, which included 2,600 individuals in a thousand households in the UK, Anderson and Tracey (2001: 16) concluded that:

there is no evidence from this data that individuals who now have Internet access in the household and who use it, are spending less time watching television, reading books, listening to the radio or engaged in social activity in the household in comparison with individuals who do not (or who no longer) have Internet access in their household. The only changes that can be associated with gaining Internet access are an increase in time spent e-mailing and web surfing—a staggeringly obvious result. The only changes that can be associated with losing Internet access are less time spent on food preparation and cooking, changes in educational circumstances and home-based paid employment.

In the US, Katz, Rice, and Aspden (2001) analyzed the relationship between use of the Internet, civic involvement, and social interaction on the basis of national probability telephone surveys conducted in 1995, 1996, 1997, and 2000. They found higher or equal level of community and political involvement among Internet users compared to non-users. They also found a positive association between Internet use and frequency of telephone calls and a greater level of social interaction. Internet users were more likely than non-users to meet with friends, and to have a social life away from home, although their networks of social interaction were more spatially dispersed than those of non-users. For both long-time and recent Internet users, on-line activity did not have much impact on time spent with family and friends. One-tenth of Internet users met new friends on-line and were active in on-line communities.

Similar findings are reported by Howard, Rainie, and Jones (2001) on the basis of a 2000 survey of a representative, national sample conducted by the Pew Institute's Internet and American Life Project (2000): use of e-mail enhances social life with family and friends, and extends overall social contacts, after controlling for possible intervening variables other than e-mail use. A survey by Uslaner in 1999 (as cited by Di Maggio, Hargittai, Neuman, and Robinson, 2001) showed that users of the Internet tend to have larger social networks than non-users. Robert Putnam, in his major book on the decline of civic engagement in America, *Bowling Alone*, asserts that: "We also know that early users of Internet technology were no less (and no more) civically engaged than anyone else. By 1999 three independent studies (including my own) had confirmed that once we control for the higher educational level of Internet users, they are indistinguishable from non-users when it comes to civic engagement" (Putnam, 2000: 170).

If anything, the Internet seems to have a positive effect on social interaction, and it tends to increase exposure to other sources of information. Di Maggio, Hargittai, Neuman, and Robinson (2001) report findings from surveys of public participation showing that Internet users (after controlling for other variables) attended more arts events, read more literature, went to more movies, watched more sports, and played more sports than non-users. A survey of a national sample of Americans conducted by a UCLA research team, and published on-line in October 2000, found that two-thirds of the 2,096 respondents had been on-line at some point during the preceding year. Of these, 75 percent declared that they did not feel that they were ignored by family or friends as a consequence of their Internet activity. Instead, they said that the use of e-mail, websites, and chat rooms had had a moderately positive impact on their ability to make friends and communicate with their families (Cole *et al.*, 2000).

Moreover, Barry Wellman and his colleagues have shown, in a stream of studies over the past half-decade, a positive, cumulative effect between intensity of use of the Internet and density of social relationships. Perhaps the most significant findings are those reported by the Wellman team on the basis of a survey of 40,000 users in North America, conducted through the National Geographic website in the fall of 1998. They found that the use of e-mail added to social interaction face to face, by phone, and by letter, and did not substitute for other forms of social interaction. The positive impact of e-mail use on sociability was more important for interacting with friends than with kin, and was particularly relevant for keeping in touch with friends or relatives living at a distance. Higher-educated people seemed to be more eager to e-mail their friends at a distance. Younger users tended to e-mail friends, while older users privileged family connections in their e-mail practice. These patterns of sociability were similar for both men and women.

Developing this research perspective, Hampton and Wellman (2000) conducted an exemplary study in 1998–9 on the most advanced wired suburb in Canada. "Netville" is a suburb of Toronto that was sold as the "first interactive new home community". Some 120 home-owners (of lower middle class status) were offered high bandwidth, full-time connection to the Internet, free of charge for two years, in exchange for agreeing to be studied. A total of 65 percent of the households accepted the deal, making possible not only their observation, but also a comparison with those residents of the same suburb who did not have Internet connection. Residents of "Netville" who were users of the Internet were found to have a higher number of strong social ties, of weak ties, and of knowing ties within the suburb, and outside the suburb, than those without Internet connection. Internet use enhanced sociability both at a distance and in the local community. People were more aware of local news by accessing the community e-mail system that served as a tool of communication among neighbors. Internet use strengthened social relationships both at a distance and at a local level for strong and weak ties, for instrumental or emotional purposes, as well as for social participation in the community. Indeed, Internet users mobilized at the end of the period of the trial to obtain an extension of their connection, and they used the community mailing list for their mobilization. Thus, overall, in the "Netville" experiment there was a positive feedback effect between on-line and off-line sociability, with Internet usage enhancing and maintaining social ties and social involvement for most users. Patrice Riemens (personal communication, 2001) reports a similar "wired community" experiment in The Netherlands, which also led to the mobilization of the users to ask for greater connectivity beyond the level that KPN, the Internet service provider, was ready to deliver.

There are, however, conflicting reports on the effects of Internet usage on sociability. In the US, two panel studies are often cited as evidence of the isolating effect of the Internet: a Stanford University on-line survey of 4,000 users conducted by Nie and Erdring (2000), and the highly publicized Pittsburgh study, conducted by Kraut et al. (1998). Nie and Erdring observed a pattern of declining person-to-person interaction and loss of social environment among heavy users of the Internet, while reporting that for the majority of the users there was no significant change in their lives. Kraut et al. (1998), in a carefully designed panel study of a sample of 169 families during the first two years of their experience with computer-mediated communication, found that greater use of the Internet was associated with a decline in the participants' communication with family members in the household, a decline in the size of their social circle, and an increase in their depression and loneliness.

Researchers have tried to interpret these studies, in sharp contrast with most of the available evidence, without questioning the quality of the studies themselves, which originated from highly respected scholarly institutions (Stanford University and Carnegie Mellon University). In the case of the Pittsburgh study, an important factor seems to have been the fact that these households were first-time users of the Internet: indeed, they were provided with computers by the researchers in order to observe their behavior. Di Maggio, Hargittai, Neuman, and Robinson (2001) note that, on the basis of a study conducted by Neuman and co-workers in 1996, novice users of the Internet tend to experience high levels of frustration with a medium that they have not really mastered, and that requires an effort on their part to break with their habits. Thus some of the effects observed by Kraut *et al.* (1998) may have been linked to inexperience with Internet use, rather than use of the Internet itself. Indeed, in the study conducted by Katz, Rice, and Aspden (2001), on the results of national telephone surveys, in 1995 Internet users reported a sense of overload, stress, and dissatisfaction with their lives in a greater proportion than non-users did. Yet, in 2000, while still feeling "life overload" in higher proportion than non-users, Internet users reported greater satisfaction, and more intense social interaction with family and friends, than did non-users, once controlling for other variables is done. So, it may well be that the insertion of the Internet into the practice of life, and familiarity with the medium, favor adaptation to the new technological environment, canceling initial negative reactions during the period of introduction of the Internet among the non-computer literate population.

In the case of Nie and Erdring's survey (2000) the reported loss of sociability concerned only the most frequent users of the Internet, which could indicate the existence of a threshold of Internet use beyond which on-line interaction takes a toll on off-line sociability. This can be better understood on the basis of another study reported by Di Maggio, Hargittai, Neuman, and Robinson (2001), according to which, while Internet users do not show declining sociability, after a certain threshold of on-line activity they do substitute Internet usage for other activities, such as housework, family care, or sleep.

Thus, overall, the body of evidence does not support the thesis that Internet use leads to lower social interaction and greater social isolation. But there are some indications that, under certain circumstances, Internet use may act as a substitute for other social activities. Since studies supporting alternative theses have been conducted at different times, in different contexts, and at different stages of the diffusion of Internet usage, it is difficult to reach definitive conclusions on the effects of the Internet on sociability. But it may be that the real issue is whether the right kind of question is being asked. This is, in fact, the position of some of the leading researchers in this field of study, such as Wellman, Haythornthwaite, Putnam, Jones, Di Maggio, Hargittai, Neuman, Robinson, Kiesler, Anderson, Tracey, and others. Namely, that the study of sociability in/on/with the Internet has to be situated within the context of the transformation of patterns of sociability in our society. This is not to neglect the importance of the technological medium, but to insert its specific effects into the overall evolution of patterns of social interaction and into their relationship to the material supports of this interaction: space, organizations, and communication technologies.

Communities, Networks, and the Transformation of Sociability

The notion of "virtual communities," advanced by the pioneers of social interaction on the Internet, had a major virtue: it called attention to the emergence of new technological supports for sociability, different from, but not necessarily inferior to, previous forms of social interaction. But it also induced a major misunderstanding: the term "community", with all its powerful connotations, confused different forms of social relationship, and prompted ideological discussion between those nostalgic for the old, spatially bounded community and the enthusiastic supporters of Internet-enabled communities of choice. Indeed, for urban sociologists, this is a very old discussion, which reproduces previous debates between those seeing the process of urbanization as the disappearance of meaningful forms of community life, to be replaced by selective, weaker ties between households scattered in the anonymous metropolis, and those identifying the city with the liberation of people from traditional forms of social control. It is highly doubtful whether such culturally homogeneous and spatially bounded communities ever existed, as argued in the devastating critique by Oscar Lewis of Robert Redfield's classic work on the Mexican village of Tepoztlan (now a fashionable hang-out place for cosmopolitan elites), which was the cornerstone of the anthropological view of community as a folk society. Yet, place-based sociability was indeed an important source of support and social interaction, both in agricultural societies, and in the early stages of the industrial era—with the additional caveat that this sociability was based not only on neighborhoods, but on workplaces. This form of territorially defined community has not disappeared in the world at large, but it certainly plays a minor role in structuring social relationships for the majority of the population in developed societies, as studies by Fischer (1982), among others, showed many years ago. Furthermore, based on my own observations of Latin American squatter settlements, as well as on other studies, geographical proximity lost its pre-eminence in patterning social relationships in many of these poverty-stricken areas at least twenty-five years ago (Castells, 1983; Espinoza, 1999; Perlman, 2001).

The fading away of the residential community as a meaningful form of sociability seems to be unrelated to the settlement patterns of the population. Claude Fischer (2001) has shown that in the land of geographical mobility, the United States, residential mobility in fact decreased between 1950 and 1999. So, people do not build their meaning in local societies, not because they do not have spatial roots, but because they select their relationships on the basis of their affinities. Furthermore, spatial patterns do not tend to have a significant effect on sociability. A number of studies by urban sociologists (including Suzanne Keller, Barry Wellman, and Claude Fischer) showed years ago that networks substitute for places as supports of sociability both in suburbs and in cities.

This is not to say, however, that there is no longer placed-based sociability. Societies do not evolve toward a uniform pattern of social relationships. In fact, it is the growing diversity of sociability patterns that constitutes the specificity of social evolution in our societies. Immigrant communities in North America and Europe continue to rely strongly on placed-based social interaction (Waldinger, 2001). But it is the immigrant status, and the spatial concentration of people with this status in certain areas, that determine the pattern of sociability, rather than mere spatial contiguity in a locality. So, what is critical is the shift from the spatial boundary as the source of sociability to the spatial community as the expression of social organization.

Perhaps the necessary analytical step to understanding the new forms of social interaction in the age of the Internet is to build on a redefinition of community, de-emphasizing its cultural component, emphasizing its supportive role to individuals and families, and de-linking its social existence from a single kind of material support. Thus, a useful working definition in this respect is the one proposed by Barry Wellman: "Communities are networks of interpersonal ties that provide sociability, support, information, a sense of belonging, and social identity" (2001: 1). Naturally, the key matter here is the displacement from community to network as the central form of organizing interaction. Communities, at least in the tradition of sociological research, were based on the sharing of values and social organization. Networks are built by the choices and strategies of social actors, be it individuals, families, or social groups. Thus, the major transformation of sociability in complex societies took place with the substitution of networks for spatial communities as major forms of sociability. This is true for friendships, but it is even more so for kinship ties, as the extended family shrunk in size, and new means of communication made it possible to keep in close touch at a distance with a small number of family members. Thus, the pattern of sociability evolved toward a core of sociability built around the nuclear family in the household, from where networks of selective ties were built according to the interests and values of each member of the household.

According to Wellman and Giulia (1999), in the North American context people have more than one thousand interpersonal ties, of which only half a dozen are intimate, and less than fifty are significantly strong. The nuclear family does play a major role in the construction of these intimate ties, but the place of residence does not. On average, North Americans know only about twelve neighbors, but no more than one represents a strong tie. Work situations, on the other hand, have kept an important role in constructing sociability, according to Arlene Hochschild's observations (1997). Yet, the composition of the intimate core of sociability seems to be a function of both the few surviving nuclear family ties and of highly selective friendships, for which distance is a factor, but not an overriding factor. However, the fact that most ties people have are "weak ties" does not mean that they are unimportant. They are sources of information, of work performance, of leisure, of communication, of civic involvement, and of enjoyment. Here again, most of these weak ties are independent of spatial proximity and must be served by some means of communication. Claude Fischer's (1992) social history of the telephone in the US showed how the telephone strengthened pre-existing patterns of sociability, so that people used it to stay in touch with their families and friends, as well as with those neighbors they used to be acquainted with. And Anderson and Tracey (2001), Tracy and Anderson (2001), and Anderson *et al.* (1999), in their studies of the use of the Internet in households in the UK, emphasize how people adapt the Internet to their lives, rather than transforming their behavior under the "impact" of the technology.

Now, the dominant trend in the evolution of social relationships in our societies is the rise of individualism, in all its manifestations. This is not simply a cultural trend. Or, rather, it is cultural in the sense of material culture; that is, a system of values and beliefs informing behavior that is rooted in the material conditions of work and livelihood in our societies. From very different perspectives, social scientists, such as Giddens, Putnam, Wellman, Beck, Carnoy, and myself, have emphasized the emergence of a new system of social relationships centered on the individual. After the transition from the predominance of primary relationships (embodied in families and communities) to secondary relationships (embodied in associations), the new, dominant pattern seems to be built on what could be called tertiary relationships, or what Wellman calls "personalized communities," embodied in me-centered networks. It represents the privatization of sociability. This individualized relationship to society is a specific pattern of sociability, not a psychological attribute. It is rooted, first of all, in the individualization of the relationship between capital and labor, between workers and the work process, in the network enterprise.

It is induced by the crisis of patriarchalism, and the subsequent disintegration of the traditional nuclear family, as constituted in the late nineteenth century. It is sustained (*but not produced*) by the new patterns of urbanization, as suburban and exurban sprawl, and the de-linking between function and meaning in the microplaces of megacities, individualize and fragment the spatial context of livelihood. And it is rationalized by the crisis of political legitimacy, as the growing distance between citizens and the state stresses the mechanisms of representation, and fosters individual withdrawal from the public sphere. The new pattern of sociability in our societies is characterized by networked individualism.

The Internet as the Material Support for Networked Individualism

So, how do the possibilities (and limitations) of the Internet play out in this context? Available evidence, particularly from the studies conducted by Barry Wellman and his colleagues, and by the Pew Institute's Internet and American Life Project (2000), seems to indicate that the Internet is effective in maintaining weak ties, which otherwise would be lost in the trade-off between the effort to engage in physical interaction (including telephone interaction) and the value of the communication. Under certain conditions it can also create new kinds of weak ties, such as in the communities of interest that spring up on the Internet, with variable fates. Networks such as SeniorNet, bringing elderly people into contact for the instrumental exchange of information and emotional and personal support, are characteristic of this type of interaction. They are supports of weak ties in the sense that they rarely build lasting, personal relationships. People go on- and off-line, they switch their interests, they do not necessarily reveal their identity (although they do not fake another one), they migrate to other on-line partners. But if the specific connections are not durable, the flow lasts, and many participants in the network use it as one of their social manifestations.

Similar observations could be made about the various on-line communities studied by Steve Jones and his colleagues. These are indeed the kind of virtual communities that Rheingold popularized. But, unlike the WELL community in San Francisco, or Nettime in The Netherlands, most on-line communities are ephemeral communities, and they rarely articulate on-line interaction with physical interaction. They are better understood as networks of sociability, with variable geometry and changing composition, according to the evolving interests of social actors and to the shape of the network itself. To a large extent, the theme around which the on-line network is constructed defines its participants. An on-line support network for cancer patients is likely to attract primarily cancer patients and their loved ones, perhaps with the addition of some medical observers and social researchers, but usually excluding voyeurs, except those of the worse kind. In contrast with the notorious cartoon published by *The New Yorker* in the pre-history of on-line communication, on the Internet you better make sure that everyone knows that you are a dog, and not a cat, or you will find yourself immersed in the intimate world of cats. Because on the Internet, you are what you say you are, as it is on the basis of this expectation that a network of social interaction is constructed over time.

The Internet seems also to play a positive role in maintaining strong ties at a distance. It has often been observed that family relationships, stressed by growing disparity of family forms, individualism, and, sometimes, geographical mobility, are being helped by the use of e-mail. Not only does e-mail provide an easy tool to "just be there" at a distance, but it makes it easier to mark a presence without engaging in a deeper interaction for which the emotional energy is not available every day.

But the most important role of the Internet in structuring social relationships is its contribution to the new pattern of sociability based on individualism. Indeed, as Wellman writes, "complex social networks have always existed but recent technological developments in communications have afforded their emergence as a dominant form of social organization" (2001: 1). Increasingly, people are organized not just in social networks, but in computer-communicated social networks. So, it is not the Internet that creates a pattern of networked individualism, but the development of the Internet provides an appropriate material support for the diffusion of networked individualism as the dominant form of sociability.

Networked individualism is a social pattern, not a collection of isolated individuals. Rather, individuals build their networks, on-line and off-line, on the basis of their interests, values, affinities, and projects. Because of the flexibility and communicating power of the Internet, on-line social interaction plays an increasing role in social organization as a whole. On-line networks, when they stabilize in their practice, may build communities, virtual communities, different from physical communities, but not necessarily less intense or less effective in binding and mobilizing. Furthermore, what we observe in our societies is the development of a communication hybrid that brings together physical place and cyber place (to use Wellman's terminology) to act as the material support of networked individualism.

Thus, just to mention one of the many studies supporting this pattern of interaction between on-line and off-line networks, the investigation conducted by Gustavo Cardoso (1998) on PT-net, one of the earlier virtual communities in Portuguese, showed a closed interaction between off-line and on-line sociability, each one with its own rhythm, and specific features, yet forming an indissoluble social process. As Cardoso reports: "We are in the presence of a new notion of space, where physical and virtual influence each other, laying the ground for the emergence of new forms of socialization, new life styles, and new forms of social organization" (1998: 116, my translation).

Vivienne Waller (2000) has shown the role of the Internet in the development of new forms of individualized family life in her pioneering study of household uses of the Internet in Canberra. She builds on the findings of the Pew Institute Internet and American Life Project (2000) that Americans often use the Internet to "celebrate" family: one-third of them used it to look for a lost relative, over 50 percent used it to increase contact with family members, and many display information about their families in their web pages. In fact, one American in ten was a member of a family in which someone had created a family website. But, having established the relevance of the Internet in family relationships, both in America and in Australia, Waller goes beyond this observation to argue that the Internet is being used to redefine family relationships in a society in which people are experimenting with new forms of family. She shows how e-mail enabled a number of households to perform what she calls "families of choice," by incorporating into the daily life of the family strangers that became acquainted via the Internet, or whose contact was developed and enriched by Internet-based interaction over a period of time. So, the practice of networked individualism may be redefining the boundaries and meaning of traditional institutions of sociability, such as the family.

In other instances, these on-line networks become forms of "specialized communities;" that is, forms of sociability constructed around specific interests. Since people may easily belong to several of these networks, individuals tend to develop their "portfolios of sociability," by investing differentially, at different points in time, in a number of networks with low entry barriers and low opportunity costs. There follows, on the one hand, extreme flexibility in the expression of sociability, as individuals construct and reconstruct their forms of social interaction. On the other hand, the relatively low level of commitment may induce a certain fragility of the forms of social support. At the societal level, while some observers celebrate diversity, plurality, and choice, Putnam fears "cyberbalkanization" as a way to accentuate the dissolution of social institutions and the decline of civic engagement.

New technological developments seem to enhance the chances for networked individualism to become the dominant form of sociability. The growing stream of studies on the uses of mobile phones seems to indicate that cell-telephony fits a social pattern organized around "communities of choice," and individualized interaction, based on the selection of time, place, and partners of the interaction (Kopomaa, 2000; Nafus and Tracey, 2000). The projected development of the wireless Internet increases the chances of personalized networking to a wide range of social situations, thus enhancing the capacity of individuals to rebuild structures of sociability from the bottom up.

These trends are tantamount to the triumph of the individual, although the costs for society are still unclear. Unless we consider that individuals are in fact reconstructing the pattern of social interaction, with the help of new technological affordances, to create a new form of society: the network society.

Reading Links

Anderson, Ben and Tracey, Karina (2001) "Digital living: the impact (or otherwise) of the Internet on everyday life," unpublished research report, Ipswich, Suffolk, Adastral Park: BTaxCT Research.

—— McWilliam, Anabel, Lacohee, Hazel, Clueas, Eileen, and Gershuny, Jay (1999) "Family life in the digital home: domestic telecommunication at the end of the twentieth century," *BT Technology Journal*, 17 (1): 85–97.

Barlow, John Perry (1995) "What are we doing on-line?," *Harper*, August.

Baym, Nancy (1998) "The emergence of on-line community," in Steve Jones (ed.), *Cybersociety 2.0: Revisiting Computer Mediated Communication and Community*, pp. 35–68. Thousand Oaks, CA: Sage.

Cardoso, Gustavo (1998) *Para una sociologia do ciberespaco: comunidades virtuais em portugues*. Oeiras, Portugal: Celta Editora.

Carnoy, Martin (2000) *Sustaining the New Economy: Work, Family and Community in the Information Age*. Cambridge, MA: Harvard University Press.

Castells, Manuel (1983) *The City and the Grassroots*. Berkeley, CA: University of California Press.

Di Maggio, Paul, Hargittai, Eszter, Neuman, W. Russell, and Robinson, John P. (2001) "The Internet's effects on society," *Annual Reviews of Sociology*, forthcoming.

Dutton, William (2000) *Society on the Line: Information Politics in the Digital Age*. Oxford: Oxford University Press.

Espinoza, Vicente (1999) "Social networks among the urban poor: inequality and integration in a Latin American city," in Barry Wellman (ed.), *Networks in the Global Village*, pp. 147–84. Boulder, CO: Westview Press.

Fischer, Claude (1982) *To Dwell Among Friends*. Chicago, IL: University of Chicago Press.

—— (1992) *America Calling*. Berkeley, CA: University of California Press.

—— (2001) "Ever-more rooted Americans," unpublished research paper, University of California, Department of Sociology/Russell Sage Foundation, USA: A Century of Difference Project.

Hampton, Keith and Wellman, Barry (2000) "Examining community in the digital neighborhood: early results from Canada's wired suburb," in Toru Ishida and K. Katherine Isbister (eds), *Digital Cities: Technologies, Experiences, and Future Perspectives*. Berlin: Springer Verlag.

Hiltz, S. R. and Turoff, M. (1995) *Network Nation*, rev. edn. Cambridge, MA: MIT Press.

Hochschild, Arlene (1997) *The Time Bind: When Work Becomes Home and Home Becomes Work*. New York: Metropolitan Books.

Howard, Philip E., Rainie, Lee, and Jones, Steve (2001) "Days and nights in the Internet: the impact of diffusing technology," *American Behavioral Scientist*, 45 (special issue on the Internet and everyday life).

Jones, Steve (ed.) (1997) *Virtual Culture*. London: Sage.

—— (ed.) (1998) *Cybersociety 2.0: Revisiting Computer Mediated Communication and Community*. Thousand Oaks, CA: Sage.

Katz, James E., Rice, Ronald E., and Aspden, Philip (2001) "The Internet 1995–2000: access, civic involvement, and social interaction," *American Behavioral Scientist*, 45 (special issue on the Internet and everyday life).

Kopomaa, Timo (2000) *The City in your Pocket: Birth of the Mobile Information Society*. Helsinki: Gaudeamus.

Kraut, Robert *et al.* (1998) "Internet paradox: a social technology that reduces social involvement and psychological well-being?," *American Psychologist*, 53: 1011–31.

Nafus, Dawn and Tracey, Karina (2000) "The more things change: mobile phone consumption and concepts of personhood," unpublished research paper, University of Cambridge, Department of Social Anthropology and British Telecom.

Perlman, Janice (2001) "Urban marginality: from myth to reality. The Favelas of Rio de Janeiro, 1969–2001," paper delivered at the Annual Meeting of the American Sociological Association, Anaheim, California, August 16.

Pew Institute for the People and the Press (1995) *Technology in the American Household*. Washington, DC: Pew Institute.

—— (1999) *The Internet News Audience Goes Ordinary*. Washington, DC: Pew Institute.

—— (2000) *Internet and American Life Project*. Washington, DC: Pew Institute.

Putnam, Robert (2000) *Bowling Alone: The Collapse and Revival of American Community*. New York: Simon and Schuster.

Rheingold, Howard (1993) *The Virtual Community: Homesteading on the Electronic Frontier*. Reading, MA: Addison-Wesley; rev. edn, 2000, Cambridge, MA: MIT Press.

Tracey, Karina (2000) "Virtual communities: what's new?," paper delivered at the First Conference of the Association of Internet Researchers, Lawrence, University of Kansas, September 16.

—— and Anderson, Ben (2001) "The significance of lifestage and lifestyle transitions in the use and disuse of Internet applications and services," *American Behavioral Scientist*, 45 (special issue on the Internet and everyday life).

Turkle, Sherry (1995) *Life on the Screen: Identity in the Age of the Internet*. New York: Simon and Schuster.

Waldinger, Roger (ed.) (forthcoming) *The New Urban Immigrants*.

Waller, Vivienne (2000) "Families courting the web: the Internet in the everyday life of household families," paper delivered at the First Conference of the Association of Internet Researchers, Lawrence, University of Kansas, September.

Wellman, Barry (1979) "The community question," *American Journal of Sociology*, 84: 1201–31.

—— (ed.) (1999) *Networks in the Global Village*. Boulder, CO: Westview Press.

—— (2000) "Living networked in a wired world," keynote address to the First Conference of the Association of Internet Researchers, Lawrence, University of Kansas, September 14.

—— (2001) "Physical place and cyberplace: the rise of networked individualism," *International Journal of Urban and Regional Research*, 1 (special issue on networks, class, and place).

—— and Giulia, Milena (1999) "Netsurfers don't ride alone: virtual communities as communities," in Barry Wellman (ed.), *Networks in the Global Village*, pp. 331–66. Boulder, CO: Westview Press.

—— and Haythornthwaite, Carolyne (eds) (forthcoming) *Internet in Everyday Life*. Oxford: Blackwell.

—— *et al.* (2000) "Does the Internet increase, ignore, decrease or replace contact with friends and relatives? The evidence from the National

Geographic Web Survey," paper delivered at the First Conference of the Association of Internet Researchers, Lawrence, University of Kansas, September 14–17.

Zhou, Gaea (2000) "The Well as a counterculture online community and as business," unpublished research paper for CP 229, University of California, Department of City and Regional Planning, Berkeley, California.

e-Links

Cole, Jeffrey *et al.* (2000) "Surveying the digital future," at www.ccp.ucla. edu/ucla-internet.pdf
The UCLA study on Internet use in the United States.

Nie, Joseph and Erdring, R. (2000) "Internet and social life survey," at www.stanford.edu/group/siqss
Stanford University Institute for the Quantitative Study of Society Survey of the Internet and social life.

Chapter 5

The Politics of the Internet I: Computer Networks, Civil Society, and the State

Societies change through conflict and are managed by politics. Since the Internet is becoming an essential medium of communication and organization in all realms of activity, it is obvious that social movements and the political process use, and will increasingly use, the Internet as well, making it a privileged tool for acting, informing, recruiting, organizing, dominating and counter-dominating. Cyberspace becomes a contested terrain. However, does the Internet play a purely instrumental role in expressing social protests and political conflicts? Or is there a transformation of the rules of the socio-political game in cyberspace that ultimately affects the game itself—namely, the forms and goals of movements and political actors?

I shall succinctly analyze the interaction between the Internet and processes of socio-political conflict, representation, and management by focusing on four distinct, albeit related, areas in which this interaction takes place: the new dyamics of social movements; the computer networking of local communities and their relevance for citizen participation; the uses of the Internet in the practice of informational politics; and the emergence of "noopolitik" and cyberwarfare on the geopolitical stage.

Networked Social Movements

Twenty-first century social movements, purposive collective actions aiming at the transformation of values and institutions of society, manifest themselves on and by the Internet. The labor movement, a survivor of the industrial era, connects, organizes, and mobilizes with and on the Internet. And so do the environmental movement, the women's movement, various human rights movements, ethnic identity movements, religious movements, nationalist movements, and the defenders/proponents of an endless list of cultural projects and political causes. Cyberspace has become a global electronic agora where the diversity of human disaffection explodes in a cacophony of accents.

In the mid-1990s the *Zapatista* movement in Chiapas, Mexico, captured the imagination of people around the world by building support for its cause over electronic networks of faxes and the Internet—related to the media world and to a decentralized structure of solidarity groups. As I reported earlier (Castells, 1997), at the origin of this electronic network of solidarity was La Neta, an Internet-based network organizing Mexican women, supported by the San Francisco Institute of Global Communication, an NGO of socially responsible "techies." Throughout the 1990s, major social movements around the world became organized with the help of the Internet. Perhaps the most notorious case is/was *Falun Gong*, the Chinese spiritualist/political movement, with tens of millions of supporters, which dared to challenge the power of the Communist Party. The leader of the movement, Li Hongzhi, while living in New York, kept in touch with a core network of its supporters via the Internet, and it was also by the Internet·that thousands of determined members of *Falun Gong* found the spiritual support and the information enabling them to converge in person, at a given place and time, in a series of well-organized protests that were met with harsh repression because of the Chinese government's concern about the potential influence of this movement (Bell and Boas, 2000; O'Leary, 2000).

In other instances, the technological vulnerability of the Internet offers the opportunity for individual or collective expressions of protest to disrupt the websites of the electronic networks of government agencies or corporations targeted as representatives of oppression or exploitation. This is the case with "hacker-activist protests," which range from individual sabotage to breaking into the restricted websites of military agencies or financial companies to underscore their insecurity and to protest against their goals (Langman *et al.*, 2000). In the fall of 2000, during the confrontation between Israelis and Palestinians, pro-Palestinian hackers (allegedly from Pakistan) broke into the websites of American pro-Israel organizations, posted political propaganda on the website, and retrieved and posted on the Net the credit card numbers of the site's members, in a symbolic protest that prompted a strong reaction from public opinion.

But the Internet is more than just a handy tool to be used because it is there. It fits with the basic features of the kind of social movements emerging in the Information Age. And because these movements found their appropriate medium of organization, they developed and opened new avenues of social change, which, in turn, enhanced the role of the Internet as their privileged medium. To build on an historical analogy, the constitution of the labor movement in the industrial era cannot be separated from the industrial factory as its organizational setting (although some historians insist on the equally important role of the pub in this respect). We know, from the preceding chapters, that the Internet is not simply a technology: it is a communication medium (as the pubs were), and it is the material infrastructure of a given organizational form: the network (as the factory was). On both counts, the Internet became the indispensable component of the kind of social movements emerging in the network society. This is so for three reasons.

First, social movements in the Information Age are essentially mobilized around cultural values. The struggle to change the codes of meaning in the institutions and practice of society is the essential struggle in the process of social change in the new historical context, as I argued in my book *The Power of Identity* (Castells, 1997)—a view that builds on a broad stream of research on social movements (Touraine, Melucci, Calhoun, Tarrow etc.). In this sense, I concur with Cohen and Rai (2000) that the distinction between old and new social movements is largely misleading. Movements from the industrial era, for example, the labor movement, persevere nowadays by redefining themselves in terms of social values, and broadening the meaning of these social values: for instance, social justice for all, rather than the defense of class interests. On the other hand, some of the most important social movements of our time, such as nationalist or religious movements, are very old in their principles, but they take on a new meaning when they become trenches of cultural identity to build social autonomy in a world dominated by homogeneous, global information flows.

In this context, communication of values, mobilization around meaning, become fundamental. Cultural movements (in the sense of movements aimed at defending or proposing specific ways of life and meaning) are built around communication systems—essentially the Internet and the media—because they are the main way in which these movements can reach out to those who would adhere to their values, and from there to affect the consciousness of society as a whole.

The second feature characterizing social movements in the network society is that they have to fill the gap left by the crisis of vertically integrated organizations inherited from the industrial era. Mass political parties, when and where they still exist, are empty shells, barely activated as electoral machines at regular intervals. Trade unions survive only by abandoning their traditional forms of organization, historically built as replicas of the rational bureaucracies characteristic of large corporations and state agencies. Formal civic associations, and their organizational conglomerates, are in full decline as forms of social engagement, as

Putnam (2000) has documented for the United States, and other observers have reported in other areas of the world. This is not to say that people do not organize and mobilize in defense of their interests or in the affirmation of their values. But loose coalitions, semi-spontaneous mobilizations, and *ad hoc* movements of the neo-anarchist brand substitute for permanent, structured, formal organizations. Emotional movements, often triggered by a media event, or by a major crisis, seem often to be more important sources of social change than the day-to-day routine of dutiful NGOs. The Internet becomes an essential medium of expression and organization for these kinds of manifestation, which coincide in a given time and space, make their impact through the media world, and act upon institutions and organizations (business, for instance) by the repercussions of their impact on public opinion. These are movements to seize the power of the mind, not state power.

The December 1999 protest against the World Trade Organization in Seattle was a paradigmatic example of this new kind of social movement. It brought together a vast coalition of extremely different, and even contradictory, interests and values, from the battalions of the American labor movement to the swarms of eco-pacifists, environmentalists, women's groups, and a myriad of alternative groups, including the pagan community. The activists of Direct Action Network provided the training and organizational skills for many protesters. But the movement was based on the exchange of information, on previous months of heated political debate over the Internet, that preceded the individual and collective decisions to go to Seattle and to try to block the meeting of what was perceived as an institution enforcing "globalization without representation."

The media linkage to worldwide public opinion was enhanced by the Seattle "Independent Media Center." Its effective role in the Seattle protest has spawned a global network of temporary (event-specific) or permanent "independent media centers," which are the information backbone of the anti-globalization movement (www.indymedia.org). This model of protest was re-enacted months later in Washington, DC, in Bangkok, in Melbourne, in Prague, in the

Hague, in Nice, in Quebec, and may wander around the world in the coming years, closely shadowing the periodic landing of global flows of wealth and power in their meeting places. The anti-globalization movement does not have a permanent, professional organization, does not have a center, a command structure, or a common program. There are hundreds, thousands of organizations, and individuals, around the world, converging in some symbolic protests, then dispersing to focus on their own specific issues—or just vanishing, to be replaced by new contingents of newly born activists. The effectiveness of this movement comes precisely from its diversity, which reaches out as far as the violent, enraged margins of society on one side, and to the heights of moral and religious authority on the other. Its influence, already measurable in terms of a significant change of attitude in institutions as important as the World Bank, comes from the ability to raise issues, and force a debate, without entering into a negotiation because no one can negotiate on behalf of the movement. It is pure movement, not the precursor of new institutions. This is not new in history, by any means. In fact, this informality and relative spontaneity are what have usually characterized the most productive social movements. The novelty is their networking via the Internet, because it allows the movement to be diverse and coordinated at the same time, to engage in a continuing debate, and yet not be paralyzed by it, since each one of its nodes can reconfigure a network of its affinities and objectives, with partial overlappings and multiple connections. The anti-globalization movement is not simply a network, it is an electronic network, it is an Internet-based movement. And because the Internet is its home it cannot be disorganized or captured. It swims like fish in the net.

There is a third major factor specifying social movements in our age. Because power increasingly functions in global networks, largely bypassing the institutions of the nation-state, movements are faced with the need to match the global reach of the powers that be with their own global impact on the media, through symbolic actions. In other words, the globalization of social movements is a distinct, and much more important, phenomenon than the movement against globalization—which is only one specific manifestation of the emergence of a global contested terrain. Cohen and Rai (2000) have coordinated a research program on this process of globalization of social movements. What appears from their findings, and from other studies (Keck and Sikkink, 1998; Langman *et al.*, 2000), is that the most influential social movements are, at the same time, rooted in their local context and aiming at a global impact. They need the legitimacy and support provided by their reliance on local groups, yet they cannot remain local or they lose their capacity to act upon the real sources of power in our world. Reversing the popular motto of twenty-five years ago, social movements must think local (relating to their own concerns and identity) and act global—at the level where it really matters today.

Cohen and Rai (2000) identify six major social movements that have engaged in a global form of coordination and action: human rights, women's, environmental, labor, religious, and peace movements. In all cases the need to build global coalitions, and their reliance on global information networks, makes the movements highly dependent on the Internet. However, it must be added that relatively cheap air transportation also plays a role in the globalization of social movements since physical meetings, and joint, localized actions, are indispensable tools in enacting social change.

The processes of conflictive social change in the Information Age revolve around the struggles to transform the categories of our existence, by building interactive networks as forms of organization and mobilization. These networks, emerging from the resistance of local societies, aim at overcoming the power of global networks, thus reconstructing the world from the bottom up. The Internet provides the material basis for these movements to engage in the production of a new society. By so doing, they transform the Internet as well: from organizational business tool and communication medium, it becomes a lever of social transformation as well—although not always in the terms sought by the social movements or, for that matter, in defense of the values that you and me would necessarily share.

Citizen Networks

From the mid-1980s to the late 1990s, a wide array of local communities around the world went on-line. They often linked up with local institutions and municipal governments, grassrooting citizen democracy in cyberspace. Generally speaking, three different components converged in the formation of these community-based computer networks: the pre-Internet grassroots movements in search of new opportunities for self-organizing and consciousness-raising; the hacker movement in its most politically oriented expressions; and municipal governments trying to strengthen their legitimacy by creating new channels of citizen participation. Social entrepreneurs emerged as leaders of many of these projects, usually community activists who became aware of the possibilities offered by computer networks. Occasionally, telecommunications operators or high-technology companies would pitch in to promote the promise of the information society for all. National governments in Europe and Japan, and international agencies in the developing world, also contributed to some of the efforts, both as experiments and as symbolic gestures of modernity, well publicized with their constituencies.

In the United States, some of the earliest and most successful experiments were the Cleveland Freenet, supported by Case Western Reserve University, and the Public Electronic Network (PEN) organized by the City of Santa Monica, California, both in 1986. The Seattle Community Network, developed under the initiative of Douglas Schuler in the late 1980s, was another pioneer experience. In Europe, the Iperbole Program, launched by the City of Bologna, and Amsterdam's Digital City, both started in 1994, became major points of reference. But throughout the world, and particularly in the developing world, hundreds of lesser known experiences brought on-line the interests, concerns, values, and voices of citizens, until then isolated among themselves and from their local institutions. These community-based networks were diverse in their constituencies and in their orientation, but they shared three major characteristics. First, they provided information from local authorities, as well as from a variety of civic associations—in other words, they became a technologically updated bulletin board of city life. Secondly, they organized the horizontal exchange of information and electronic conversation among the participants in the network. Thirdly, and most importantly, they allowed access to on-line networking to people and organizations that were not into the emerging Internet, and would otherwise not have been connected for quite a long time. In fact, there were two different agendas among the people coming into these citizen networks. As Steve Cisler, one of the pioneers of this movement, writes: "The driving interest in organizing groups was divided between those who wanted a focus on local life, community, and networking, and those who wanted access to the global Internet. In effect, these people wanted to get out of town, and the civic networks were the only choice for most" (Cisler, 2000: 1). Probably this ambiguity, indeed tension, between the desire to connect to the global Internet and the fostering of local community, present in these early computer networks, is what made their development possible. They became the testing ground for thousands of activists operating their transition to a new technological environment of social mobilization. But they were also the entry point in the Internet Age for many uneducated, poor, uninformed people, or, simply, for many who did not have adequate or affordable access to the Internet.

Therefore, as soon as the world wide web diffused globally, and Internet access became relatively affordable and easy to operate, community computer networks differentiated themselves along the lines of their original components: social activists concentrated on fostering citizen participation in an attempt to redefine local democracy; social service agencies provided access, training, and help with education and jobs to people in need, in a new expansion of the non-profit, or third sector, of the economy. This induced the development of what came to be known as community technology centers (Servon, 2002). On the other hand, many people who were interested in access to the Internet for personal use, rather than in broader issues of social change, migrated to the commercial websites, which they had discovered, in many cases, via community networks.

Lessons from History in the Making: The Constitution of the Amsterdam Public Digital Culture

A brief account of the trajectory of the most famous citizen computer network, Amsterdam's Digital City—or *De Digitale Stad* (DDS) in Dutch—may illustrate the analysis presented here. The DDS experience radiated beyond the community network itself to become the anchoring element of what is known internationally as the "Amsterdam public digital culture," a new form of public sphere combining local institutions, grassroots organizations, and computer networks in the development of cultural expression and civic participation (Patrice Riemens, personal communication and private archives, 1997–2001; Caroline Nevejan, personal communication, 1997, 1999, 2001; Marleen Stikker, personal communication, 1997, 1999; Lovink and Riemens, 1998; Van Bastelaer and Lobet-Maris, 2000; Van den Besselaar, 2001).

The Digital City was launched in January 1994, originally as a ten-week experiment to set up an electronic dialogue between the city council and the citizens of Amsterdam, and as a social experiment in interactive communication. Given its success, it was expanded to a fully fledged "networked community" which provided information resources and free communication capability to its users. Some of them were "residents" of the city, after complying with the registration procedures. Others were visitors. Most of the information was in Dutch, but English could be used for communication in chat rooms. Although originally aimed at Amsterdam's residents, it was of course accessed globally. Indeed, the proportion of Amsterdam-based users dropped from 45 percent in 1994 to 22 percent in 1998. The city metaphor materialized in the structure of the site. There was a municipal bulletin board, so that citizens could check all relevant municipal documents and deliberations of the city council, and express their opinion. The city of Amsterdam was the first local administration to agree to link its internal networks to the Internet, in an effort of controlled transparency. DDS was virtually organized in homes, squares, cafés, digital kiosks, digital houses of culture and the arts, and even a digital sex-shop. A central station offered access to the global Internet.

DDS instantly became an extraordinary success in terms of its public appeal, as well as in terms of the interest aroused in the global Internet community. Residents would take up residence in one "home," post their family photos on the Net, express their feelings, voice their opinions, organize protests, and vote on issues. There was a squatting law: if a home had not been used by its owner for three months, it could be taken up by another owner. Residents of the city also came up with their own alternative to cope with scarcity of space (disk capacity): they would transform a home into a flat, to be shared by several residents, therefore sharing the computer capacity assigned to the home. One year after its beginning, DDS had 4,000 daily users, with a monthly request for one million web pages. In only three years, it reached 50,000 residents, and in 2000 claimed about 140,000. Not only was DDS the European pioneer of citizen networks, but it became the largest community-based computer network in Europe. In spite of the fact that only a minority of residents were living in Amsterdam, the language boundary gave DDS a distinctive Dutch character.

For the experience to be analytically meaningful it is necessary to reconstruct the process of formation of DDS, and to place it in the historical context of Amsterdam's digital culture tradition. DDS was the result of the convergence of two very different networks: on the one hand, artists and people from the media scene interested in experimenting with new media; on the other hand, the hacker community, interested in diffusing access to the Internet. Two women were at the origin of the connection between these two groups in the conception of a shared project. Marleen Stikker (who would become the first virtual "mayor" of the Digital City) was organizing cultural events, experimenting with new media as a tool for new forms of people-based communication and expression. In the early 1990s she organized major cultural events, such as Van Gogh TV and the Wetware Convention. She was also influenced by the Freenet experience in the US, and was acquainted with the early Internet. The cultural center De Balie (sponsored by the social-democratic municipality of Amsterdam) invited Stikker to include multimedia and computer communication events in the center's program.

Caroline Nevejan was also working on new media at another cultural center, Paradiso, where she came into contact, in the late 1980s with the HackTic group, a key actor in Amsterdam's hacker culture. A participant in the squatters movement (she founded *Bluff*, one of the movement's magazines), Nevejan connected with the hackers by inviting the Hamburg-based Chaos Computer Club to Paradiso in 1988. Rop Gonggrijp, the founder of HackTic, and Patrice Riemens, cooperated with Nevejan to organize international events such as the 1989 "Galactic Hackers Party," in which they were joined by a network of political techno-activists. In 1990, when the International Conference on AIDS in San Francisco was disrupted by the refusal of visas to anti-AIDS activists by US authorities, the same group organized an alternative event in Amsterdam: the Sero-Positive Ball. It was a major gathering, including hackers, academics, NGOs, with the support of public institutions and companies, such as Apple. The event launched a campaign of on-line organizing and information activities on AIDS issues, such as HIV-net. A series of similar events continued to take place throughout the 1990s and into 2001, benchmarking the rise of the Amsterdam public digital culture. It is worth mentioning activities such as the three successive 'Next Five Minutes' Conferences on 'Tactical Media' at Paradiso and De Balie in 1993, 1996, and 1999. There were two international summer gatherings of hackers: "Hacking at the End of the Universe" in 1993 (where the DDS plan was first conceived) and "Hacking in Progress" in 1997. Planned for 2001 was 'HAL' ("Hackers at Large"), organized by the XS4all Foundation and the usual HackTic/hippy suspects.

Amsterdam's hacker culture and the techno-activist networks did not develop in a social vacuum. There is in The Netherlands a long tradition of interest in cybernetics and alternative computer development, rooted in the strong academic community of physics researchers. Some prominent academics, such as Herschberg at Leiden University and De Zeeuw, a social scientist at the University of Amsterdam, protected and helped these rebellious computer geeks. Some of them were essentially interested in computers, and created a BBS culture in the 1980s, with groupings such as the Hobby Computer Club. Others came from a more political tradition, participating in the squatter movement and in the peace movement. They sought information and support for their struggles from alternative computer networks, such as PeaceNet and GreenNet, making use of the FIDONET infrastructure. One of the most active members of this culture was Michael Polman, the founder of Antenna, a connectivity and resources center for NGOs working on North/South solidarity. On the other hand, the most political hackers, with the support of a system's administrator from Delft Polytechnicum, constituted a social movement: HackTic, led by Rop Gonggrijp.

Then, through Caroline Nevejan, in 1993 Marleen Stikker met the leaders of HackTic, Felipe Rodriguez and Rop Gonggrijp, and invited them to participate in her cultural program at De Balie. They conceived the formation of a citizen network that would provide an open platform for cultural expression and community debate on public issues, besides experimenting with the new medium of communication. The result of their joint project became the Digital City when the city of Amsterdam decided to support the experiment at a time when the March 1994 municipal elections were approaching. Financial support (150,000 ecus) came from the city of Amsterdam, the Ministry of Economic Affairs, and the Ministry of Internal Affairs.

The origins of the Digital City are meaningful both for analytical purposes and for its subsequent development. It epitomized the origins of European citizen networks in the countercultural movements and in the hacker culture, a theme recurrent throughout this book. This hacker culture sprang from the university world, both through the inspiration of academic researchers, and as an expression of student politics. But this historical background also shows how the ability of citizen networks to reach out to a broader user base is highly dependent on institutional support from an open-minded administration—in spite of the divergence of goals.

These differences between the components of Amsterdam's community network would reflect in its development. Having concluded a positive experiment, the HackTic network went its own way in 1995 and became an Internet access provider, under a new name: XS4all (access for all). It was so successful that in 1998 it was bought by the Dutch telecommunications company KPN, with the proviso of a three-year period of "independence." The six former owners of XS4all became very rich, and many of its employees reasonably wealthy. They used some of their money to support worthy Internet causes. Yet the independent hackers' network is alive and well, as exemplified by the vitality of the "Hippies from Hell" network, still meeting virtually on e-mail, and physically in "The Hang Out," a meeting place and cultural activities center in East Amsterdam.

The original media-oriented network scattered itself into alternative local cultural scenes, including radio and television. Marleen Stikker and Caroline Nevejan created a new group to support cultural experimentation, the Society for Old and New Media, symbolically housed in the historical building The Waag, property of the city of Amsterdam. They also parted company later on: Marleen Stikker continued to be active in Amsterdam's cultural scene; Caroline Nevejan became a senior information technology adviser at Amsterdam Polytechnic.

DDS restructured itself as a foundation in 1995, and assumed a managerial structure. It streamlined decision procedures, limiting citizen participation, and offering better services. In 2000, new communication possibilities, such as a digital living room and DDS broadcasting, were introduced. The interface provided by DDS developed substantially over time. DDS 1.0 (until October 1994) started as a bulletin board system and was text-based only. As soon as the world wide web became available, DDS adopted it. In October 1994, under DDS 2.0, a new graphic interface, based on Mosaic, was introduced, but at the price of eliminating interactivity, except for e-mail. Then DDS 3.0 restored interactivity, and DDS 4.0, in 1999, improved the design of the site. However, overall, DDS was behind new commercial Internet sites in both technology and design.

Indeed, the major issue that DDS had to confront was the competition from the spread of Internet use to which it had contributed so much in The Netherlands. This was reflected in the changing uses and the changing composition of DDS users. In the early period, 1994–7, users participated in the building of the city, and engaged in debates about its management, as well as on broader political issues. Later on, DDS came into competition with several websites, including the city of Amsterdam's own website. Data from a log-file analysis over time showed that the ten most visited websites accounted for 85 percent of all hits, while 75 percent of the sites were not visited at all. There was also a major discrepancy between the supply of information and the use of information depending on content category: in the politics category, there was much more supply than use; while in the information-technology category, there was much more use than supply. This may imply that the majority of users are more interested in information about technology than in politics. It could still be that the input in political debates would be very high. But this is not the case: the level of activity in political forums declined over the years, and in 2000 very little of such activity was visible (Van den Besselaar, 2001).

The contradictory evolution of DDS was reflected in its recurrent financial problems. At the outset, there was a launching grant, but it was used for the building of the infrastructure. It was expected that DDS would become self-sufficient over time, by providing free service to individuals but having institutions and NGOs pay for the service. Financial autonomy was not only a condition of the government, but the desire of the community network in order to assert its independence. However, the success of DDS, coupled with the explosion of the Internet, and the sudden commercial interest in it, created major contradictions among the idealistic activists at the origin of the network and the managers of the foundation. In addition, as is often the case in social movements, personal problems between some of the key actors, and disputes about the use of financial resources, permeated into organizational conflicts (for instance in the split between the De Balie center and the XS4all network). As for the municipality, the diffusion of the Internet among the general population made it unnecessary to use countercultural experiments to inform citizens and request their opinion on local matters, so it took the web design and provision of municipal information into its own hands by building its own citizen website, the City of Glass. This greatly diminished the financial support for DDS. Over time, members of the cultural and artistic circles of Amsterdam became more deeply involved in DDS, as on-line distribution of audio and image were among the most important expressions of electronic community in the city.

DDS existed in ambiguity, and perhaps contradiction, between its image as a democratic, networked community and its reality as a top-down managed foundation, only accountable to the foundation's board, and to its managers who ended up accumulating all decision-making power. As DDS expanded, there was an increasing split between managers of the foundation and residents of the virtual city. After some shouting matches (both physical and virtual), most active members of the community gave up and used it just as a service. As for the management of DDS, their attitude could be summarized by a statement from the coordinator in one of the heated exchanges with the city dwellers: "the fact that the telephone system is the property of the people does not entitle them to occupy the telephone exchange" (reported by Patrice Riemens, personal communication, 2000).

The commercialization of the Internet put increasing pressure on the Digital City. Seeing the opportunity for a profit-making operation, the two DDS managers transformed DDS into a holding business, and divided its activities into four different organizations to cross-subsidize the Digital City from services and advertising in the other segments of the holding. As a result, there was growing tension between the new role of DDS as a commercial Internet content provider and the original goals of the community network. Finally, on October 5, 2000, a press release issued in Amsterdam bluntly stated that:

The Digital City Holdings Pvt Ltd (DDS) has decided to terminate the editorial activities pursued through its subsidiary DDS City Ltd. Over this past half year, there has been a dramatic shift in the investing environment concerning the Business to Consumer (B2C) Internet industry. At the moment, activities that were taking place in the subsidiary DDS City are showing a loss, and with no fresh investment money forthcoming they must be curtailed.

In only a few years, there had been a dramatic shift from the dreams of the electronic free commune to the harsh world of a dot.com business in crisis.

Patrice Riemens, a long-time observer of the Digital City, summarized the rise and fall of the experiment in December 2000:

the DDS had quite a few stakeholders which were not lacking influence. After all, the concept of the Amsterdam Public Digital Culture, of which DDS has been a central feature, is not entirely a figment of the spirit. But in the end, it either proved a transient phenomenon or did not have very much substance to begin with. Not enough in any case to forestall its—with the benefit of hindsight—foreseeable and irresistible demise. And its resurrection in very much different guises. (personal communication)

Another leading expert on the matter, Van den Besselaar (2001) goes even further in his pessimistic assessment:

The DDS will not survive 2001, the Digital City will be abolished and the commercial part may continue, or the whole thing will be taken over. The experiment of the DDS as an independent non-profit approach has failed; we may have to rethink the role of the public sector for guaranteeing and regulating the electronic public domain. As with physical public space, virtual public space requires care and maintenance, and resources to do this. The main question is whether there is room left for non-commercial Internet culture and social interaction.

History never ends, though. In early 2001, a netizen take-over of the bankrupt DDS was being attempted by a newly created "Association in constitution (for the DDS"—*vio DDS*) led by Reinder Rustema. Its aim was to recover control of DDS community-oriented services from DDS Holdings, and to reconstruct the experience on new grounds. Ironically, by providing hope of the revaluation of the assets of the defunct DDS, the netizens increased its financial value, making it more difficult to transfer the remnants of DDS to its original citizens. For the moment, the struggle goes on . . .

Thus, whither citizen networks as neo-anarchist fantasies of the early Internet era? In fact, as usual, the process by which historical change muddles through is far more complex. At about the same time as the great Dutch experiment was spiraling down from its high hopes, in Paris, on December 15, 2000, there was a major gathering of "digital countercultures" (the ZeligConf); and in Barcelona, on November 2, 2000, about five hundred representatives from citizen networks from around the world (mainly from

Europe and Latin America) met to build a global network of citizen networks. Many were sponsored by local governments, feeling that their turn to enter the Internet Age had finally come, and trying to find a formula to fight political skepticism among their citizens. Others came from revamped NGOs feeling the pinch of competition from religious groups, and the pain from the growing apathy of charitable donors, in search of a new magic to help the people. Still others were the heroic survivors of networked communities that were finally in the social mainstream, after years of effort to put the new technologies at the service of society. There were also the militants of the new social movements, academics committed to diffusing their knowledge, government officials in a learning process, international agencies updating their programs, journalists reporting on on-line reporting, and even participants from the business world, looking for a taste of corporate social responsibility.

Altogether, the gathering, to be re-convened one year later in Buenos Aires, appeared to foreshadow a new, global civil society, built by the networking of community-based computer networks and civic associations. If this embryo, and similar efforts currently sprouting in different areas of the world, could actually develop, it would add a new, meaningful layer of social organization. They would not necessarily be social movements, since most of them seem to be linked in one way or another to the local state. Nor would they be oblivious to commercial interests, since Internet business takes place wherever people are on-line. Yet, by connecting globally, they could strengthen their autonomy and representativeness in their local settings. This is because they would benefit from information, support, resources, and legitimacy from global sources of solidarity and connection, rather than being exclusively dependent on their local ties. Furthermore, local institutions may connect to the world through their community networks, thus engaging in organizational cooperation and public image-making. And the local state, looking for a breathing space, may find it tactically useful to side with civil society as a counterpoint to the merger between the nation-state and global capitalism. It is still unclear if a global civil society is emerging, or if it could emerge in the years to come. But if it does, local/global citizen computer networks will undoubtly be one of its essential components.

The Internet, Democracy, and Informational Politics

The Internet was expected to be an ideal instrument to further democracy—and still is. Political information can be easily accessed, so citizens can be almost as well informed as their leaders. With government goodwill, all public records, as well as a wide range of non-classified information, could be made available online. Interactivity makes it possible for citizens to request information, voice their opinion, ask for a personalized answer from their representatives. Instead of the government watching people, people could be watching their government—which is actually their right, since in theory people are the masters of the place. And yet, most studies and reports describe a bleak picture—with the possible exception of Scandinavian democracies.

Governments at all levels use the Internet, primarily, as an electronic billboard to post their information without much effort at real interaction. Parliamentary representatives often have their own websites, but they do not pay excessive attention to them, either in their design or in their response to citizens' requests. Their answers are processed by their members of staff, in general with little difference from what they were doing earlier in responding to written letters. Indeed, on some of the websites of British MPs, in 2000, citizens were encouraged to write by regular mail and were warned that answers would take at least a week. According to an informal survey by the Institute of Economic Affairs in the UK of the websites of 97 MPs, in November 2000, their design and maintenance were extremely poor and indicated considerable neglect.

An interesting and well-documented international study of the use of the Internet in the parliaments of OECD countries documented the rapid increase of Internet use, both by the parliament and in its relationship with the electorate, but it also showed, generally speaking, a great deal of continuity with traditional political practices (Coleman, Taylor, and Van den Donk, 1999). Docter,

Dutton, and Elberse (1999) studied the California Democracy Network (DNET), an on-line voters' guide. They found it instructive and useful, and it seemed to play a functional role in informing citizens about their choices. However, its use was very limited: it had less than 4,000 visitors just before the gubernatorial election, suggesting that "DNET's role in the political arena is at the margins" (Doctor, Dutton, and Elberse, 1999: 187). Political parties routinely go on the web, and, during election campaigns, their candidates, or their surrogates, dutifully cater to the web. Yet, television, radio, and newspapers are still the preferred media since they fit better in the one-to-many communication pattern that is still the norm in politics.

In fact, it would be surprising if the Internet reverses, by means of its technology, what is a deep-seated political distrust among the majority of citizens throughout the world. Thus, at the time of the California gubernatorial election of 1998, to which the study by Docter and co-workers refers, the Public Policy Institute of California conducted a poll of a representative sample of California voters, according to which 54 percent of the voters thought that "public officials don't care what people like me think" (the proportion for the US as a whole was of 60 percent) (Baldassare, 2000: 43).

In a world of widespread crisis of political legitimacy, and citizens' disaffection *vis-à-vis* their representatives, the interactive, multi-directional channel of communication provided by the Internet finds few active takers on both sides of the link. Politicians and their institutions post their announcements and respond bureaucratically—except when election time comes. Citizens do not see much point in spending their energy on political queries, except when struck by an event that arouses their indignation or touches their personal interests. The Internet cannot provide a technological fix to the crisis of democracy.

Yet, the Internet does have a significant role in the new political dynamics, characterized by what I have called "informational politics" (Castells, 1997). Access to government in our societies is largely based on media politics, and on information systems that provoke the support or rejection of people's minds, thus influencing their electoral behavior. Because people do not trust programs, only persons, media politics is highly personalized, and organized around the image of the candidates. Thus, media politics leads to the prevalence of "scandal politics" (Rose-Ackerman, 1999; Thompson, 2000). This is because leaking information to the media to discredit the opponent, or producing counter-information to restore the image of an embattled politician, has become a critical weapon of latter-day politics. The media are the necessary intermediaries, and for access to the media it is necessary to know the right channels, and in some cases to have the money to produce and diffuse the appropriate information. Not that the media control politicians. Rather, the media form the space of politics, and politicians are the ones who, in order to free themselves of the control of party bureaucracies, choose to relate directly to citizens at large—thus using the media as their channel of mass communication. However, all this is changing because of the Internet.

The Internet provides, in principle, a horizontal, non-controlled, relatively cheap, channel of communication, from one-to-one as well as from one-to-many. As I stated, there is still only limited use of this channel by politicians. Yet, there is a growing use of the Internet by maverick journalists, political activists, and people of all kinds as a channel to diffuse political information and rumors. Precisely because of its openness, many of these rumors never find credibility, as witness the innumerable conspiracy theories that populate the Internet's chat rooms and radical websites of all sorts. But there are also instances of relevant political information diffused over the Internet that could not have reached the same level of diffusion, or with the same speed, if they had circulated through the mainstream media. This was the case for the first information concerning the Monica Lewinsky affair, diffused by a freelance Los Angeles journalist via his Internet newsletter, while the main media were still evaluating the story. Or else, the memoirs of François Mitterrand's doctor, barred from diffusion by the French courts, which found their way to the French people via the Internet—prompting a strong reaction from the French government, as I will analyze in Chapter 6. There are no more political secrets in the Internet Age, once they have gone beyond a very small circle of insiders. Because of the speed of diffusion of the news, the media have to be on guard, and react to these rumors, evaluate them, decide how to report them—they cannot dismiss them any longer. The borderline between gossip, fantasy, and valuable political information becomes increasingly blurred, thus further complicating the use of information as the privileged political weapon in the Internet Age.

Therefore, for the time being, rather than strengthening democracy by fostering the knowledge and participation of the citizens, use of the Internet tends to deepen the crisis of political legitimacy by providing a broader launching platform for the politics of scandal. The problem, naturally, is not with the Internet, but with the kind of polity our societies are generating. A polity that ultimately shapes the power of the state at a time when states are confronting a transformation of their security environment.

Security and Strategy in the Internet Age: Cyberwar, Noopolitik, Swarming

We know from Sun Tze and Clausewitz that war is the pursuit of politics by other means. Thus, informational politics naturally leads to the possibility of informational warfare and, more broadly, to the emergence of a new security doctrine appropriate to the Internet Age. Several related issues must be considered. I will try to disentangle them with the help of the research conducted on these matters at the Rand Corporation for a number of years by John Arquilla and David Ronfeldt, in my view the leading analysts of security affairs in the informational paradigm (1999, 2000).

Much has been made of the vulnerability of military installations and strategic command centers of government to cyber-attack from hostile hackers. Indeed, the ability to retrieve critical information, pollute databases, or create havoc with key communication systems becomes a weapon of choice in the new technological environment. The more a government and a society depend on their advanced communications network, the more they become exposed to such attacks. Furthermore, unlike conventional or nuclear warfare, these attacks could be launched by individual hackers, or by small, able groups who could escape detection or retaliation—and such attacks have indeed taken place on a limited scale, for instance against NATO computers by Serbian hackers during the Kosovo war, or against Russian command centers by pro-Chechen hackers.

Nevertheless, it appears that, at least in the case of the United States' government, the fears of vulnerability are somewhat over-blown. While some computers at NASA or the Pentagon have indeed been broken into by hackers, electronic defenses for the key nodes of the system seem to be reasonably robust. I would assume that major world powers have similarly efficient systems of protection. However, the system is indeed vulnerable, not at its center, but at its periphery. This is for two reasons. The first is because the critical security issue for any country is not necessarily the computers at the defense department, but the entire electronic network on which the daily life of people and the functioning of the economy depend. Because the Internet, and computer networks in general, have interconnected the entire country, indeed the world, avenues for the penetration of security systems are nearly unlimited. There is a powerful counter-measure that could strengthen security throughout the system: the diffusion of advanced encryption technology for organizations and for people at large. With the entire network able to protect itself at the point of its individual components, intrusions into the network become much more difficult. However, governments are barring the diffusion of encryption technology, claiming that this would empower criminal activities. In fact, as I will discuss in Chapter 6, it is a last ditch attempt by states to keep some level of control over information flows, on which their power has been founded for centuries. In one of the greatest historical ironies, the attempt to control information by forbidding distribution of encryption capacity leaves the state—and society—vulnerable to attacks from the periphery of the network.

There is a second major source of a state's vulnerability to cyber-attack. The emergence of a global network state, formed by cooperation between governments around the world on a number of issues, including security matters, and the extension of this network to an increasing number of NGOs, has created an electronic network of shared governance. Under such conditions the security of one particular node, including a powerful one, is only as good as the security of the network as a whole—which, of course, is not very good on average. States react by differentiating their openness to cooperation and networking by levels, so that only the most trusted partners have access to the most strategic networks. Yet, this distrustful cooperation limits partnership, and ultimately undermines joint security efforts—for instance in international police work, the only effective way to counter the global criminal economy or international terrorism. In other words, the more the state refuses to limit its sovereignty (either by encryption or international cooperation), the more it becomes vulnerable to cyber-attack.

There is a more fundamental transformation of international security issues: the rise of "noopolitik," using the terminology proposed by Arquilla and Ronfeldt. "Noopolitik" refers to the political issues arising from the formation of a "noosphere," or global information environment, which includes cyberspace and all other information systems—the media, for instance. Noopolitik can be contrasted with realpolitik, the traditional approach in terms of fostering the power of the state in the international arena, by negotiation, force, or the potential use of force. Realpolitik does not disappear in the Information Age. But it remains state-centric, in an era organized around networks, including networks of states. In a world characterized by global interdependence and shaped by information and communication, the ability to act on information flows, and on media messages, becomes an essential tool for fostering a political agenda. Indeed, social movements and NGOs have become much more adept at acting on people's minds around the globe by intervening in the noosphere; that is, in the system of communication and representation where categories are formed, and models of behavior are constituted.

Public diplomacy aimed at societies, and not just at governments, becomes an essential national security strategy, which may prevent confrontation, increase the opportunity for alliances, and foster cultural and political hegemony. This is distinct from propaganda or public relations. It is the actual capacity to intervene in the process of mental representation underlying public opinion and collective political behavior. It requires a technological infrastructure—the Internet, and global networked media. It also demands a liberal information order, ensuring the free movement of ideas and images. But it also implies the flexibility of states and political leaders to change their own ideas, to correct their views in order to connect with their changing global environment. In other words, cultural hegemony is not persuasion: it requires the acceptance of co-evolution. However, because political strategy is a medium for power-making, there is a double game taking place: on the one hand, the opening up of a global information and communication space, as open as possible to its diverse participants (governments, international organizations, business firms, and NGOs); on the other hand, from the point of view of a specific government or organization, an information strategy will be needed to further its own interests and values within the rules of the game. Thus, shaping global views as much as possible in a mold favorable to a given set of national or social interests becomes the new, and most effective, frontier of the exercise of power on the world stage.

Yet, as long as states exist, their *raison d'être* remains, in the last resort, their ability to exercise violence in defense of the interests they represent—including their own. But warfare is also being transformed by computer networks. First, technologically: electronic communications, surveillance systems, unmanned aircraft, and satellite-guided munitions are the decisive weapons in military confrontation. Secondly, strategically. A new strategic thinking is rapidly gaining favor among defense think-tanks in the US and in NATO. It is called "swarming." It represents a sharp departure from military concepts based on massive build-ups of fire power, armored hardware, and large concentrations of troops. It calls for small, autonomous units, provided with high fire power, good training, and real-time information. These "pods" would form "clusters" able to concentrate on an enemy target for a small fraction of time, inflicting major damage, and dispersing again. This "non-linear" warfare eliminates the notion of a front line, and represents a high-tech version of the old tradition of guerrilla struggles. This "network-centric" warfare, in Pentagon terminology, is entirely dependent on robust, secure communications, able to maintain constant connection between the nodes of an all-channel network. A combination of satellite transmission and mobile computer networking would enable platoon-size units to coordinate their actions, with the support of air power, and logistical units, out-maneuvering the enemy by their advantage in information as a result of knowing where they are, where they are going to be, and what they have to accomplish in the episodes of combat. Furthermore, their self-reliant character allows them a superior level of initiative, without losing the coordination of their purpose.

The US Marine Corps has already successfully experimented with these new tactics in its Hunter Warrior/Sea Dragon war-fighting exercises. The US armed forces seemed to be moving in the direction of a hybrid of the still dominant air–land battle strategy and the swarm battle strategy. An indication of the new mode of thinking was the tentative decision, in 2000, of gradually replacing tanks with light armored vehicles, better suited to the mobility required for the new way of fighting. If this new strategy were to be adopted, the implications for the armed forces are enormous. The entire organization of large-scale corps, divisions, regiments, and battalions would have to be undone. So would the functional division between different specialties: infantry, armored units, communications, artillery, engineering. Units should be largely multi-functional, and rely on their networking capacity for mutual support. They would also be entirely dependent on intelligence-gathering and information-processing. The entire military structure should in fact be shaken up. Furthermore, as the military increasingly act in political and functional cooperation with the armed forces of other countries, the polyvalence of small units could provide the building blocks of a fighting force to be assembled on an *ad hoc* basis, depending on the objectives and circumstances of each military mission. On the other hand, the compatibility of communications and computing systems and of networking procedures becomes a necessary condition for any kind of joint military operation. As Arquilla and Ronfeldt (2000: 46) point out,

this doctrinal vision cannot be effected in the absence of a fully integrated surveillance and communication system. The vision must help turn the military into a "sensory organization," while the system will be crucial for internetting the operational units. The command, control, communications, computers, intelligence, surveillance, and reconnaissance (C4ISR) system may generate so much information that it will be necessary . . . to retain "topsight"—a big picture of what is going on.

The combination of autonomy and topsight is obtained by computer-based inter-networking on the ground, between the autonomous units, and between the units and command and control centers. These centers become providers of a broad operational perspective, rather than micro-managers of the actual operations.

Swarming appears to be the new frontier of strategic thinking and military practice, one that could match the security threats posed by the swarming ability of international terrorism, and unpredictable hostile forces around the world. Several experimental programs were under way in the US military in 2000: the "Army After Next" program to empower light forces; the Navy "Fleet Battle" experiments, based on the concept of "network-centric warfare"; the Marines' "Chechen swarming" concept, modeled on the successful tactics of Chechen fighters against the Russian troops; the Marine "infestation teams," designed to operate in a decentralized but internetted fashion, and so on. Interestingly enough, thirty years after its inception, the Pentagon seems to have found a real use for Internet-related technologies, but not so much for the original, much-vaunted, Paul Baran goal of surviving a nuclear strike, as for adapting to the new forms of warfare—savage, individualized confrontations between swarming networks of small bands powered by information technology. "Swarming," conclude Arquilla and Ronfeldt (2000: 26), "provides an important alternative vision of the future for the American military—and it may well do so for other militaries, too, if they begin looking for innovations that may enable them to outwit the Americans. Whoever gets there first may find in swarming the doctrinal catalyst for waging cyberwar—the military end of the information-age conflict spectrum." Whether by information-based technology, by swarming military tactics, or by building ideational hegemony, the means and goals of state power in our world depend on communication and networking. By assuming these new means, states do not fade away, but they are deeply transformed in their structure and in their practice.

The Politics of the Internet

In the co-evolution of the Internet and society the political dimension of our lives is being deeply transformed. Power is primarily exercised around the production and diffusion of cultural codes and information content. The control of communication networks becomes the lever by which interests and values are transformed in guiding norms of human behavior. This movement proceeds, as in previous historical contexts, in a contradictory manner. The Internet is not an instrument of freedom, nor is it the weapon of one-sided domination. The Singapore experience is a case in point. Guided by a strong, capable government, Singapore has fully embraced technological modernization as a development tool. At the same time, it is widely considered to be one of the most sophisticated authoritarian systems in history. Attempting to steer a narrow path between these two policies, the government of Singapore has tried to expand the use of the Internet among its citizens, while retaining political control over this use by censoring Internet service providers. And yet the study by Ho and Zaheer (2000) shows how, even in Singapore, civil society has been able to use the Internet to broaden its space of freedom, to articulate the defense of human rights, and to propose alternative views in the political debate.

In fact, freedom is never a given. It is a constant struggle; it is the ability to redefine autonomy and enact democracy in each social and technological context. The Internet offers extraordinary potential for the expression of citizen rights, and for the communication of human values. Certainly, it cannot substitute for social change or political reform. However, by relatively leveling the ground of symbolic manipulation, and by broadening the sources of communication, it does contribute to democratization. The Internet brings people into contact in a public agora, to voice their concerns and share their hopes. This is why people's control of this public agora is perhaps the most fundamental political issue raised by the development of the Internet.

Reading Links

Arquilla, John and Ronfeldt, David (1999) *The Emergence of Noopolitik: Toward an American Information Strategy*. Santa Monica, CA: RAND National Defense Research Institute.

—— and —— (2000) *Swarming and the Future of Conflict*. Santa Monica, CA: RAND National Defense Research Institute.

Baldassare, Mark (2000) *California in the New Millennium: The Changing Social and Political Landscape*. Berkeley, CA: University of California Press.

Bell, Mark R. and Boas, Taylor C. (2000) "Falun Gong and the Internet: evangelism, community, and the struggle for survival", paper delivered at the Annual Meeting of the American Academy of Religion, Nashville, Tennessee, November 19.

Calhoun, Craig (ed.) (1994) *Social Theory and the Politics of Identity*. Oxford: Blackwell.

Castells, Manuel (1997) *The Power of Identity*. Oxford: Blackwell.

—— Yazawa, Shujiro, and Kiselyova, Emma (1996) "Insurgents against the global order: a comparative analysis of *Zapatistas* in Mexico, the American Militia and Japan's *Aum Shinrikyo*," *Berkeley Journal of Sociology*, 40: 21–60.

Cohen, Robin and Rai, Shirin M. (eds) (2000) *Global Social Movements*. London: The Athlone Press.

Coleman, Stephen, Taylor, John, and Van den Donk, Wim (eds) (1999) *Parliament in the Age of the Internet*. Oxford: Oxford University Press.

Docter, Sharon, Dutton, William, and Elberse, Anita (1999) "An American democracy network: factors shaping the future of on-line political campaigns," in Stephen Coleman *et al.* (eds), *Parliament in the Age of the Internet*, pp. 173–90. Oxford: Oxford University Press.

Dutton, William H. (1999) *Society on the Line: Information Politics in the Digital Age*. New York: Oxford University Press.

Giddens, Anthony (1994) *Beyond Left and Right: The Future of Radical Politics*. Cambridge: Polity Press.

Graham, Stephen and Aurigi, Alessandro (1997) "Urbanising cyberspace?," *City*, 7 (May): 18–39.

Grossman, Lawrence K. (1995) *The Electronic Republic: Reshaping Democracy in the Information Age*. New York: Penguin.

Ho, K. C. and Zaheer, Barber (2000) "Sites of resistance: charting the alternative and marginal websites in Singapore," Singapore: National University of Singapore, Department of Sociology, paper delivered at the First Conference of the Association of Internet Researchers, Lawrence, University of Kansas, September 14–17.

Juris, Jeffrey S. (forthcoming) "Transnational activism and the Movement for Global Resistance in Spain," unpublished PhD dissertation, University of California, Department of Anthropology, Berkeley, California.

Keck, Margaret E. and Sikkink, Kathryn (1998) *Activists Beyond Borders: Advocacy Networks in International Politics*. Ithaca, NY: Cornell University Press.

Langman, Lauren, Morris, Douglas, Zalewski, Jackie, Ignacio, Emily, and Davidson, Carl (2000) "Globalization, domination, and cyberactivism," paper delivered at the First Conference of the Association of Internet Researchers, Lawrence, University of Kansas, September 14–17.

Lesser, Ian, *et al.* (1999) *Countering the New Terrorism*. Santa Monica, CA: RAND, Project Air Force.

Lovink, Geert and Riemens, Patrice (1998) "The monkey's tail: the Amsterdam Digital City three and a half years later," in Richard Wolff *et al.* (eds), *Possible Urban Worlds: Urban Strategies at the End of the Twentieth Century*, Proceedings of the Seventh Conference of the International Network for Urban Research and Action (INURA). Basel and Boston: Birkhaeuser.

Melucci, Alberto (1989) *Nomads of the Present: Social Movements and Individual Needs in Contemporary Society*. Philadelphia, PA: Temple University Press.

O'Leary, Stephen D. (2000) "Falun Gong and the Internet", *USC Annenberg Online Journalism Review*.

Presidencia da Republica do Portugal (2000) *Os Cidadaos e a sociedade de informacao*, Proceedings of an International Conference. Lisbon: Imprenta Nacional.

Putnam, Robert (2000) *Bowling Alone: The Decline of Community in America*. New York: Basic Books.

Rose-Ackerman, Susan (1999) *Corruption and Government*. Cambridge: Cambridge University Press.

Schuler, Douglas (1996) *New Community Networks: Wired for Change*. New York: Addison-Wesley.

Servon, Lisa (2002) *Bridging the Digital Divide*, Oxford: Blackwell.

Sklair, Leslie (2000) *The Transnational Capitalist Class*. Oxford: Blackwell.

Smith, Jackie, *et al.* (eds) (1997) *Transnational Social Movements and World Politics: Solidarity Beyond the State*. Syracuse: Syracuse University Press.

Starhawk (2000) "Comment nous avons bloqué l'OMC," *Multitudes*, 1 (March): 102–7.

Tarrow, Sidney (1995) *Power in Movement: Social Movements and Contentious Politics*. Cambridge: Cambridge University Press.

—— (1996) *Fishnets, Internets and Catnets: Globalization and Transnational Collective Action*. Madrid: Instituto Juan March de Estudios e Investigaciones.

Thompson, John (2000) *Political Scandals*. Cambridge: Polity Press.

Touraine, Alain (1989) *Le retour de l'acteur*. Paris: Fayard.

Van Bastelaer, Beatrice and Lobet-Maris, Claire (2000) "The Digitale Stad (DDS), Amsterdam: between public domain and private enterprise", Edinburgh, University of Edinburgh, SLIM Project, unpublished research report.

Van den Besselaar, Peter (2001) "E-community versus e-commerce: the rise and decline of Amsterdam Digital City," *AI and Society: the Journal of Human-centered Systems and Machine Intelligence*, 1 (forthcoming).

e-Links

Cisler, Stephen (2000) http://home.inreach.com/cisler, posted 7 November
www.memoire-vivante.org
On citizen networks.

www.heise.de/tp/english/inhalt/co/6972/1.html (posted August 18, 2000)
http://squat.net.ascii
On the Amsterdam Digital City.

http://ojr.usc.edu
On Falung Gong and the Internet.

Chapter 6

The Politics of the Internet II: Privacy and Liberty in Cyberspace

Created as a medium for freedom, in the first years of its worldwide existence the Internet seemed to foreshadow a new age of liberty. Governments could do little to control communication flows able to circumvent geography, and thus political boundaries. Free speech could diffuse throughout the planet, without depending on mass media, as many could interact with many in an unfettered manner. Intellectual property (in music, in publications, in ideas, in technology, in software) had to be shared since it could hardly be enclosed once these creations were placed on the Net. Privacy was protected by the anonymity of communication on the Internet, and by the difficulty of tracing back the sources and identify the content of messages transmitted using Internet protocols.

This paradigm of freedom was based on both technological and institutional grounds. Technologically, its architecture of unrestricted computer networking, based on protocols that interpret censorship as a technical failure, and simply go around it in the global network, made it difficult—albeit not impossible—to control it. This is not in the "nature" of the Internet: this is the Internet itself, as designed by its original creators, as documented in Chapters 1 and 2.

Institutionally, the fact that the Internet developed first in the United States meant that it came under the constitutional protection of free speech enforced by the US courts. Because the backbone of the global Internet was largely based in the United States, any restriction to servers in other countries could generally be bypassed by re-routing through a US server. To be sure, authorities in a given country could detect the recipients of certain types of message by exercising their surveillance capabilities, and then punish the offenders according to their laws, as Chinese dissidents have often experienced. Yet, the surveillance/punishment process was too cumbersome to be cost-effective on a large scale, and, in any case, it did not stop Internet communication, simply imposed penalties upon it. The only way to control the Internet was not to be in the network, and this rapidly became too high a price to pay for countries around the world, both in terms of business opportunities and access to global information.

In this sense the Internet decisively undermined national sovereignty and state control. But it could only do so because of the judicial protection it received in the core of its global backbone, the US. Indeed, for all their talk about the Internet and freedom, the US Congress and the Clinton administration tried to arm themselves with legal tools of control over the Internet. After all, control of information has been the essence of state power throughout history, and the US is no exception. This is why one of the exemplary values of the American Constitution is precisely to place the right to free speech as the First Amendment of the Constitution. In their attempt to exercise control over the Internet, the US Congress and the US Justice Department used the argument that strikes a chord in every one of us: the protection of children from the sexual evils roaming the Internet. To no avail. The 1995 Communications Decency Act was declared unconstitutional by a US federal court in Pennsylvania, on June 12, 1996, stating that "Just as the strength of the Internet is chaos, so the strength of our liberty depends upon the chaos and cacophony of the unfettered speech the First Amendment protects" (quoted in Lewis, 1996). This "constitutional right to chaos" was upheld by the Supreme Court on June 26, 1997. A new attempt by the Clinton administration to enable government to censor the Internet, the 1998 Child On-line Protection Act, was again struck down in June 2000 by the US Court of Appeals in Philadelphia. Because of the difficulty of bringing the US on the side of government regulation of computer communication, given the global nature of the network the *direct* attempt by the state to control the Internet by traditional means of censorship and direct repression appears to have failed.

However, these two foundations of liberty on the Internet could be challenged, and are indeed being challenged, by new technologies and new regulations (Lessig, 1999; Samuelson, 2000*a*). Software applications can be layered on top of Internet protocols, making it possible to identify communication routes and content. By using these technologies, privacy can be breached, and once individuals can be related to specific communication processes in specific institutional contexts, all traditional forms of political and organizational control can be unleashed upon the networked individual. This is the powerful, convincing argument put forward by Lawrence Lessig in his influential book *Code and Other Laws of Cyberspace* (1999). Although my views diverge somewhat from his interpretation (and more so from his normative position), Lessig's thesis should be taken as the starting-point of this analysis. The transformation of liberty and privacy on the Internet is a direct result of its commercialization. The need to secure and identify communication on the Internet to make money out of it, and the need to protect intellectual property rights on the Net, have led to the development of new software architectures (which Lessig calls "the code") that make it possible to control computer communication. Governments around the world both support these technologies of surveillance and eagerly adopt them to claim back some of the power they were losing (Lyon, 2001a, b). Yet, new technologies of freedom are being opposed to these technologies of control, civil society comes to the trenches of new battles for liberty, and the judiciary offers a degree of protection against blatant abuses, at least in some contexts (not in the workplace). The Internet is no longer a free realm, but neither has it fulfilled the Orwellian prophecy. It is a contested terrain, where the new, fundamental battle for freedom in the Information Age is being fought.

Technologies of Control

A variety of technologies of control have emerged from the intertwined interests of commerce and governments. There are technologies of identification, of surveillance, and of investigation. All rely on two basic assumptions: the asymmetrical knowledge of codes in the network; and the ability to define a specific space of communication susceptible of control. Let us review succinctly these issues, as a step in analyzing the processes of restriction of freedom at work on the Internet.

Technologies of identification include the use of passwords, "cookies," and authentication procedures. "Cookies" are digital markers automatically placed by websites in the hard disks of the computers that connect to them. Once the "cookie" is set in the computer, all on-line movements from that computer are automatically recorded by the server of the website that placed the "cookie." Authentication procedures use digital signatures that allow other computers to verify the origin and features of the interacting correspondent. They often rely on encryption technology. Authentication often works in layers, with individual users being identified by servers that are themselves identified by networks. One of the earliest examples of security protocols on the Internet was the "secure socket layer" (SSL) introduced by Netscape. Other standard security protocols have been adopted by consortiums of credit card companies and by e-commerce companies.

Surveillance technologies are of a different kind, but often rely on identification technologies to be able to locate the individual user. Suveillance technologies intercept messages, place markers that allow tracking of communication flows from a specific computer location, and monitor machine activity around the clock. Surveillance technologies may identify a given server at the origin of a message.Then, by persuasion or coercion, governments, companies, or courts may obtain from the Internet service provider the identity of the potential culprit by using identification technologies, or simply by looking up in their listings when the information is available (as electronic addresses match real addresses for the clients of most Internet service providers).

Technologies of investigation refer to the building of databases from the results of both surveillance and storage of routinely recorded information (Garfinkel, 2000). Once data are collected in digital form, all the information items contained in the database can be aggregated, disaggregated, combined, and identified according to purpose and legal capacity. Sometimes, it is simply aggregate profiling, as in market research, either for commerce or for politics. In other cases, it is individualized targeting, as a given person may be characterized by a large body of information contained in his or her electronic records, from credit card payments to websites visits, electronic mail, and telephone calls. In the current technological environment, any electronically transmitted information is recorded, and can eventually be processed, identified, and combined, in either a collective or an individual unit of analysis.

Encryption is the fundamental technology that protects the privacy of the message (although not of the messenger, since the originating computer will be identified by the point of entry in the electronic network) (Levy, 2001). This is particularly true for public key encryption (PKI), with two keys for decoding, one of which is privately held. However, as Lessig (1999) points out, encryption is an ambiguous technology because, while it can preserve confidentiality, it is also the basis for advanced identification technologies. It allows the development of certified digital signatures which, once their request becomes generalized, will cancel anonymity on the Internet, since every dog will be required to register as a dog in order to have access to a dog's life—or else it will end up with the cats of its cyber-neighborhood.

These technologies operate their controls under two basic conditions. First, the controllers know the codes of the network, the controlled do not. Software is confidential, and proprietary, and cannot be modified except by its owner. Once on the network, the average user is the prisoner of an architecture he or she does not know. Secondly, controls are exercised on the basis of a space defined on the network, for instance, the network around an Internet service provider, or the intra-network in a company, a university, or a government agency. Yes, the Internet is a global network, but points of access to it are not. If filters are placed on this access, the price of global freedom is local submission. Let us now see these technologies of control in action.

The End of Privacy

There has been so much enthusiasm about the freedom brought by the Internet that we have forgotten the persistence of authoritarian, surveillance practices in the environment that remains the most important in our lives: the workplace. With workers becoming increasingly dependent on computer networking in their activity, most companies have decided that they have the right to monitor the uses of their networks by their employees. In the US, a study released in April 2000, showed that 73.5 percent of US firms conduct some form of surveillance of the use of the Internet by their employees on a regular basis. There have been innumerable cases of workers fired for what was deemed improper use of the Net (Howe, 2000: 106). Programs such as Gatekeeper display in a server all of the Internet activity taking place in any organization suscribing to the server. Shopfloor control of the worker by management was a traditional source of conflict in the Industrial Age. It seems that the Internet Age is bound to heighten this tension—as it becomes more insidious because of its automated pervasiveness.

But even beyond the glass walls of the company world, "you already have zero privacy—get over it," proclaims Scott McNealy, the charismatic CEO of Sun Microsystems, in a widely noted statement (quoted in Scheer, 2000: 100). Here, the fundamental development has been the technologies of data-gathering associated with the economics of e-commerce. In many cases, the main revenue for e-commerce companies is advertising and marketing, as noted in Chapter 3. On the one hand, they receive the proceeds from the advertising banners they can post for their users. On the other hand, the data from their users are sold to their clients for marketing purposes, or used by the company itself to better target its customers. In all cases, precious information must be collected from each click to the website. In the United States, 92 percent of websites collect personal data from their users, and process them according to their commercial interests (Lessig, 1999: 153). Companies swear that they only use data in an aggregated form for marketing profiles. And, after all, most consumers do not exercise their right of opting out by clicking away the use of their personal data. Consumer advocates have shown how inconvenient in practice is the exercise of the opt-out clause, proposing instead an opt-in, affirmative decision. Yet, in the US, Congress, under strong lobbying efforts from advertisers and the e-commerce industry, rejected the obligation of the opt-out formula. In the European Union, stronger government action in favor of consumer protection led to a privacy law under which companies cannot use data from their customers without their explicit consent. However, the issue then becomes the exchange of data against the privilege of access to websites. Most people waive their rights to privacy in order to be able to use the Internet. Once this privacy protection right has been waived, personal data become the lawful property of Internet firms, and of their clients.

To illustrate this process, consider the case of Double Click, the Internet's largest advertising-placement company. Its business is to place "cookie" files by the million in the computers that connect with websites equipped with Double Click technology. Once a computer receives a "cookie," it will be targeted with specific commercials in any visit to the thousands of websites that employ the services of Double Click. As many other Internet companies, Double Click regularly tests the limits of further taking away privacy. Thus, in November 1999 Double Click bought Abacus, a database of names, addresses, and information concerning the shopping patterns of 90 million households in the US. Using this database, Double Click created profiles linking individual's real names and addresses with their on-line and off-line shopping. The protests from privacy advocates forced Double Click to put on hold its profiling business until an agreement could be reached between the government and the industry on standards to deal with privacy issues (Rosen, 2000*a*).

As reported by Rosen (2000*b*), technologies that make it possible to download digitally stored books and magazines, music, and movies directly on to hard drives make it possible for publishers and entertainment companies to record and monitor browsing habits, and target their customers. The largest electronic communication publishing conglomerate in the world, AOL–Time Warner, is a case in point. The integrated multimedia box of the future (eagerly sought after by Microsoft and ATT) may have substantial surveillance capabilities. Globally unique identifiers (GUID) make it possible to link every document, e-mail message or chat posted with the real identity of the person who sent it. In November 1999, Real Jukebox was challenged by privacy advocates when they noted that the music player could send information to its parent company, Real Networks, about the music each user downloaded, and this could be matched with a unique ID number that pinpointed the user's identity. Fearing bad publicity, Real Networks disabled the GUID. Remember, however, that digital identification is the rule rather than the exception in the industry: Microsoft software products, such as Word97 and Powerpoint97, include identifiers into every document that we produce with the help of these programs. The identity of these documents is traceable to the computer that originated them.

Privacy in e-mail does not receive adequate legal protection. According to Rosen (2000*a*: 51):

In an entirely circular legal test, the Supreme Court has held that constitutional protections against unreasonable searches depend on whether citizens have subjective expectations of privacy that society is prepared to accept as reasonable . . . More recently, courts have held that merely by adopting a written policy that warns employees that their email may be monitored, employers will lower expectations of privacy in a way that gives them unlimited discretion to monitor whatever they please.

Business opportunities are unlimited in this new industry of marketing private behavior. In the 2000 elections in the US, a company created a database, named Aristotle, which, using data from different sources, provided political profiling of as many as 150 million citizens, selling these profiles to the highest bidder, usually the campaign offices of political candidates.

Piggybacking on the technological breakthroughs from commercial Internet companies, governments have stepped up their own surveillance programs, combining heavy-handed, traditional methods with new technological sophistication. Internationally, the Echelon program, created by the United States and the UK during the Cold War, seems to have been converted into industrial espionage, according to French government agencies, by combining traditional eavesdropping and interference of telecommunications, with interception of electronic messages. The FBI's Carnivore program works in cooperation (voluntary or not) with Internet service providers, recording all e-mail traffic, then sorting out the desired information on the basis of automated sampling and key-wording. In 2000 the FBI asked Congress for 75 million dollars to finance surveillance programs, including "Digital Storm," a new version of recording telephone communication combined with computerized programs to mine keywords in the messages.

The potential emergence of an electronic surveillance system is on the horizon. The irony is that it was, by and large, the Internet firms, ardent libertarians in their ideology, that provided the technology for breaking anonymity and curtailing privacy, and they were the first to use it. So doing, they let government surveillance roar back with a vengeance in the space of liberty that had been carved out by the Internet pioneers by taking advantage of the ignorant indifference of traditional bureaucracies. Yet, history is contradictory, and the counter-offensive of freedom lovers is under way. But before considering this alternative trend, we must examine the consequences of the undermining of privacy for the other dimensions that together constitute the Internet's kingdom of freedom.

Sovereignty, Liberty, and Property when Privacy Fades Away

In the year 2000, governments around the world took seriously the threat from what they labeled "cybercrime." It had become clear that the computer communications infrastructure, on which wealth, information, and power in our world depend, was highly vulnerable to intrusion, interference, and disruption. Relentless waves of viruses and worms roam the Internet, crackers break through fire walls, credit card numbers are stolen, political activists take over websites, files of military computers are transferred around the world, and confidential software is retrieved from even Microsoft's internal network. In spite of billions of dollars spent on electronic security, it became evident that, in a network, security is only as good as the security of its weakest link. Break into the network at any point, and you can go around its nodes with relative ease.

In fact, real damage, whether in property or personal harm, was very limited—and customarily overstated: nothing comparable with the loss in human lives, environmental degradation, and even money inflicted by the misadventures of, say, the automobile industry (remember Firestone/Ford?) or the chemical industry (please remember Bhopal). Yet, the notion of insecure computer networks is literally untenable for the powers that be in our world—everything depends on these networks, and control over these networks is an essential principle of remaining in control.

But there was something else. Hacking and cracking, practiced from anywhere to anywhere in the global network, revealed the powerlessness of traditional forms of policing, rooted in the powers of the state within its national boundaries. It heightened the anxiety already present in all governments around the world because of their inability to stop the communication flows that they had banned within their borders—be it Falun Gong messages in China, the memoirs of Mitterrand's doctor in France, or the auctioning of valid absentee ballots for American elections over the Net in the United States (the website was moved to Germany). The sovereignty of the state always began with the control of information, and this control was now being slowly but surely eroded. Because of the global character of the Internet, it became necessary for the most important governments to act together, creating a new, global space of policing. In fact, by doing so they were losing sovereignty, since they had to share power and agree on common standards of regulation—they became a network themselves, a network of regulatory and policing agencies. But sharing sovereignty was the price to pay to collectively retain some degree of political control. So, dumping together legitimate and illegitimate practices, the state struck back. The meeting of the G-8 club in Paris in June 2000 led the charge, and the Council of Europe echoed the concern with a convention against cybercrime, drafted by the security agencies of European countries, with the advice of global software companies—the most far-reaching, comprehensive attempt to control communication over the Internet to that date. Many countries around the world, such as Russia, China, Malaysia, Singapore, and others, applauded this new, deliberate attitude of major governments to clamp down on the Internet. An attitude that they saw, rightly, as a vindication of their own earlier distrust.

The provisions of all these concerted policies are at the same time too vague and too technical to be discussed here in detail. Besides, they will soon be technologically obsolete, so they will have to be constantly updated. What really counts is the intent and the methodology of intervention. In a nutshell, they try to neutralize encryption power in the hands of citizens by restricting or banning encryption technology. They ban software personal security tools of the kind I will discuss below. They greatly extend government's power on wiretapping and interception of data traffic. And they establish the obligation for Internet service providers to set traceability techniques for their users, as well as forced notification of users' identities at the request of government agencies, in a very broad range of situations, and in circumstances vaguely defined. Notice that, overall, it all amounts to a curtailment of privacy of communication on the Internet—to shift the Internet from being a space of freedom to becoming a glass house. Communication will still flow unfettered because this is the architecture of the Internet. But by redefining the space of access, through the control of

Internet service providers, and by setting up special protocols of surveillance layered on top of the Internet for specific networks, control (and punishment) may be exercised *ex post facto*. Lessig is right. The new Internet architecture, the new code, becomes the fundamental tool of control, making it possible to exercise regulation and policing by traditional forms of state power.

The first victim of this repossession of cyberspace is sovereignty itself. To exercise global regulation, states have to merge and share power. Not under the old-fashioned dream of a world government, but as a network state, the political creature engendered by the Information Age (Carnoy and Castells, 2001). The second victim is liberty; that is, the right to do as one pleases. Why so? Why does the threat to privacy translate into the potential curtailment of liberty? Partly, this stems from the mechanism through which sovereignty is enforced in a global context. For states to be partners in this network of control they must agree on common standards, and these standards are patterned on the lowest common denominator. If a given government is to cooperate in enforcing control over child pornography websites located in its territory, it will do so only on condition that it has access to data retrieved from intercepting traffic between its country and countries out of its reach—or else, why should it cooperate? The very notion of international policing is based upon sharing the effort of information-gathering.

A different matter is the ability of a given state to act upon behavior conducted in another jurisdiction—this will be restrained by the old forms of power based on territoriality. Yet, sharing global access to information networks is a decisive form of imposing collective state power over all citizens everywhere, as the consequences of the information obtained will guide repression in specific contexts. While repression will be differential, according to the degree of liberty in each country, the informational basis of the repression will be adjusted to standards of reasonable suspicion shared by all the governments participating in the network of police surveillance. For instance, legal methadone or marijuana consumption in The Netherlands by an American citizen may be exposed, and potentially repressed (by law or by norms), in the US as a consequence of joint surveillance on drug distribution. To be gay or lesbian is still punished by law in some countries (for example, Malaysia, Saudi Arabia), so joint surveillance of sexual preference chat rooms (looking for child pornography), once it is related to the real identity of citizens of these countries, may result in serious consequences for them, in spite of the legal tolerance of their sexuality in other countries. Furthermore, global surveillance encroaches on free speech. This is less so in countries, such as the United States, with strong legal protection of this fundamental right. But once traffic is jointly intercepted by agencies of various countries, the uses of the data obtained by surveillance will not be confined to the jurisdiction of the US courts.

There is a more fundamental threat to liberty under the new global policing environment: the structuring of everyday behavior by the dominant norms of society. Free speech was the essence of the right to unfettered communication at the time when most daily activities were not related to personal expression in the public realm. But in our age, a significant proportion of everyday life, including work, leisure, personal interaction, takes place on the Net. As I have shown in preceding chapters, most economic, social, and political activity is in fact a hybrid of on-line interaction and in-flesh interaction. In many cases, one cannot exist without the other. Thus, life in an electronic panopticon is tantamount to having half of our lives permanently exposed to monitoring. Because we live composite existences, this exposure may lead to a schizophrenic self between being ourselves off-line and an image of ourselves on-line, thus internalizing censorship.

The issue is not the fear of Big Brother because, in fact, most surveillance will have no directly damaging consequences for us—or, for that matter, no consequences at all. The most worrisome aspect is, in fact, the absence of explicit rules of behavior, of predictability of the consequences of our exposed behavior, depending upon the contexts of interpretation, and according to the criteria used to judge our behavior by a variety of actors behind the screen of our glass house. It is not Big Brother, but a multitude of little sisters, agencies of surveillance and processing of information that record our behavior for ever, as databases surround us throught our life— soon starting with our DNA and personal features (our retina, our thumbprint as digitalized marks). Under conditions of authoritarian states this surveillance may directly affect our lives (and this is in fact the situation for the overwhelming majority of humankind). But even in democratic societies where civil rights are respected, the transparency of our lives will decisively shape our attitudes. No one has ever been able to live in a transparent society. If this system of surveillance and control of the Internet develops fully, we will not be able to do as we please. We may have no liberty, and no place to hide.

The great historical irony is that one of the key institutions in the defense of liberty, the free enterprise, is the essential ingredient in the construction of this system of surveillance—in spite of the general goodwill and libertarian ideology of most Internet companies. Without their help, governments would not have the know-how, and, more fundamentally, the possibility of intervening on the Internet: it all depends on the capacity to act on Internet service providers and specific networks everywhere. For instance, the company Internet Crimes Group Inc. (ICG) specializes in revealing the identity of anonymous posters, with the cooperation of Internet service providers. EWATCH, a service of PR Newswire, will find the identity of any name on the screen for a fee of 5,000 US dollars: it has hundreds of corporate clients. And the surveillance can be retroactive: Deja.com has gathered a database on Usenet newsgroups that can be searched in all their postings since 1995 (Anonymous, 2000).

Why do information-technology businesses cooperate so eagerly in the reconstruction of the old world of control and repression? There are two main reasons besides occasional opportunistic attitudes. The first one, concerning mainly dot.com firms, is that they need to crack the privacy of their customers in order to sell their information. The second is that they need government support to preserve their property rights in the Internet-based economy. The Napster affair in 2000 was a turning-point. Faced with the possibility of a technology (MP3) that allows people (and particularly young people) to share and exchange their music on a global scale, without paying anything, music companies mobilized both the courts and government legislation to restore property rights (see Chapter 7). Publishing houses, and media companies in general, face a similar threat. Intellectual property rights are a fundamental source of profit-making in an information economy. Indeed, their protection is paramount to keep the value difference between the knowledge economy, based in the dominant, global networks, and the commodities and manufacturing economies, which are the prevailing feature of developing countries. As Lessig (1999) points out, the "fair use" of information, customarily protected by copyright laws, is being substantially reduced in the context of the enforced protection of this information as an incentive to producers of information to keep producing it. Yet, the balance between stimulating production and allowing the public use of information is being lost, as information is commodified and increasingly geared toward high-paying markets. To enforce this protection, information-producing business needs to control access and identity on the Internet, where most information is distributed. Therefore, it has a vested interest in supporting government efforts to restore control by building a glass house on the basis of an architecture of controlled software—a code, in Lessig's terminology.

The global attack on privacy to restore control in a pattern of shared sovereignty ensures property rights of information at the expense of the public use of this information. In order to assert their interests, commerce and governments jointly threaten liberty by breaching privacy in the name of security. Yet, this is only one side of the story.

The Internet Freedom Barricades

Codes versus codes. Technologies of control can be counteracted by technologies of freedom. And there is an abundance of them, often produced and commercialized by firms that have found a new market niche; in other instances, invented by determined freedom fighters ready to take up the challenge. Here is a sample, probably outdated within a year or so, yet indicative of the technological battle under way.

Firms such as Disappearing Inc. and ZipLip have created self-deleting e-mail that uses encryption technology. The Canadian company Zero-knowledge Systems decomposes identities with a software package called Freedom, which provides five digital pseudonyms that can be attributed to different activities. On the Freedom system, no one can trace the pseudonyms back to the real identity. Freedom makes traceability difficult by encrypting e-mail and web-browsing requests and sending them through at least three intermediary routers to their final destination. Each router can only take one layer of the encryption. Zero-knowledge uses the same technology, so the company itself cannot link pseudonyms to individual suscribers. The company has only a list of names of clients, without relationship to pseudonyms. Anonymizer.Com offers free anonymizers, in exchange for its advertising. Anonymizers are extra servers that buffer the customer's browser from its final destination. Idzap.com offers similar services (Anonymous, 2000; Rosen, 2000*a*). The fast development of privacy protection technologies is exactly what worries governments, prompting their attempts to forbid the private use of encryption technology, and outlaw its use and sale (Levy, 2001).

There is a second level of fight over the code: the development of open source codes, in the terms discussed in Chapter 2. If software codes are open, then they can be altered, either by the informed user or by a service firm or a non-profit organization, or a hackers' network, working for the common good of the Information Age. Proprietary control over software codes paves the way for the restriction of uses of information, and to the end of privacy on the Internet. You may think this the correct way to go. But for those who do not, the critical issue is the ability to know and modify the source code, and all software for that matter. In a world of open source software, the ability of government and corporations to control the founding architecture of Internet applications is vastly reduced.

Which way societies will go does not certainly depend on the code itself, but on the ability of societies and their institutions to impose, resist, and modify the code. At the dawn of the twenty-first century there is an unsettling combination in the Internet world: pervasive libertarian ideology with increasingly controlling practice. Social movements in defense of freedom on the Internet, such as the coalition formed around the Electronic Privacy Information Center in the United States, are essential sources for the preservation of the original Internet as a realm of freedom. But resistance will not suffice. Laws, courts, public opinion, the media, corporate responsibility, and political agencies will be the decisive areas where the future of the Internet will be shaped. Global networks cannot be controlled, but people using them, can, are, and will be—unless societies opt for the freedom of the Internet by acting from and beyond the barricades of their nostalgic libertarians.

Internet and Liberty: Whither Governments?

In much of this analysis, as in the ideology of most of the grassroots of early Internet users, there is an implicit assumption that governments are not the allies of liberty. And yet, we know from history that institutional democracy, not libertarian ideology, has been the main rampart against tyranny. So, why not entrust governments, at least democratic governments, with regulating the proper uses of the Internet? For instance, the European Union's regulation of data gathered by dot.com companies from their users protects privacy to a much greater extent than the *laissez-faire* environment in the United States. However, at the same time, European governments are adamant in retaining as much control as they can over information and communication, leading the charge, for instance, against the diffusion of encryption technology, the most effective way for people to control their communication.

In the last analysis, and on a variety of pretexts, governments distrust their citizens—they know better. And citizens distrust their governments—they know enough. In 1998 in the US 60 percent of citizens thought that "public officials don't care what people like me think," and 63 percent that "government is run by a few big interests." In California, the respective percentages of citizens supporting these statements were 54 percent and 70 percent (Baldassare, 2000: 43). Similar data can be found in many countries in the world, with the notable exception of the Scandinavian democracies. So, if people do not trust their governments, and governments do not trust their people (after all, political parties try all kinds of tricks to win elections), it is only logical that the emergence of the Internet as a space of freedom would epitomize this cleavage, with the advocates of liberty trying to preserve this new land of opportunity, while governments mobilize their considerable resources to close this leak in their control systems.

And yet, the story could be different. One could think of a strategy of mutually guaranteed disarmament, of a restoration of reciprocal trust. But because governments are still on top of the institutions of society, they should start the process: they bear the burden of social responsibility. Indeed, the Internet could be used by citizens to watch their government, rather than by the government to watch its citizens. It could become an instrument of control, information, participation, and even decision-making, from the bottom up. Citizens could have access to government data files, as in fact is their right. And governments, not people's private lives, should become a glass house—save for some essential national security matters. Only under such conditions of transparent political institutions could governments legitimately pretend to set up a limited control over the Internet to detect the few instances of the manifestation of the perverse side that inhabits us all. Unless governments stop fearing their people, and therefore the Internet, society will resort once again to the barricades to defend freedom and this will mark a stunning historical continuity.

Reading Links

Agree, Philip E. and Rotenberg, Marc (eds) (1998) *Technology and Privacy: The New Landscape*. Cambridge, MA: MIT Press.

Anonymous (2000) "The invisible man," *Yahoo! Internet Life*, October: 108–10.

Baldassare, Mark (2000) *California in the New Millennium: The Changing Social and Political Landscape*. Berkeley, CA: University of California Press.

Borgman, Christine L. (2000) *From Gutenberg to the Global Information Infrastructure: Access to Information in the Networked World*. Cambridge, MA: MIT Press.

Carnoy, Martin and Castells, Manuel (2001) "Poulantzas at the millennium: globalization, the knowledge society, and the state," *Global Networks: A Journal of Transnational Studies*, 1(1).

Garfinkel, Simson (2000) *Database Nation*. Sebastopol, CA: O'Reilly.

Howe, Jeff (2000) "Big boss is watching," *Yahoo! Internet Life*, October: 105–7.

Lessig, Lawrence (1999) *Code and Other Laws of Cyberspace*. New York: Basic Books.

Levy, Stephen (2001) *Crypto. How the Code Rebels Beat the Government: Saving Privacy in the Digital Age*. New York: Viking.

Lewis, Peter H. (1996) "Judge temporarily blocks law that bars indecency on the Internet," *New York Times*, February 16: C1.

Lyon, David (1994) *The Electronic Eye: The Rise of Surveillance Society*. Cambridge: Polity Press.

—— (2001*a*) *Surveillance Society: Monitoring Everyday Life*. Milton Keynes: Open University Press.

—— (2001*b*) "Everyday surveillance: personal data and social classification," *Information, Communication and Society* (forthcoming).

Rosen, Jeffrey (2000*a*) "The eroded self," *New York Times Sunday Magazine*.

—— (2000*b*) *The Unwanted Gaze: The Destruction of Privacy in America*. New York: Random House.

Rosenberg, Marc (ed.) (2000) *The Privacy Law Sourcebook: United States Law, International Law, and Recent Developments*. Washington, DC: Electronic Privacy Information Center.

Samuelson, Pamela (2000*a*) "Five challenges for regulating the global information society," in Chris Marsden (ed.), *Regulating the Global Information Society*. London: Routledge.

—— (2000*b*) "Privacy as intellectual property," *Stanford Law Review*, 52: 1125.

Scheer, Robert (2000) "Nowhere to hide", *Yahoo! Internet Life*, October: 100–2.

Scheer, Robert *et al.* (2000) "Privacy: a special report," *Yahoo! Internet Life*, October: 98–100.

Schneier, Bruce (1996) *Applied Cryptography*. New York: John Wiley.

—— (2000) *Secrets and Lies: Digital Security in a Networked World*. New York: John Wiley.

Whitaker, Reg (1999) *The End of Privacy*. New York: The New Press.

e-Links

epic.org
One of the leading organizations and resource centers on Internet privacy in the US.

eff.org
ftc.gov/bcp/conline/pubs/online/sitesee
Information on threats to privacy and forms of resistance.

cnetdownload.com
junkbusters.com
silentsurf.com
anonymizer.com
Websites providing technological resources to protect privacy.

http://qsliver.queensu.ca/sociology
Website of the Surveillance Project at Queen's University, one of the leading academic research projects in the sociology of electronic surveillance.

Chapter 7

Multimedia and the Internet: The Hypertext beyond Convergence

The Elusive Magic Box

Throughout the 1990s futurologists, technologists, and media tycoons pursued the dream of convergence between computers, the Internet, and the media. The key word was "multimedia," and its materialization was the magic box that would sit in our living room and could, at our command, open a global window to endless possibilities of interactive communication in video, audio, and text format. Between 1998 and 2000 Microsoft invested 10 billion dollars in cable companies around the world, laying the ground for its market control of the new software technology embedded in the future, interactive TV set-top box. It failed to deliver the software as scheduled because of its insistence on powering the boxes with its

Window CE operating system, but the project is indicative of the strategy of convergence being pursued by Internet and software business and traditional media companies. On January 12, 2001, the US federal government regulatory authority, the Federal Communications Commission (FCC), approved the 100 billion dollar merger of AOL and Time Warner, hailed as the corporate foundation to unleash the promise of multimedia.

Yet, the business experiments on media convergence carried on since the early 1990s have ended in failure, often technologically, and always in terms of consumer demand, especially regarding video on demand (Owen, 1999; Castells, 2000; *The Economist*, 2000). First, there was the unsuccessful merger between the PC and interactive video on demand, of which the collapse of Time Warner's Full Service Network in Orlando was the most notorious example. Then, the attempt to broadcast video via the Internet, although technically possible, could not proceed with comparable quality to television (analog or digital), and found few takers, with Web TV (acquired by Microsoft in 1997) being the main victim of the ill-conceived project.

Before trying to understand the reasons for the provisional demise of this multimedia vision, it would be useful to clarify what exactly is meant by the technological convergence between television and the Internet. In his authoritative analysis of the matter, Owen (1999) provides a succint enumeration of convergence mechanisms, as of 1999 (the situation had not substantially changed by the end of 2000):

- Broadcasting of regular TV signals over the Internet. This was not possible with 2000 bandwidth and compression technology, but will become technologically possible in the first decade of this century.
- Internet-transmitted video information inserted in web pages. This is already usual practice.
- A TV can be used as display, and connected to the Internet by a computer and a phone line (the Web TV concept).
- The interval in video signals broadcast (by airwaves or cable) can be used to transmit information to personal computers, including Internet access (for example, Intel's Intercast).

Multimedia and the Internet

- Web pages can be transmitted by telephone lines to a television screen to provide complementary information (for example, Gateway 2000 or Net TV).
- Internet-transmitted information can be coordinated with conventional TV broadcasting by servers maintained by TV stations, with display in different monitors (this is the Time Warner "City Web" concept).
- Cable or wireless communication can be used to transmit Internet content to computers (for example, @Home service in the US). Microsoft, in cooperation with ATT, has bet on a major cable company, MSO, using cable modem connections and set-top boxes working on Microsoft software.
- Narrow band non-video material transmitted over the Internet, able to provide animating icons on Web pages—such as Dynamic HTML software.
- TV channels can be used, when they are off the air, to transmit information, including video, to storage devices to be accessed by computers.

I would also add that the development of wireless Internet access provides the possibility of accessing any video or text material available on-line, although the quality of the transmission and reception of the image still raises daunting problems. At any rate, Owen (1999: 313) reminds us that "each of these alternatives, except for the first, is being experimented with at present. No one is going to send broadcast quality video programming over the Internet anytime soon . . . When and if that happens, it will be primarily a video medium carrying Internet content, not the reverse."

Upon further review, in 2001, none of these forms of convergence is practiced on a large scale, and none of them is making money. Indeed, traditional media companies are not generating any profits from their Internet ventures. And the prospects are unlikely to change in the near future. Even Bob Pittman, Chief Operating Officer (COO) of AOL–Time Warner, thinks so: according to him "the newest stuff," such as interactive TV and video-on-demand, will not take hold for seven to ten years (meaning until 2007–2010) (quoted in *Business Week*, 2001: 64).

Let me be clear. The media world is in the midst of an extraordinary transformation, going glocal (globalizing and narrowcasting at the same time), and finding economies of scale and synergy between different modes of expression. Satellite-broadcast, digital television is exploding around the world, particularly in Europe. In the US, cable television viewers equalled the network television audience in 2000, and are projected to overtake the open broadcast networks in the coming years. Furthermore, young Americans are watching less television: between 1985 and 2000 the average number of hours of TV watched by people under 18 declined by 20 percent. Part of this trend was attributed to increasing time spent by young people surfing the Internet (*The Economist*, 2001: 60).

The newsrooms in all media are also being retooled around the Internet. They work in a continuous stream of information-processing, on Internet time, along the model pioneered by *The Chicago Tribune/Los Angeles Times* in 2000. The cable industry is investing staggering sums to deliver everything everywhere (at a price). Radio broadcasting is enjoying a renaissance, actually becoming the most pervasive communication medium in the world. And book publishing is, overall, doing well, thanks. This profound restructuring is associated with mergers and consolidation between major companies, so that seven multimedia mega-groups control most of the global media, and in each country a few corporations (stand alone or globally connected) determine what is published and broadcast (Schiller, 1999). However, other than as a working tool, the Internet is, so far, a very minor factor in all this transformation, the AOL–Time Warner merger notwithstanding. In a nutshell, for the time being there is very limited convergence between the Internet and multimedia—and therefore there is no interactivity, the key feature of the authentic multimedia vision. Why so?

The most obvious reason is insufficient bandwidth. In 2000, less than one-fifth of US households had access to digital subscriber line (DSL) transmission. But even for those privileged few, this bandwidth was not enough. Quality video television requires about 3 megabits per second transmission capacity. In 2000, DSL transmission speeds varied between 300 kilobits and 1.5 megabits per second. In principle, cable transmission had an edge on its carrying capacity, at 10 megabits per second. However, because of the layout of cable wires, this theoretical capacity is shared in the local area, so if your neighbor decides to download his dose of porno video for the weekend you will need to go to the local sports bar to enjoy your football game. Moreover, at the turn of the century there was no installed communications capacity able to sustain a large-scale video transmission using the Internet. In 2001, what Owen reported in 1999 is still relevant: "Almost any scenario in which standard-quality video is offered interactively (that is, on demand) to millions of ordinary viewers results in the collapse of present distribution systems. The interactive integrated video future requires much more capacity than we have, not only in national backbones but in local distribution systems that link up with individual households" (Owen, 1999: 313).

This could change, taking into consideration new technological developments, especially in the area of compression technology. Yet, it would require an extraordinary investment by multimedia companies and communication companies, in the hundreds of billions of dollars. This gigantic bet would be undertaken only if potential demand were there. Indeed, it was with this potential demand in mind that media companies, communication operators, and computer companies positioned themselves during the 1990s. It never materialized, not even in prospective marketing studies. While people massively adopted the Internet, they kept it separate from television, and, in general terms, from most of the media world—except for news reporting. The main reason for this seems to be the saturation of entertainment demand by television, radio, and portable video-games. The mid-1990s' experiments showed that consumers were not ready to pay additional money to expand their choice of video within the same genre. Sports and customized programming was an exception, but this could be offered by digital TV at a much lower investment cost: indeed, this was the basis for the booming European digital TV business, with sports events being appropriated by the media world and transformed into the driver of the pay-per-view television industry. Beyond that, the main unsatisfied demand was for general information, education, and cultural programming, which was simply not available on a large scale (Castells, 2000: 394–403).

The flawed hypothesis of the media business world seems to have been that demand for entertainment was unlimited, and that it was all that mattered for consumers—save a cultural elite that could be satisfied with up-market magazines, subsidized art exhibitions, and "high-culture" performances. In fact, what people did was to accept TV and video as entertainment, keep radio as a companion, and use the Internet for their content-oriented interests. Thus, fig. 7.1 offers an illustration of the uses of the Internet in

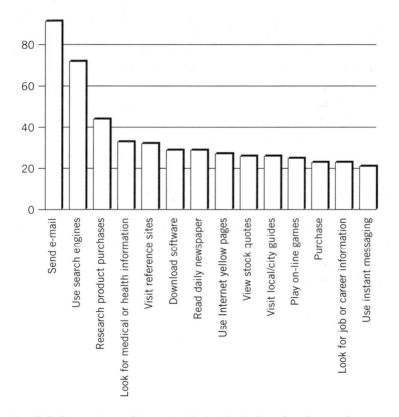

Fig. 7.1 Percentage of households in North America that perform on-line activities weekly by activity

Source: Based upon data from Forrester Research.

2000 in the United States. Except for a small percentage of activity related to on-line games, there is no entertainment-related practice. And the relationship to the media world is limited to reading daily newspapers—an interesting observation on which I will elaborate below. So, as we have observed elsewhere in this book, the use of the Internet as a communication medium is woven into the multi-dimensional practice of life. It is characterized by an active use, linked to a variety of interests, in most instances very practically oriented, while the world of media entertainment is confined to the available time for passive relaxation. A time that is, in fact, shrinking for most people, and for which television (particularly in its new modalities of customized broadcasting by cable or satellite) seems to be well suited.

Isn't the AOL–Time Warner business project a proof to the contrary? Not really. Remember who bought whom: AOL bought Time Warner. It was Steve Case's genius business strategy to buy one of the largest multimedia businesses in the world with AOL's highly valued stock, just a few weeks before the price of its shares dwindled, so that by the time the merger was finally approved, Time Warner's shareholders were at a loss. Also, by taking a stake in both the Internet and multimedia worlds, the new group could pre-empt any future transformations of the communication industry, including the unlikely event of the much-vaunted convergence between the Internet and audiovisual communication. This strategic move came at a price: AOL reported losses in excess of 1 billion US dollars for 2000.

But who knows? Perhaps the technological visionaries are right, and they just have the timing wrong (they usually mistime their predictions, and timing is essential, in business, war, politics, and personal lives). It may well be after all that broader bandwidth diffuses in every domain of life, compression technology solves some of the transmission problems, and people finally come to realize all the wonderful opportunities offered by our digital environment. I frankly do not know. I have never known how to predict the future. What I do know is that the only serious way to think about the future is to have a clear idea, empirically grounded, of our present, and of our past—particularly of our recent past. In other words, the way to understand the potential relationship between the Internet and the media world is to reflect on the few success stories of their integration around the turn of the century. I now turn to this analysis.

The Uses of the Internet in the Multimedia System

The wonderful thing about technology is that people end up doing with it something different from what was originally intended. It is this serendipity that underlies creativity in society and innovation in business. As we saw, the Internet is the result of the social appropriation of its technology by its users/producers. A similar story may be developing in the interaction between the media and the Internet. Let us take, one after the other, the areas of communication and cultural expression in which the Internet is becoming a privileged medium, leading to the transformation of cultural practices (Jankowski *et al.*, 1999; Jones, 1999; UNESCO, 1999; Croteau and Hoynes, 2000; *The Economist*, 2000). On the basis of these observations, I will formulate some hypotheses on the meaning of emerging, Internet-based media practices.

Music delivery over the Internet is a technologically feasible and widely practiced activity, particularly in the form of the free sharing of stored music, allowed by MP3/Napster, Gnutella or Freenet technologies. Streaming is also becoming a popular technology; that is, the delivery of content in real time over the Internet using applications such as Realplayer or Quicktime, although in this latter case storage and recording of the exchanged files is technically difficult. Millions of young people in the world have enthusiastically adopted these technologies, exchanging their favorite music over the Net, and rocking the foundations of the music recording industry. Companies are still trying to cope with the phenomenon, simultaneously developing security technologies (such as electronic watermarks), going to court to protect their property rights, and envisioning new business models. In December 2000, the BMG Group made an agreement with Napster, the pioneer MP3-based company, under which Napster would prevent illegal copying and charge a fee for its sharing service. In exchange, BMG would offer its entire catalog to Napster users for 4.95 dollars a month. Nelson and Jones (2001) are skeptical about the success of this new business model. About one-half of Americans do not consider that free downloading of music over the Internet is stealing. In March 2001, a San Francisco court ordered Napster to block access to copyrighted material. But if Napster is shut down or if it joins the commercial world, alternative technologies, such as Gnutella and Freenet, will attract many users. And, unlike the case of MP3, there is no one company that could be identified as the purveyor of the technology (as Napster is). The power of the network makes effective control of the free sharing of music unlikely, and so the march towards free music delivery is likely to proceed, turning the entire music recording industry upside-down (Suarez, 2001).

The second major development is porno video and the posting of offensive material over the Internet; that is, the kind of content usually banned over mass media. So, here the Internet offers a real alternative. However, the intriguing matter here is that there is plenty of porno on pay TV and neighborhood video stores. Most Internet porno sites are also paid sites (although cheaper than porno TV or phone sex), so the use of the Internet for this matter does not seem to be determined by the economics of perversion. Privacy and ubiquity seem to be the key factors. Porno Internet can be accessed from anywhere—particularly from the workplace, often a delightful transgression for the disgruntled worker. And because most people still do not think (or know) that they are being watched in their on-line surfing, the Internet is perceived as providing a better safe haven for sexual fantasies than TV offerings dutifully recorded in the monthly bill. So, the added value of porno over the Internet is the supposedly free expression of people's desires.

Then, on-line video-games seem to be picking up as a favorite activity, particularly for men, and predominantly for the younger ages (but not only teenagers). Here is where entertainment directly connects with the Net. The off-line video-game industry is doing very well, particularly because of major technological improvements in interactivity, graphics, and image quality. The computer power of Sony's Playstation consoles surpasses that of most personal computers. Desktop virtual reality machines are coming up, and new gaming devices (such as Dreamcast), with high-quality resolution and interactivity, are becoming networked, allowing on-line, interactive gaming.

The possibility of socializing through game-playing gives the Internet-based games an edge over stand-alone video-games. Role-playing games revive in a commercial form the early Internet tradition of the MUDs (multi-user dungeons) culture, bringing interactivity and open-ended gaming together in a winning formula. In other words, on-line games are characterized by the relative control of the players over the rules of the game, and by their discovery of new possibilities through their interaction, as used to be the case with the social games of our pre-digital past.

Radio listening is flourishing over the Internet, both for open broadcast stations and for radios transmitting over the Internet. MIT's radio listing in the US shows over 10,000 radio stations broadcasting on the Internet. Two factors seem to influence this development. On the one hand, interest in local events is difficult to satisfy on a global scale outside the reach of local information networks. If you want to know what happened in your city from the other side of the world, only the Internet is able to provide you with the information, either on text (local newspapers) or on audio (local radio stations). So, the freedom to bypass the global culture to reach your local identity depends on the Internet, the global network of local communication. On the other hand, the commercial success of radio has led to its oligopolistic control by major media conglomerates in every country—in a direct effect of deregulation, which in fact has led (as in many other areas of the economy) to increasing concentration. Therefore, while radio is locally targeted (you need to know the traffic in your city, not anywhere else), its content is increasingly syndicated and largely homogenized. Alternative radio stations, focused on narrow-casting, find a cheap, easy way to broadcast on the Internet, beyond the limits of the licensed spectrum. Here again, the Internet offers freedom in a world of increased control by large media groups.

Newspapers are on-line, and people often read them on-line. One-third of Americans read news on-line at least once a week. However, they are not ready to pay for it. The only newspaper with a succesful on-line paid subscription service is the *Wall Street Journal*, which falls into the category of what people need for their work and money-making. Newspapers are not being undermined by the Internet because in a world of endless information, credibility is an essential ingredient for information-seekers. So, established newspapers have to be on-line in order to be always there ready for their readers, to keep them under their authoritative mantra. So doing, the newspapers hope that the physical contact with a very portable and user-friendly format of the printed newspaper (or, for that matter, magazine) will still fill a need, and ultimately benefit from its on-line ubiquitous presence.

Books offer a dual story. On the one hand, reference books and encyclopedias in print are being put out of business by the Internet, in a trend that underlines the importance of the educational and information-seeking uses of the Internet over its entertainment function. Textbooks offer extraordinary potential for electronic publishing, among other things because libraries do not have the physical space to cope with the information explosion, and are gearing up to offer books and journals on-line. In principle, this is for eligible readers, provided with a password, but it will be difficult to limit electronic distribution of texts once they are accessed. So, overall, textbooks are going on-line, although the formation of a mass market (with new business models) will largely depend on the speed and form of the major revolution taking place in education: e-learning and distance education (Borgman, 2000; Dumort, 2000).

Another growth area of electronic publishing is that of scholarly journals (Ekman and Quandt, 1999). It is likely that academic and scientific journals, aimed at a relatively small audience, almost entirely Internet-literate, will increasingly be published on-line, and sold to specialized institutions on the basis of a subscription service. Since publication in these journals is motivated by reputation and professional promotion, it really does not matter for the authors which form publication takes. Thus, overall, strictly academic publishing, except for some prestige publications suitable for Christmas gifts and special occasions, is likely to go on-line.

On the other hand, for books of broader scope (including, in fact, much of so-called academic publishing), the Internet is working only as an advertising/marketing platform, Stephen King's novel notwithstanding. And it does not seem that demand is fading for the classic, printed book—after all, it is a very user-friendly and portable device. The process of conception, production, and publication of printed material is being entirely transformed by the Internet, but the product itself (the book you have in your hands) is unlikely to change substantially in the foreseeable future, as the negligible demand for the first versions of electronic pocket books seems to indicate.

There is, however, a major realm of cultural expression being profoundly transformed by digital technology and by the Internet: art (Boyd *et al.*, 1999). Computerized graphic design is renewing the forms of artistic expression, as virtual art brings into shapes, colors, sounds, and silences the deepest manifestations of human experience. The Internet offers the possibility of collective, interactive, joint artistic creation, through groupware practices that allow people at a distance to paint, sculpt, design, compose, and produce together, in interaction, and often in contradiction. In most instances, these co-artists do not know each other, except in their art—and this is all that matters. Open source art is the new frontier of artistic creation. Furthermore, the openness of the web truly democratizes art, at last. Websites offer the legacy of art, as well as on-going creations, with netizens from around the world being invited to learn, propose, and participate in the creation. One example: the Internet has popularized in recent times the extraordinary work of Escher, and particularly his graphic design creations of geometric patterns, known as tessellations. Escher World is an extremely popular website, and people from around the planet participate in competitions to create new shapes of tessellations, opening up new domains of graphic experimentation with the help of digital technologies and virtual reality models.

In fact, rather than converging with the media, the Internet is asserting its specificity as a communication medium. For instance, instant messaging is one of its most popular applications. In its wireless form, it is the most widely diffused practice in the early mobile Internet world, a favorite tool for young people to build their networks, enjoy their autonomy, yet relying on their back-up systems. It is symptomatic that one of the key conditions imposed by the FCC on AOL to approve its merger with Time Warner was to preserve the inter-operability of its instant messaging service with similar services of its competitors. The argument from Kennard, the FCC chairman, was that instant messaging was essential for the existence of the Internet's autonomous communities, and that the formation of these communities could not be impeded by the enclosure of their communication within corporate bounds.

The Internet is, indeed, as I have documented in previous chapters, a communication medium with its own logic and its own language. But it is not confined to one particular area of cultural expression. It cuts across all of them. Furthermore, its communication is usually embedded in social practice, not isolated in some kind of imaginary world, the domain of role-playing and fake identities. It is used to post political messages, to communicate by e-mail with the networks of life, to convey ideas and search for information. It is communication, but not entertainment, at least not predominantly. And since the audiovisual media, and particularly television, have become dominated by the logic of entertainment, including infotainment, the Internet interprets it as a failure of communication, and goes around it. The kind of communication that thrives on the Internet is that related to free expression in all its forms, more or less desirable according to each person's taste. It is open source, free posting, decentralized broadcasting, serendipituous interaction, purpose-oriented communication, and shared creation that find their expression on the Internet. If convergence takes place one day, it will be when the investment required in setting up broadband capabilities beyond the instrumental uses of the corporate world is justified by a new media system willing and ready to satisfy the most important latent demand: the demand for interactive free expression and autonomous creation—nowadays largely stymied by the sclerotic vision of the traditional media industry.

Toward a Personalized Hypertext? Real Virtuality and Protocols of Meaning

Perhaps the most innovative line of thinking on cultural transformation in the Information Age is the tradition built around the concept of the hypertext and the promise of multimedia—in its original sense (Levy, 1995; de Kerckhove, 1997). Packer and Jordan (2001) have shown the intellectual continuity from Wagner to Berners-Lee, through Vannevar Bush and William Gibson, in rethinking communication on the basis of interactivity and multi-dimensional expression. In their interpretation, which I largely share, the emergence of a new communication pattern, indeed a new culture, can be identified by the simultaneous workings of five processes:

Integration: the combining of artistic forms and technology into a hybrid form of expression. Interactivity: the ability of the user to manipulate and affect her experience of media directly, and to communicate with others through media. Hypermedia: the linking of separate media elements to one another to create a trail of personal association. Immersion: the experience of entering into the simulation of a three-dimensional environment. Narrativity: aesthetic and formal strategies that derive from the above concepts, and which result in nonlinear story forms and media presentation. (Packer and Jordan, 2001: xxviii)

Convergence between the media and the Internet and the utilization of digital virtual reality technologies were supposed to fulfill the promise of multimedia: the emergence of an electronic hypertext on a global scale. However, as far as we can observe, this is not happening at the start of the twenty-first century. And, for the reasons exposed above, I doubt that it will happen soon (although I can certainly be proved wrong, and the futurologists' chorus right in this matter—but the jury is still out on this one). Let us assume, for the sake of analysis, that we can extrapolate current trends and that the Internet continues to be the Internet, while the multimedia system continues to inter-operate its one-directional communication components without actually integrating the Internet, except as a working tool and a platform for referral—save for some virtual reality interactive games on-line.

Does this mean that there is no hypertext? That the vision of an interactive, cross-referred communication system was a technological dream? Maybe cultural transformation is more complex than we used to think. Perhaps the hypertext does not exist outside us, but within us. We probably created an excessively material image of the hypertext (myself certainly included in this error—since for once I believed too much in the predictions of futurologists). That is: a hypertext as an actual interactive system, digitally communicated and electronically operated in which all the bits and pieces of cultural expression, present, past, and future, in all their manifestations, could coexist and be recombined. This could exist technologically in the age of the Internet. But it does not exist because there is no interest in it (ask Ted Nelson). And particularly there is no interest from the multimedia business world unless/ until there is a viable business that could be built around the hypertext. And since multimedia business has a proprietary hold on much of the cultural products and processes, there is no passage from the reality of multimedia to the vision of the hypertext. So, in terms of an electronically operated, material artefact, there is no hypertext.

Yet, this is too primitive a vision in the understanding of cultural processes. Our minds—not our machines—process culture, on the basis of our existence. Human culture only exists in and by human minds, usually connected to human bodies. Therefore, if our minds have the material capability to access the whole realm of cultural expressions—select them, recombine them—we do have a hypertext: the hypertext is inside us. Or, rather, it is in our inner ability to recombine and make sense inside our minds of all the components of the hypertext that are distributed in many different realms of cultural expression. The Internet enables us to do precisely that. Not multimedia, but the Internet-based inter-operability of accessing and recombining all kinds of text, images, sounds, silences, and blanks, including the entire realm of symbolic expression enclosed in the multimedia system. So, the hypertext is not produced by the multimedia system using the Internet as a medium to reach all of us. It is, instead, produced by us, by using the Internet to absorb cultural expression in the multimedia world and beyond. Indeed, this is what Ted Nelson's Xanadu explicitly meant, and this is what we should have understood.

So, because of the Internet, and in spite of multimedia, we do have a hypertext: not *the hypertext*, but my hypertext, your hypertext, and everybody else's hypertext. These hypertexts, however, are limited for the time being because bandwidth and access are limited. And they may remain so, unless this decentralized form of cultural expression can be either marketized or universally decommodified. So, we have a personalized hypertext, a modest hypertext, as modest or as sophisticated as everyone can afford. But it is indeed an individual hypertext made of multi-modal, cultural expressions recombined in new forms and new meanings.

In this sense, we indeed live in the kind of culture that in my previous writings I have called "the culture of real virtuality" (Castells, 1996/2000). It is virtual because it is constructed primarily through electronically based, virtual processes of communication. It is real (and not imaginary) because it is our fundamental reality, the material basis on which we live our existence, construct our systems of representation, practice our work, link up with other people, retrieve information, form our opinions, act in politics, and nurture our dreams. This virtuality is our reality. This is what is distinctive of culture in the Information Age: it is primarily through virtuality that we process our creation of meaning.

But if virtuality is the language through which we construct meaning, and the hypertext is personalized, a fundamental question arises: how can we share meaning in social life? If cultural expressions are gathered in a vast, diverse constellation that can be accessed individually, and then reconstructed in its specific codes by each one of us, how can we speak a common language? If the hypertext would exist outside us, internalized in the multimedia system, we would endure systemic cultural domination, but at least we would all be processed under the same formula—multi-faceted, but based on similar codes. But if, as seems to be the case, outside the multimedia world (with decreasing capacity to include decentralized networks of communication), we build our own systems of interpretation, with the help of the Internet, we are free, but potentially autistic.

So, how is common meaning, and therefore society, reconstituted under the conditions of a distributed, personalized hypertext? The most obvious process is through shared experience. Our minds are not single, isolated worlds; they are wired in their social environment, so we process signals, and we look for meaning, according to what we perceive through the experience of everyday life. But in a social structure—the network society—that induces structural individualism, and increasingly distinct social experiences, some of this shared meaning through practice is lost, so that areas of cognitive dissonance may grow proportionally to the extent of self-construction of meaning. The more we select our personal hypertext, under the conditions of a networked social structure and individualized cultural expressions, the greater the obstacles to finding a common language, thus common meaning.

This is why, in addition to the traditional mechanism for the sharing of cultural codes, derived from the simple fact of living together, in the culture of real virtuality communication largely depends on the existence of protocols of meaning. These are bridges of communication, independent of common practice, between personalized hypertexts. In our context, the most important of these protocols is art, in all its manifestations (including, of course, literature, music, architecture, and graphic design). Indeed, art has always been a tool to build bridges between people from different countries, cultures, classes, ethnic groups, genders, and power positions—bridges of meaning, sometimes through the expression of the social conflicts between the people on both sides of a meaningful contradiction. Art has always been a communication protocol to restore the unity of human experience beyond oppression, difference, and conflict. The paintings of the powerful in their human misery, the sculpting of the oppressed in their human dignity, the bridges between the beauty of our environment and the inner hells of our psyche—as in Van Gogh's landscapes—are all media to go beyond the inescapable labors of life, to find the expression of joy, of pain, of feeling, that reunites us, and makes this planet liveable after all.

Art has always been a builder of bridges between the diverse, contradictory expressions of human experience. More than ever this could be its fundamental role in a culture characterized by fragmentation and potential non-communication of codes, a culture where multiplicity of expressions may in fact undermine sharing. Lack of common meaning could open the way for widespread alienation among humans—everybody speaking a different language, built around his or her personalized hypertext. In a world of broken mirrors, made of non-communicable texts, art could be, without any deliberate agenda, just by being, a protocol of communication and a tool of social reconstruction. By suggesting, through disarming irony or sheer beauty, that we are still capable of being together, and enjoying it. Art, increasingly a hybrid expression of virtual and physical materials, may be a fundamental cultural bridge between the Net and the self.

Reading Links

Borgman, Christine L. (2000) *From Gutenberg to the Global Information Infrastructure: Access to Information in the Networked World.* Cambridge, MA: MIT Press.

Boyd, Frank, Brickwood, Cathy, Broeckman, Andreas, Haskel, Lisa, Kluitenberg, Eric, and Stikker, Marleen (eds) (1999) *New Media Culture in Europe.* Amsterdam: Uitgeverij de Balie and the Virtual Platform.

Business Week (2001) "Showtime for AOL/Warner," January 15: 57–64.

Cafassi, Emilio (ed.) (1998) *Internet: politicas y comunicacion.* Buenos Aires: Biblos.

Castells, Manuel (1996/2000) *The Rise of the Network Society,* 2nd edn, pp. 355–406. Oxford: Blackwell.

Croteau, David and Hoynes, William (2000) *Media/Society: Industries, Images, and Audiences,* 2nd edn. Thousand Oaks, CA: Pine Forge Press.

Dumort, Alain (2000) "New media and distant education: an EU–US perspective," *Information, Communication and Society,* 3(4): 546–56.

The Economist (2000) "E-entertainment survey," October 7.

The Economist (2001) "Television takes a tumble," January 20.

Ekman, Richard and Quandt, Richard E. (eds) (1999) *Technology and Scholarly Communication.* Berkeley, CA: University of California Press.

Jankowski, Nicholas, Jones, Steve, Samarajiva, Rohan, and Silverstone,

Roger (eds) (1999) *What's New about New Media?*, special issue *of New Media and Society*, vol. 1. London: Sage.

Jones, Steve (ed.) (1999) *Cybersociety 2.0*. London: Sage.

de Kerckhove, Derrick (1997) *Connected Intelligence: The Arrival of the Web Society*. Toronto: Somerville House.

Levy, Pierre (1995) *Qu'est-ce que le virtuel?* Paris: La Decouverte.

Nelson, Chris and Jones, Steve (2001) "Revolutionary times for music," *Boston Globe*, January 16: A11.

Owen, Bruce M. (1999) *The Internet Challenge to Television*. Cambridge, MA: Harvard University Press.

Packer, Randall and Jordan, Ken (eds) (2001) *Multimedia: From Wagner to Virtual Reality*. New York: W. W. Norton.

Schiller, Dan (1999) *Digital Capitalism: Networking the Global Market System*. Cambridge, MA: MIT Press.

Silverstone, Roger and Hirsch, Eric (1992) *Consuming Technologies. Media and Information in Domestic Spaces*. London: Routledge.

Suarez, Manuel (2001) "Free music, the music industry, and the Internet," University of California, Berkeley, unpublished research paper for CP229 seminar.

UNESCO (1999) *World Communication Report, 1999–2000*. Paris: UNESCO.

e-Links

www.artmuseum.net
On electronic art.

www.worldofescher
On Escher and tessellations.

Chapter 8

The Geography of the Internet: Networked Places

The Internet Age has been hailed as the end of geography. In fact, the Internet has a geography of its own, a geography made of networks and nodes that process information flows generated and managed from places. The unit is the network, so the architecture and dynamics of multiple networks are the sources of meaning and function for each place. The resulting space of flows is a new form of space, characteristic of the Information Age, but it is not placeless: it links places by telecommunicated computer networks and computerized transportation systems. It redefines distance but does not cancel geography. New territorial configurations emerge from simultaneous processes of spatial concentration, decentralization, and connection, relentlessly labored by the variable geometry of global information flows.

I will explore the contours of this space by focusing first on the geography of the Internet itself. I will then analyze the influence of information and communication technologies on the spatial transformation of cities and regions. I will also address a myth of our time: the end of the workplace thanks to telecommuting, by reporting on the actual developments in metropolitan mobility. I will consider the potential changes brought by the Internet in our home environment, and in our relationship to public space. Finally, I will examine the social differentation induced by this networking geography.

The Internet's Geography

The geographical dimension of the Internet can be analyzed from three perspectives: its technical geography, the spatial distribution of its users, and the economic geography of Internet production. The *technical geography* refers to the telecommunications infrastructure of the Internet, the connections between the computers that organize Internet traffic (routers), and the distribution of the Internet's broad bandwidth; that is, the telecommunication lines dedicated to Internet data packet traffic. A number of pioneering researchers have been working on mapping the Internet for some time, most notably John Quaterman, head of MIDS.com, as well as the work conducted around the consulting firm Telegeography (2000), founded by John Staple. Cheswick and Burch (2000), working from Bell Laboratories, have built a remarkable, evolving database on the topography of connections between Internet nodes. Martin Dodge (1998–2001) (Cybergeography.com) and Townsend (2001) have also contributed to the mapping of the Internet's infrastructure, while other researchers, including Cukier (1999) and Abramson (2000), have analyzed the meaning of this spatial configuration. The graph on the cover of this book, produced by Cheswick and Burch, reflects the topography of the Internet, based on trace routes in January 2000. I take the liberty of referring the reader to the websites listed at the end of the chapter to visualize, with the help of beautiful images, the structure and evolution of the Internet's technical network.

These studies show the complexity, pervasiveness, and global reach of the Internet backbone. Every node is connected to every node through a myriad of possible routes. However, because the US has much greater bandwidth capacity than the rest of the world, the US plays a central role in the connections between countries. According to Cukier, in 1999 the Internet's technical structure "resembled a star with the United States at its center" (1999: 53). It is often the case that connections between two European or Asian cities, let alone African or Latin American ones, are first routed through a US node. However, according to Telegeography, this is changing, as bandwidth increases in other areas of the world, particularly in Europe. Most traffic is still routed through the United States but new nodes emerge as key routers. Townsend (2001) observes that major metropolitan areas rely on a backbone made up of a network of networked cities. In sum, technically speaking, the Internet backbone is global in its reach, but territorially uneven in its layout in terms of capacity. While inter-country differences are declining, dependency upon the United States is gradually being replaced by technical dependency upon connection to a large, broad bandwidth network of networks linking the major metropolitan centers around the world, with the main nodes still predominantly located in the United States.

Concerning the *geography of users*, figs 8.1 and 8.2, elaborated by Matthew Zook on the basis of NUA surveys, show the highly uneven territorial distribution of the Internet in September 2000, both in terms of the number of users and of the penetration rate relative to the population of each country. Thus, North America, with over 161 million users, was the dominant region of the world, and, together with Europe's 105 million users, constituted the bulk of the total 378 million Internet users, in sharp contrast to the distribution of the population in the planet. Thus, the Asia Pacific region, with over two-thirds of the world's population, only accounted for 90 million users, some 23.6 percent of the total; Latin America had only about 15 million users; the Middle East 2.4 million; and Africa 3.11 million, of which the majority was in South Africa. In terms of density of use of the Internet, Scandinavia, North America, Australia, and (interestingly enough) South Korea, came clearly above all other countries, followed by the UK, The Netherlands, Germany, Japan, Singapore, Taiwan, Hong Kong, then Southern

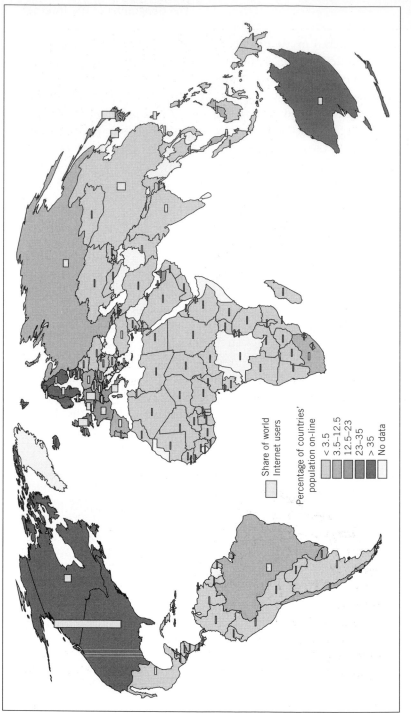

Fig. 8.1 Share of world Internet users and percentage of countries' population on-line worldwide, September 2000

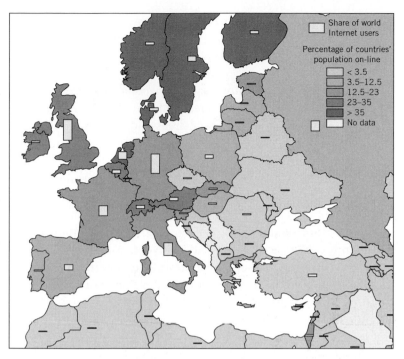

**Fig. 8.2 Share of world Internet users and percentage of countries'
population on-line in Europe, September 2000**

Source: Zook (2001*a*)

Europe; at a greater distance came the rest of Asia, Latin America,
the Middle East, and, at the very bottom, Africa.

I shall elaborate on the implications of this differential diffusion
of the Internet in Chapter 9. However, while exploring its geography, it is essential to emphasize that the use of the Internet is
highly differentiated in territorial terms, following the uneven distribution of technological infrastructure, wealth, and education in
the planet. This geographical pattern evolves over time. Thus,
according to NUA surveys, in the first global surveys of Internet use
at the end of 1996, of a total of 45 million users, North America
accounted for 30 million, with another 9 million in Europe, and
the rest of the world sharing the other 6 million (most of them in

Australia, Japan, and East Asia). Internet use is diffusing fast, but this diffusion follows a spatial pattern that fragments its geography according to wealth, technology, and power: it is the new geography of development.

Within countries, there are also major spatial differences in the diffusion of Internet use. Urban areas come first, both in developed and developing countries, and rural areas and small towns considerably lag behind in their access to the new medium, in a blatant denial of the futurologists' image of the electronic cottage, working and living in the countryside. Retardation in the diffusion of the Internet in rural areas has been observed in the United States, in Europe, and even more so in developing countries. For instance, in China, the three largest cities, Beijing, Shanghai, and Guangzhou, in September 2000, according to NUA surveys, accounted for about 60 percent of Internet users. In contrast, the penetration rate for the country as a whole remained at less than 2 percent of the population. Within urban areas, major metropolitan areas, and particularly the most important cities, tend to be the ones with the fastest and largest adoption of the Internet. There are, however, exceptions in countries with a decentralized urban structure, such as Germany, where Munich, Berlin, and Hamburg adopted the Internet faster, or the United States, where dynamic areas, such as Austin or Seattle, were intensive users at an earlier time than older industrial cities, such as Chicago or Philadelphia. Yet, overall, there is a strong correlation between metropolitan dominance and early adoption of Internet use. So, Internet diffusion proceeds unevenly over time and space, by successive layers of incorporation that may reflect in a diversity of social geographies in the future.

However, while the use of the Internet is expected to diffuse broadly in the coming years, at least in the most developed countries and in the metropolitan areas of the developing world, a more selective, *economic geography is emerging concerning the production of the Internet*. This is certainly the case with the Internet's equipment manufacturing and technology design. Silicon Valley and its global networks, together with the Ericsson world network centered on Sweden, the Nokia world network centered on Finland, the NEC world network centered on Japan, and perhaps a few other networks built around mighty corporations of the pre-Internet era (ATT, IBM, Microsoft, Motorola, Phillips, Siemens, Hitachi) continue to concentrate in a few milieux of innovation most of the technological know-how on which the Internet is based. Indeed, Cisco Systems, controlling over 80 percent of the market for Internet routers, was planning by the end of 2000 to build a giant campus in Coyote Valley, near San Jose, in Silicon Valley, to house 20,000 employees, on top of the thousands already working for Cisco in the area, so that the majority of its global labor force would be concentrated in a few miles.

While new centers of Internet-related technological innovation, such as Austin, and Denver–Boulder, were growing fast, the overall geography of Internet-related hardware closely follows the pattern identified years ago by Peter Hall and myself in our worldwide scanning of technopoles (Castells and Hall, 1994): dense spatial concentrations of major companies and innovative start-ups, as well as their ancillary suppliers, located in a few technological nodes, usually in the periphery of large metropolitan areas, then linked up with each other by telecommunications and air transportation. No undifferentiated spatial diffusion, but highly selective, metropolitan concentration, and global networking. A similar locational pattern seems to be followed by Internet software companies, Internet media services, and Internet service providers. However, the metropolitan areas that host the leading firms reflect the diverse origins of each company: for instance, Washington, DC, home of AOL, or Seattle, home of Amazon. Yahoo!, e-Bay, e*Trade, and a long list of leaders of the early Internet industry were spin-offs from Silicon Valley's and San Francisco's entrepreneurial milieux.

Nevertheless, as I emphasized in Chapter 3 on e-business, it would be too narrow a vision to consider the Internet industry as made up exclusively of Internet manufacturers, Internet software companies, Internet service providers, and Internet portals. The commercial Internet is not just about web companies, it is about companies in the web. Thus, we need an assessment of the geography of Internet content providers at large; that is, of the Internet domains of all kinds that generate, process, and distribute information. Since information is the key product of the Information Age, and the Internet is the fundamental tool for the production and communication of this information, the economic geography of the Internet is, by and large, the geography of Internet content providers.

Matthew Zook has conducted the most rigorous, analytical effort to date to map Internet content providers, and to make sense of their spatial patterning in the world, within countries, within regions, and within cities, between 1996 and 2001 (Zook, 2000*a*, *b*; 2001*a*, *b*). To do so, he constructed a database locating a random sample of Internet domains, on the basis of their registration postal addresses, according to a methodology that can be checked on his website (see the Appendix to this chapter). He also mapped the thousand top websites (ranked by Alexa.com), measured by the number of hits from users, and ranked them by numbers of webpages consulted. Figs 8.3–8.6 display the location of Internet content providers, measured by the location of domain addresses, in the world, in Europe, in the United States, and in New York City as of July 2000. Zook calculated both the number of domains in the world and in each country, and the density of domains, standardizing by population for each country, and by the number of businesses for the commercial Internet in the United States. Reading from Zook's tables for his July 2000 sample (which are not given here for simplicity's sake), he found the United States to account for the lion's share of Internet domains, with about 50 percent of the total, followed by Germany with 8.6 percent and the UK with 8.5 percent. Canada (3.6 percent), South Korea (2.5 percent) and France (2.1 percent) were in the middle, with all other countries below 2 percent.

Standardizing by population, the dominance of the developed world is still more accentuated, with the US showing a ratio of 25.2 Internet domains per thousand population, compared to Brazil's 0.5, China's 0.2, and India's 0.1. Europe shows a strong internal diversity, with Switzerland, Denmark, Finland, and The Netherlands ranking at the top, with over 15.0 per thousand population, and Southern Europe at the bottom, with Spain, for instance, showing a ratio of 3.4 per thousand, representing only

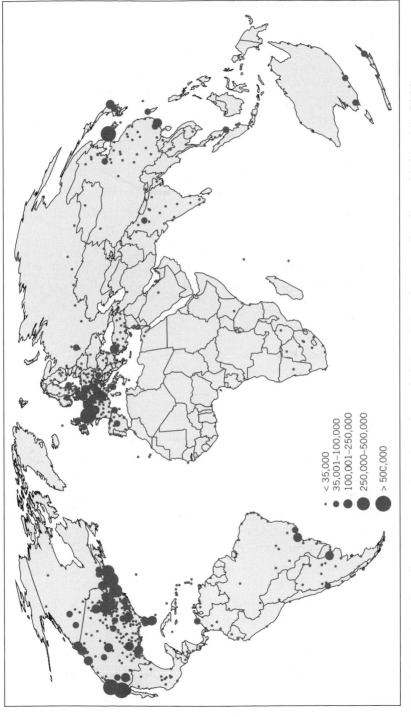

Fig. 8.3 Total number of .com, .org, .net, and country code Internet domain names by city worldwide, July 2000

Source: Zook (2001a)

Fig. 8.4 Total number of .com, .org, .net, and country code Internet domain names by city in Europe, July 2000

Source: Zook (2001*a*)

1 percent of world domains. The case of Japan is significant, accounting for only 1.6 percent of world domains, with a domain/population ratio of only 1.7 per thousand, although this is probably changing rapidly with the expansion of Do-Co-Mo.

What these data say is that Internet domains are highly concentrated by country, with substantial dominance by the US. This concentration is much higher than the concentration of Internet users, suggesting a growing asymmetry between production and consumption of Internet content, with the US producing for everybody else, and the developed world producing for the rest of the world—

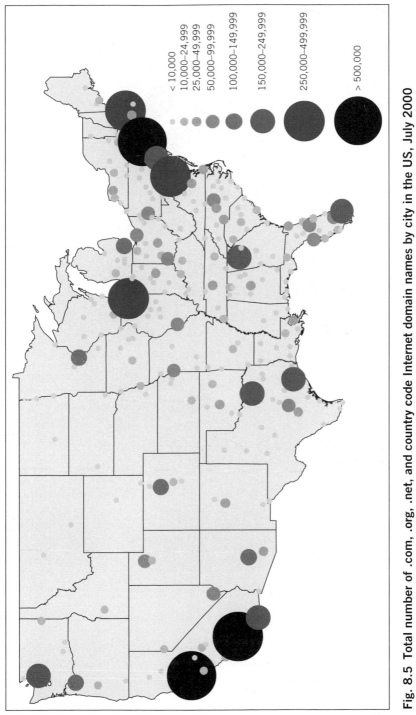

Fig. 8.5 Total number of .com, .org, .net, and country code Internet domain names by city in the US, July 2000

Source: Zook (2001*a*)

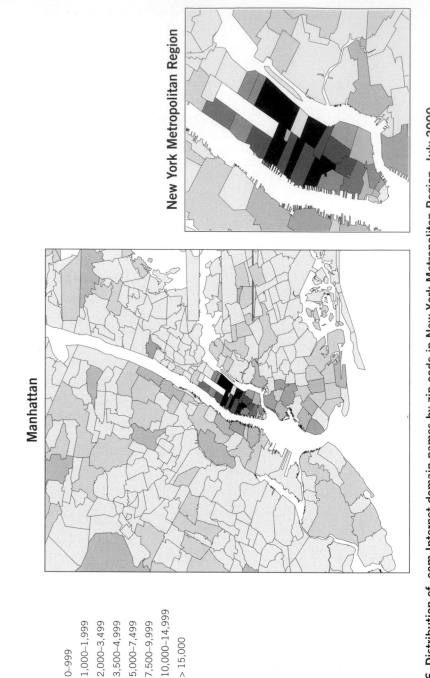

Manhattan

New York Metropolitan Region

0–999
1,000–1,999
2,000–3,499
3,500–4,999
5,000–7,499
7,500–9,999
10,000–14,999
> 15,000

Fig. 8.6 Distribution of .com Internet domain names by zip code in New York Metropolitan Region, July 2000

Source: Zook (2001a)

with the exception of Japan which consumes much more than it produces. South Korea represents an interesting case as it displays one of the highest penetration rates in the world both in the production and consumption of Internet content. Although there is no convincing explanation for this Korean specificity, the South Korean anomaly should introduce caution against a hasty cultural interpretation of the reason why Japan lags behind in Internet content provision.

These data should be interpreted in a time-dynamic perspective. In 1997, Quaterman reported that 83 percent of all dot.com domains were located in the US, while the US, Canada, and the UK represented 90 percent of all dot.com domains. In January 2000, the relative figures had declined to 67 percent and 74 percent (remember that Zook's database refers to all domains, and not just dot.com domains). So, there is indeed a trend toward greater diffusion of the commercial Internet's content provision. But this geographical diffusion starts from a very high level of spatial concentration in a few countries, whose dominance in designing and distributing content will be felt for a considerable period of time. Furthermore, many of these content providers entered foreign markets with expertise and capital (for example, Yahoo! was the most widely used portal in Europe in 2000).

The US dominance is even greater when measured in terms of top sites and pageviews. In 2000, the US accounted for 65 percent of the top thousand websites, and 83 percent of the total pageviews of Internet users. Again, South Korea is the surprise phenomenon here, ranking second after the US in its percentage of total pageviews—a tribute to the high level of use of the Korean Internet by Koreans. South Korea only accounted for 5.6 percent of total pageviews but this percentage was well above the 2.9 percent for the UK or the 1.1 percent for Germany. Since Japan also fared better in top websites and pageviews than in content provision, it may be that the language barrier in accessing English sites favors nationally based Internet content.

Zook's data also allow analysis of the location of Internet domains by city, with a database of 2,500 cities worldwide. The results are highly significant. In January 2000, the top five cities, accounting for 1 percent of world population, accounted for 20.4 percent of Internet domains. The top fifty cities, with only 4 percent of world population, contained 48.2 percent of Internet domains, and the top 500 cities, with 12.4 percent of the population, represented 70 percent of Internet domains. Moreover, the concentration of Internet domains between 1998 and 2000 increased for the top five cities by 2.7 percentage points, and for the top ten cities by 1.3 percentage points. This is in contrast to the phenomenon of the diffusion of the Internet from its original location. In other words, Internet content provision is increasingly, and overwhelmingly, a metropolitan phenomenon.

Where are these Internet concentrations located? According to Zook's data, in January 2000, seventeen out of the top twenty cities in the ranking of Internet domains were in the United States. The largest concentration was in the Greater New York area (CMSA), followed by Greater Los Angeles (CMSA), and San Francisco–Oakland–San Jose. London came fourth in the ranking, Seoul seventh, and Hong Kong nineteenth. Within countries, the general rule is the metropolitan concentration of Internet domains, particularly in the largest metropolitan areas. Thus, London accounts for 29 percent of Britain's domains, and the highest density in the UK relative to its population. This predominance of London in Internet content provision has also been verified in the study by Dodge and Shiode (2000) on the Internet's "real estate" in Britain, by calculating the spatial distribution of IP addresses. Birmingham, Cambridge, Oxford, and Nottingham, completed the upper tier of Britain's Internet geography. In France, Paris accounted for 26.5 percent of Internet domains. In Spain, Madrid and Barcelona together represented over 50 percent of Internet domains. Stockholm concentrated the largest share of Internet content provision in Sweden, and so did Helsinki in Finland, and Copenhagen in Denmark. Only Germany has a decentralized system of Internet content provision, with Berlin, Munich, and Hamburg sharing relatively low percentages of concentration, ahead of other areas. This reflects the flat hierarchy of the German urban system, suggesting that Internet content provision adapts to the pre-existing metropolitan structure, rather than reversing it. However, when domain sites were adjusted for population, Zurich and Munich appeared at the top of the European ranking, reflecting Zurich's role in finance and Munich's role in high-technology and media industries.

In the United States, there is an overwhelming metropolitan dominance in Internet content provision, with a particularly concentrated structure at the top of the ranking. In terms of Internet domains, New York, Los Angeles, and San Francisco/Silicon Valley top the rest of the cities by far. Adding the fourth and fifth largest areas (Seattle and Washington, DC), these areas together accounted for 18.7 percent of domains worldwide, and 38.1 percent of the top thousand sites in the world, as well as for 64.6 percent of pageviews of the top thousand sites. In contrast, the rest of the US represented only 27 percent of the world's top websites and 16.9 percent of pageviews. In other words, the concentration of Internet content providers in the US reflects in fact its concentration in a few metropolitan areas, and particularly at the top of this Internet metropolitan hierarchy, formed by New York, Los Angeles, San Francisco, Seattle, and Washington, DC.

Measuring the Internet content provision specialization of these areas, standardizing by population, and by the number of businesses, a new hierarchy appears, with the San Francisco Bay area at the top, Los Angeles in third place, and New York in fourteenth place, with smaller areas, highly intensive in Internet provision high on the list. This is the case for Provo-Orem (Utah), San Diego, and (of course) Las Vegas (gambling, porno, tourist information). What is important in this analysis is that the Internet domain hierarchy does not really follow population distribution in the United States. For instance, the San Francisco Bay area is much higher than Chicago in absolute numbers of domains, and in terms of specialization. San Francisco has twice the number of domain names per firm than Chicago, Philadelphia, Dallas, or Houston.

Finally, moving inside metropolitan regions, Zook shows the high level of concentration of Internet domains in certain areas. Thus, in the city of San Francisco, there is an extraordinary concentration of Internet content providers in the South of Market area. In New York, fig. 8.6 shows the overwhelming concentration in Manhattan, and inside Manhattan in a few neighborhoods: the so-called Silicon Alley, at the tip of Manhattan; and south of Central Park, on the East Side. In Los Angeles, there is also a pattern of spatial concentration of Internet content providers in a few areas, particularly around Santa Monica, the Ventura Freeway Corridor, and the San Gabriel Valley.

Thus, research shows that Internet content provision, as measured by domains addresses, follows a pattern of high spatial concentration. This supposedly footloose activity has a higher location quotient than most other industries. It is concentrated in a few countries; it is overwhelmingly located in metropolitan areas, and particularly in some of the wealthiest metropolitan areas of the world; it is usually (but not always) concentrated in the largest metropolitan areas of each country; it is concentrated in a few, leading metropolitan locations in each country with high levels of specialization in those areas that started the commercial Internet; and it is concentrated in specific areas, and neighborhoods within metropolitan areas. The geography of the Internet's content providers is characterized by taking over the world's virtual sites from a few physical places. The question is why?

Zook has investigated the matter in the United States, using both statistical analysis and case studies. There are three main answers. The first refers to the connection to the metropolitan structure of the information economy. Internet domains are related to information production organizations. The large spatial clusters of these organizations in advanced services, finance, media, entertainment, education, health, technology, and the like, are predominantly in metropolitan areas, and particularly in areas such as New York, Los Angeles, and Washington, DC. So, the spatial patterning of the Internet follows not the distribution of the population but the metropolitan concentration of the information economy. However, this is not the only answer because major information production centers, such as the Chicago area, do not rank as high as Internet content providers.

The second answer refers to the connection to pre-existing milieux of technological innovation, which provide the know-how of new technologies, and the network of suppliers, which could sustain new entrepreneurial initiatives: this is the case for the San Francisco Bay area, for Seattle, Austin, San Diego, Denver–Boulder, and for a number of high-technology hubs riding the new wave of the information-technology revolution. But this only partially explains the case of New York, the largest concentration of Internet content providers in 2000. New York was built on the design expertise accumulated in the world of media, advertising, and art, yet it had little technological base of its own. Zook found that the key missing link, which explains the prominent role of both New York and San Francisco in the provision of Internet content, is the spatial structure of the venture capital industry, including the personalized version of "angel investors" (Zook, 2001a).

Venture capital plays an essential role in financing innovation and entrepreneurialism in the Internet economy, as I showed in Chapter 3. Venture capitalists have an intimate connection to Internet start-up companies. They work with the companies on a weekly basis, they nurture and advise them, they are part of the same process of work (Gupta, 2000). In other words, venture capital is an integral component of the Internet industry. And the geography of venture capital is highly concentrated. In the late 1950s, in the first stage of the micro-electronics-led revolution, it was concentrated in the San Francisco and Boston areas, although New York-based investment banks were always a major source of capital everywhere (for instance, the emblematic micro-electronics company of Silicon Valley, Fairchild Semiconductors, was started with capital from New York investors). In the 1990s, New York became a major player in the Internet content industry, as well as Los Angeles, both financed by venture capital. The reasons for this spatial patterning of venture capital firms are two-fold. Most venture capital originated from inside the high-technology industry, from investors who had made money in the industry, knew it well, and were ready to take risks because of their insider knowledge, often with backing from outside investment, particularly from New York. However, insider knowledge was essential for the development of a dynamic and rich venture-capital sector in the San Francisco Bay area.

The process by which New York became a hub of the Internet content industry was different. Wall Street firms learned from Silicon Valley how profitable technology investments could be. They spun off specialized units to scan opportunities, at the time when New York's bursting entrepreneurial culture was discovering the potential of the Internet in its cultural/commercial dimension. The convergence of the New York information economy, New York money, New York media, New York art, and New York business savvy launched Silicon Alley, and beyond, reinventing the New York economy once again. The geography of Internet production is the geography of cultural innovation. A geography that Peter Hall (1998) has demonstrated was historically rooted in the major urban centers of the world—and still is.

The Internet Age: An Urbanized World of Sprawling Metropolises

One of the founding myths of futurology about the Internet Age refers to the end of cities. Why keep these cumbersome, congested, filthy creatures from our past when we have the technological possibility of working, living, communicating, and enjoying from our mountain top, our tropical paradise, or our little house on the prairie? And yet, while you are reading this book our blue planet will probably be crossing the threshold when 50 percent of the world's population live in cities (up from 37 percent in 1970), and the projections are for about two-thirds of the population being urbanized by 2025. Sub-Saharan Africa, the least urbanized region in the world, is the one with the fastest rate of urban growth (an annual 5.2 percent in 1975–95), so that by 2020, 63 percent of the population will be likely to live in cities. In 1998–9, Western Europe was 82 percent urban, Russia 75 percent, and the US 77 percent. In 1996, Japan and the Korean peninsula were 78 percent urban, Brazil 80 percent, South East Asia 37 percent, Pakistan 35 percent. China, with 30 percent in 1996, and India with 28 percent in 1998, were still, by and large, rural countries, and they account for over one-third of humankind. Yet, the projections are for

India's urban population to almost double between 1996 and 2020, jumping from 256 million to 499 million. China's urban population is expected to increase even faster, from 377 million in 1996 to 712 million in 2020, thus representing over half of the projected total population of China. In all likelihood, the twenty-first century will see a largely urbanized planet, with the population increasingly concentrated in very large metropolitan regions—leaving most of the planet's land mass sparsely inhabited.

At the turn of the millennium, in the rich countries, the proportion of people living in areas of over one million people was 30 percent, and one-third of Latin Americans lived in these large metropolitan areas. Moreover, the statistical categories are misleading because the functional spatial units where people live encompass much larger populations linked by fast transportation systems that shrink distance and give people the option of being in a major node of economic and social livelihood without being in the proximity of one of its centers. The entire planet is being reorganized around gigantic metropolitan nodes that absorb an increasing proportion of the urban population, itself the majority of the population of the planet.

But what has the Internet to do with it? First, the story I have just told is the opposite of the official story of Internet-based futurologists. I read, in mid-2000, one of the most prominent representatives of the trade forecasting once again the end of cities, and declaring that the Internet would be the golden opportunity for rural regions of the world, such as South America—which, of course, at the same date was already 80 percent urban, and counting. So, to consider the actual data on the spatial patterning of human settlements is a healthy reminder of the realities of our world while trying to ascertain the spatial dimension of the Internet. But, secondly, and more importantly, the Internet is in fact the technological medium that allows metropolitan concentration and global networking to proceed simultaneously. The networked economy, tooled by the Internet, is an economy made up of very large, interconnected metropolitan regions. I shall explain.

While our economy and society are built around decentralized networks of interaction, the spatial pattern of human settlements is characterized by unprecedented territorial concentration of population and activities (Borja and Castells, 1997). Why so? Why do urban and metropolitan areas continue to grow in size and complexity, in spite of increasing technological ability to work, and interact, at a distance? The fundamental reason is the spatial concentration of jobs, income-generating activities, services, and human development opportunities in cities, and particularly in the largest metropolitan areas. This is, on the one hand, because increasing productivity in the advanced sector of the economy, and the crisis of agricultural and extractive activities, eliminate jobs in rural areas and backward regions, inducing new rural–urban migrations. On the other hand, metropolitan areas concentrate the higher-value generating activities, both in manufacturing and services; because they are the sources of wealth, they provide jobs, both directly and indirectly. And because there is a higher level of income in these areas, they offer greater opportunities for the provision of essential services, such as education and health. Furthermore, even for those migrants at the bottom of urban society, the spillover of opportunities provides better chances for survival first, and for the promotion of future generations later, than anything they could find in increasingly marginalized rural areas and backward regions. As long as metropolitan areas continue to be cultural centers of innovation, their residents have access to unparalleled opportunities for cultural enhancement and personal enjoyment, thus improving the quality and diversity of their consumption.

Yet, why does the new production and management system of the Information Age favor metropolitan concentration? Knowledge generation and information-processing are the sources of value and power in the Information Age. Both depend on innovation, and on the capacity to diffuse innovation in networks that induce synergy by sharing this information and knowledge. A twenty-year-old tradition of urban and regional research has shown the importance of territorial complexes of innovation in facilitating synergy. What Philippe Aydalot, Peter Hall, and I named some time ago as "milieux of innovation" seem to be at the heart of the ability of cities, and particularly of large cities, to become the sources of wealth in the Information Age. This is certainly the case for Silicon Valley (and the San Francisco Bay area in general), the acknowledged birth-place of the information-technology revolution (Saxenian, 1994). But, as shown by Peter Hall and myself in our world survey of technopoles, the argument extends to all societies. All major centers of technological innovation have appeared in and from large metro-politan areas: Tokyo–Yokohama, London, Paris, Munich (succeeding Berlin after the war), Milan, Stockholm, Helsinki, Moscow, Beijing, Shanghai, Seoul–Inchon, Taipei–Hsinchu, Bangalore, Bombay, São Paulo–Campinas, and, in the US, the San Francisco Bay area, Los Angeles/Southern California Technopole, Greater Boston, and, lately, Seattle, although there are secondary milieux of innovation in areas such as Austin, North Carolina's research triangle, Princeton's corridor, and Denver. New York used to be a major exception (which has an historical explanation), largely compensated for by its innovative role in finance, business services, media, and cultural industries. But its ability to seize the opportunity of the Internet economy has propelled New York to the forefront of innovation. Moreover, Peter Hall extended the argument of the relationship between cities and innovation to the entire Western history of cultural creativity and entrepreneurial innovation (Hall, 1998). If so, it seems logical that when we reach the Information Age, and cultural creativity becomes a productive force, major cities enjoy more than ever their competitive advantage as sources of wealth.

But the innovative potential of cities is not restricted to information-technology industries. It extends to a whole range of activities dealing with information and communication, thus based on networking and the Internet. Innovation is essential in advanced business services, which form the leading money-making sector in our economy. Services such as finance, insurance, consulting, legal services, accounting, advertising, marketing comprise the nerve center of the twenty-first century economy. And they are concentrated in large metropolitan areas, with New York/New Jersey, and Los Angeles/Orange County being the prominent areas in the United States. Advanced services are unevenly distributed between the central business district and the new suburban centers, depending on the history and spatial dynamics of each area. What is critical is that these advanced service centers are territorially concentrated, built on interpersonal networks of decision-making processes, organized around a territorial web of suppliers and customers, and increasingly communicated by the Internet among themselves.

A third set of value-generating activities concentrated in metropolitan areas are the cultural industries: media, in all their forms; entertainment; art; fashion; publishing; museums; cultural creation industries, at large. These industries are among the fastest growing, and the highest value-generating activities in all advanced societies. They also rely on the spatial logic of territorially concentrated milieux of innovation, with a multiplicity of interactions, and face-to-face exchanges at the core of the innovation process—to be complemented, not contradicted, by on-line interaction.

Fourth, in the whole range of activities associated with the emergence of the new economy, highly educated workers and entrepreneurs are the key source of innovation and value creation. These knowledge creators are attracted to vibrant urban areas, to cities such as San Francisco, New York, London, Paris, Barcelona. And they build their networks and milieux that attract additional talent. This is the argument developed by Kotkin (2000) to explain the differential dynamics of American cities in the late 1990s.

Let us now connect these trends to Zook's observation of the increasing concentration of Internet domains in the largest metropolitan areas in the world. Since the Internet processes information, the Internet hubs are located in the main information systems which are the basis of the economy and institutions of metropolitan regions. However, this does not mean that the Internet is just a metropolitan phenomenon. Instead, it is a network of metropolitan nodes. There is no centrality, but nodality, based on a networking geometry.

It is precisely because of the existence of telecommunication networks, and computer networks, that these milieux of innovation, and these high-level networks of decision-making, can exist in a few nodes in the country, or in the planet, reaching out to the whole world from a few blocks in Manhattan, in Wilshire Boulevard, in Santa Clara County, in San Francisco's South of Market, in the City of London, in Paris' Quartier de l'Opera, in Tokyo's Shibuya, or in São Paulo's Nova Faria Lima. While concentrating much of the production and consumption capacity of a vast hinterland, these territorial complexes of knowledge generation and information-processing, link up with each other, ushering in a new global geography, made up of nodes and networks.

Wherever, and whenever, a major node of this global network is formed, it expands, and it generates a new spatial form, the metropolitan region, which is characterized by the functional connection between activities scattered in a vast territory, usually defined in terms of a specific labor market, consumer market, and media market (for example, television). The metropolitan region is not just a very large urban area. It is also a distinctive spatial form, close to what a brilliant journalist, Joel Garreau, labeled as *Edge City*, after reporting on new spatial developments in some of the largest American metropolitan areas (Garreau, 1991). In most cases, the metropolitan region does not even have a name, let alone a political unity or institutional agency. When we speak of the "Bay Area" (in my case meaning the San Francisco Bay area), we are referring to a large constellation of cities and counties, stretching at least from Santa Rosa in the North Bay to Santa Cruz in the South of the South Bay, and from the Western cliffs of San Francisco to the outer suburbs of the East Bay, all the way to Livermore; that is, almost 7 million people living in an expanse that is about 60 miles long and 40 miles wide. Indeed, the largest city in the San Francisco Bay area is not San Francisco, but San Jose, with a population close to one million in 2000. The real settlement pattern is already reaching far beyond this area, linking up with the Central Valley, and absorbing, across the Nevada border, Lake Tahoe, and towards the South, Monterey and Carmel, as secondary residences for Bay Area dwellers.

An even more striking case is the Southern California metropolitan region, which merges in one largely integrated space the area extending from Ventura in the north, to the southern tip of Orange County, with about 17 million people living, working, consuming, and travelling in this territory without boundaries, name, or identity, other than as a labor market and a consumer market.

Furthermore, the freeway links up Orange County with San Diego, and beyond the border, with Tijuana, making this area a binational, multicultural, nameless, mega-urban constellation. Outside California, the New Jersey–New York–Long Island–Rhode Island–Connecticut, the Washington, DC–Maryland–Virginia conurbation, or the New England mega-region are similar examples of new spatial agglomerations.

In Asia, some of the largest metropolitan regions in the world are being formed, such as the region in the process of articulation between Hong Kong–Shenzhen–Canton–Macau–Zuhai and the Pearl River delta, with a population of about 60 million. Or the Tokyo–Yokohama–Nagoya region, extending, via Shinkansen, to Osaka–Kobe, and Kyoto, within a 3–4-hour transportation time framework (Lo and Yeung, 1996). Seoul–Inchon, Shanghai–Pudon, Bangkok metropolitan region, Jakarta megapolis, Calcutta, Bombay (Mumbai), Greater Mexico City, Greater São Paulo, Greater Buenos Aires, Greater Rio de Janeiro, Paris–Ile de France, Greater London, and Greater Moscow, are all major areas, most of which have no clear boundaries, or defined identity, beyond the vague images of what used to be their central city. And I am not even mentioning areas of 7 million plus, such as Lima, Bogotá, or Manila, which continue to grow both as magnets *vis-à-vis* their hinterlands in crisis, and as sources of growth and survival through their connections to global networks.

In Western Europe, the building of a dense high-speed train network is integrating London with Paris, Paris with Lyons and Marseille, and with Northern Italy; Paris–Lille–Brussels with The Netherlands; and Frankfurt and Cologne with the French network; from the South, Lisbon–Seville–Madrid–Barcelona–Bilbao are scheduled to link up with the European network in 2004. Overall, in Central/Western Europe an extraordinary concentration of population, production, management, markets, and urban amenities are being connected within 3-hour transportation time-frames, let alone air shuttles with a dense network of flights between 40 minutes and 2 hours connecting most of Western Europe. Thus, the new spatial structure emerging at the heart of Western Europe is that of a series of interconnected metropolitan regions, each one connecting several conurbations, each one with millions of people, and jointly harnessing a significant share of the world's wealth and information (Hall, 1997).

These settlements blur the traditional distinctions between cities and countryside, and between cities and suburbs. They include, in spatial discontinuity, built-up areas of various density, open space, agricultural activities, natural areas, residential expanses, and a concentration of services and manufacturing activities, scattered along transportation axes, made up of freeways and mass transit systems. There is no real zoning—as workplaces, residential, and commercial areas are dispersed in various directions. Moreover, while these regions are usually centered around a major central city, smaller urban centers gradually become absorbed in intra-metropolitan networks. New nodes constantly emerge, as areas concentrate business/industrial activities decentralized from their previous locations. Other localities grow in their role of providers of services for the metropolitan population at large. This regional metropolitan structure is entirely dependent upon transportation and communications. And communication and information systems are organized by and around the Internet. Work at a distance, from home, or between spatially disjointed locations, increases considerably—but not in the form forecasted by futurologists. Rather than telecommuting, we are observing the emergence of multi-modal metropolitan mobility. I will elaborate on this fundamental point.

Telework, Tele-life, and the New Patterns of Metropolitan Mobility

Work from the electronic cottage was supposed to usher in a new kind of human settlement, with workplaces fading away, and homes becoming the center of multi-functional activity. In fact, telecommuting is not a widespread practice, and work from home is only partly related to the Internet. Thus, in the US, supposedly the most advanced area in the world in terms of flexibility of working patterns, in 1997 only about 6.43 percent of the labor force were estimated to work at home on a regular basis, with 47 percent of them working on average 15 hours a week, and the rest, about 23 hours a week (US Bureau of Labor Statistics, elaborated by Zayas, 2000). Furthermore, only a fraction of these workers worked predominantly from home, and many of them did not use computers. In a series of studies conducted by Mohktarian and by Handy in the 1990s (Mohktarian, 1991, 1992; Mohktarian, Handy, and Salomon, 1995), it was shown that the percentage of the labor force that in a given day in California worked from home was, on average, less than 2 percent. In fact, a 1991 national survey on homework in the US found that fewer than half of homeworkers used computers: the rest worked with a telephone, pen, and paper (Mohktarian, 1992: 12). A 1993 survey by Link Resources in the US estimated at 6.1 percent the proportion of US workers working at home, but on average work at home was only one or two days per week. A 1999 survey by Pratt Associates in the US estimated the percentage of homeworkers at about 10 percent, but work at home was limited to nine days per month on average (reported by Zayas, 2000).

In one of the most comprehensive overviews of the phenomenon, Gillespie and Richardson (2000) analyzed data on telecommuting, workplace, teleservices, and metropolitan travel in a comparative perspective, contrasting the UK with other European countries and with the US. In line with other researchers on teleworking, they began by differentiating distinct kinds of work at a distance, then reviewed the evidence for each form of activity. Electronic home-working was found to be limited in all contexts, and usually part-time, one or two days a week. Most electronic homeworkers still need to commute to their office most days. Some studies suggest that trips saved by working at home replaced public transportation trips, not the automobile. Indeed, other studies seem to indicate that tele-working increases the use of the automobile because it makes the car available for other members of the household, and because it cuts down "trip chaining;" that is, the process by which people drop children at school or pick up groceries on the way to work. Ability to work at home part-time, particularly for the professional labor force, leads to residential location further from workplaces, thus increasing commuting distance for those trips that are still necessary. So, overall, the study by Mohktarian, Handy, and Salomon (1991) showed that in the US, for telecommuters working an average of 1.2 days a week at home, the reduction of miles traveled per vehicle was less than 0.51 percent. Gillespie and Richardson (2000) estimate that the reduction is probably lower in the UK.

However, there are other forms of work at a distance, on the basis of the Internet, that have important spatial consequences. One is the development of remote offices, or "call centers," located on the periphery of metropolitan areas. Rather than bringing sophisticated telecommunications equipment to their workers' homes, companies build call centers and data-processing centers which concentrate workers but diffuse their calls throughout the country and throughout the world. Many of these centers, for instance in the UK, are located in lower-cost areas, generally served by women employees living in the suburbs or small towns in the area of influence of major cities (such as Edinburgh, Glasgow, Leeds, which have been attracting telebanking jobs). The reasons for the concentration of work in these telecenters have to do mainly with management procedures, but not necessarily related to control of the worker. In fact, in a fully computerized system, it would be easy to constantly monitor the worker's activity. What management of information requires is, in fact, the opposite: to give workers as much initiative as they can handle, under conditions defined and organized by management. The informal transmission of information, tacit knowledge of the company, group dynamics, and economies of scale for advanced telecommunications equipment seem to be among the key elements underlying the growth of these "electronic communication factories" that become a new form of workplace in the Internet economy.

In a striking manifestation of the new spatial concentration of telecommunicated business operations, there was a boom in "telecommunication hotels" in downtown Los Angeles in the late 1990s. Taking advantage of vacant office space in downtown, as the result of the crisis of the Los Angeles economy in 1990–94, over 150 firms specializing in telecommunications and Internet-related switching operations occupied commercial and historic buildings, and provided the use of telecommunications equipment for dozens of firms. This created a cluster of what some observers call "tele-communications factories," leading to displacement of residents, business, and cultural amenities (Horan, 2000: 4).

Another major development is mobile teleworking, which is on the verge of increasing dramatically with the explosion of wireless-based Internet access (WAP) and mobile access to the Internet. Professional workers spend more and more time in the field, relating to their clients and partners, traveling across the metropolitan area, across the country, and across the world, while keeping in touch with their office via the Internet and mobile phones (Kopomoa, 2000). Companies are now reducing desk assignment for their employees, so that they use the space they need only when they need it. So, the emerging model of work is not the home tele-worker, but the nomadic worker and the "office on the run."

What the Internet makes possible is a multiple configuration of work spaces. The overwhelming majority of people do have work-places to which they go regularly. But many also work from home (not instead of, but in addition to, their usual workplace), they work from their cars, trains, and planes, from their airports and their hotels, on their vacations and in the night—they are always on call, as their beepers and mobile phones never stop ringing. The individualization of working arrangements, the multi-location of the activity, and the ability to network all these activities around the individual worker, usher in a new urban space, the space of endless mobility, a space made of flows of information and com-munication, ultimately managed with the Internet.

The picture becomes even more complex if, in addition to pro-fessional tasks, we introduce the management of everyday life, from telebanking to teleshopping. Places do not disappear, people still go shopping to the malls—after checking options and prices on the Internet, or the other way around. This, in turn increases, not decreases, mobility and transportation needs. Summarizing their findings, Gillespie and Richardson (2000: 242) write:

the "reduced demand for travel" scenario . . . may be decidedly mislead-ing . . . Not only are communication technologies expanding the "activ-ity spaces" within which work takes place, leading to longer distances traveled, but in addition, journey patterns associated with new ways of working are becoming more diffuse and less nodal, and hence more difficult to accomplish by public transport. This effect is exacerbated by companies adjusting their premises stock to accommodate more effectively new ways of working, leading to a reduction in demand for conventional city-center offices and an increase in demand for office space in office park environments with high levels of accessibility to the motorway sytem. At the same time the substitution of tele-mediated for face-to-face banking and other services risks further undermining the role of city centers and high streets, as branch offices are closed and customers are served from large teleservices centers, themselves usually located on business parks . . . Teleworking and tele-activities are, then, perhaps best understood not as developments that suppress the demand for mobility but, rather, as forms of what might best be described as "hypermobility."

So, metropolitan regions in the Internet Age are characterized, simultaneously, by spatial sprawl and spatial concentration, by the mixing of land-use patterns, by hypermobility, and dependence on communications and transportation, both intra-metropolitan and inter-nodal. What emerges is a hybrid space, made up of places and flows: a space of networked places.

Living Places in the Space of Flows: William Mitchell's E-topia

For a few paragraphs I am going to break a basic rule I follow in most of my writing. I will explore some of the future implications for our living environment of information technologies in the making. I am going to do so by relying on the analysis of William Mitchell. I usually distrust visions of the future. Yet Mitchell's knowledge of the matter is so deep, and he is so careful in situating technological forecasting in the complexity of social and cultural interactions, that by reporting on his analysis I hope to add a new dimension to the understanding of the spatial transformations associated with the rise of the Internet, and its future expansion as a communications environment (Mitchell, 1999, personal communication, 2001).

Trends in the relationship between architecture, design, and technology seem to be moving in the direction of building "intelligent environments." Work proceeding at MIT's Media Lab, particularly by Joe Jacobson, focuses on materials sensitive to electrical stimuli, so that our daily environment could be made of sensors surrounding us like pigment in the wall. Naturally, this also extends to our clothing, our cars, our objects, our work environments. Networking technologies of the Jini type would allow these objects to communicate among themselves, and with us at our request, in a flexible environment of information. I would add myself that the "Blue Tooth" technology introduced by Nokia/Ericsson in 2000 may enhance this network of constant interconnection of our daily objects. Broadband Internet, always connected, and mobile access to it, may link us permanently with our home environment and with the world at large. The communicated home may be necessary to handle the diversity of tasks/experiences that are likely to take place within it. The home does not become the workplace, and in many cases it is the workplace that could feel like home for disaffected, lone professionals, as Arlene Hochschild (1997) found in her research on workers in a large corporation. Yet, the home becomes multidimensional, and needs to support a diversity of experiences, functions, and projects for a household whose members have a growing diversity of interests. As Mitchell (1999: 22–3) writes:

This does not mean that the majority of us will become full-time, stay-at-home telecommuters, and that traditional workplaces—particularly downtown offices—will simply disappear. Despite decades of interest in the possibility of telecommuting, there is little evidence that it will take over to such an extent. But we will certainly see increasingly flexible work schedules and spatial patterns, and many people will divide their time, in varying proportions, among traditional types of workplaces, *ad hoc* work settings that serve while they are on the road, and electronically equipped home workplaces . . . We will not have a world where there's no there anywhere. Just the opposite in fact. We will increasingly take advantage of digital telecommunications technology to stay more closely in touch with places that are particularly meaningful to us when we travel. There will still be some place we call "home."

And this home will have its *genius loci* (the genius of the place), an intranet connecting devices equipped with sensors and powerful software, able to respond to the needs of those living in the place, "focusing global resources in local tasks." Buildings will develop electronic network systems, connecting to each other and to each unit in the building. Implications for planning and zoning are considerable, starting with the end of the separation between residential and working functions in a given spatial area. Indeed, San Francisco's South of Market and New York's South of Houston are characterized by work/living spaces that reconstruct the unity of the experience of the pre-industrial era, while being linked to the world via the Internet. Urban designers are particularly inspired by the potential rich texture of this space of mixed uses and multi-dimensional activity.

Indeed, the challenge for architects and urban planners is how to avoid isolation, how to reintegrate the functional self-sufficiency of individualized spaces with the shared experience of common places on which urban life will continue to be based. As Mitchell (2000: 82) writes: "For architects and urban designers, the complementary task is to create an urban fabric that provides opportunities for social groups to intersect and overlap rather than remain isolated by distance or defended walls—the laptop at the piazza café table instead of the PC in the gated condo."

Cities are faced with a challenge: throughout history they were socio-spatial forms able to articulate synchronous and asynchronous communication, the essential process for transforming information into decision-making. The Internet substitutes for this function. Thus, place-based activities, on which cities are founded, need to compete by adding value to face-to-face experiences that can only take place in cities. It follows that public space and monumentality (museums, cultural centers, public art, architectural icons) will play a key role in marking space, and facilitating meaningful interaction. How these trade-offs between electronic flows and urban places are translated into spatial forms is a largely contingent matter, depending on history, culture, and societies: "It is a mistake to overgeneralize, as futurist gurus have been prone to do. The diverse architectural and urban forms of the future will surely reflect the balances and combinations of interaction modes that turn out to work best for particular people, at particular times and places, facing their own specific circumstance within a new economy of presence" (Mitchell, 1999: 144).

Building on Mitchell's theory, Thomas Horan has reported the development of new forms of architectural, urban, and metropolitan design that treat functionally and symbolically the specificity of these new, "fluid locations." By such he refers to "the need for place design to address the unprecedented spatial fluidity we now have to perform day-to-day activities anywhere and at anytime" (Horan, 2000: 13). He examines a number of design experiences in the United States and Europe, from home to public libraries and community networks, that show the emergence of a hybrid space of urban places and electronic networks whose understanding and treatment form the new frontier for architecture and urban design.

Indeed, as Mitchell (2000: 155) concludes: "The power of place will still prevail . . . Physical settings and virtual venues will function interdependently and will mostly complement each other within transformed patterns of urban life rather than substitute within existing ones. Sometimes we will use networks to avoid going places. But sometimes, still, we will go places to network." However, not everybody seems to be invited to the new, meaningful space promised by the Internet Age because the cities of our time are being increasingly segregated by the logic of splintering networks.

Dual Cities and Glocal Nodes: Splintering Networks

What characterizes the networking logic embedded in the Internet-based infrastructure is that places (and people) can be as easily switched off as they can be switched on. The geography of networks is a geography of both inclusion and exclusion, depending on the value attached by socially dominant interests to any given place. In a path-breaking investigation, Stephen Graham and Simon Marvin (2001) have shown how the networks of urban infrastructure are splintering urban areas around the world, both in developed and developing countries. Urban infrastructures built on the principle of universal service were the cornerstone of modern urbanization, and underlay the formation of industrial cities as integrated functional and social systems. During the 1990s, liberalization, privatization, and deregulation, together with rapid technological change, and the globalization of investment, reversed the historical trend, diversifying urban infrastructure according to market capacity, functional priorities, social privileges, and political choices. Graham and Marvin (2001) document the increasing specialization and segmentation of infrastructure in water, power, transportation (roads, rails, airports, mass transit), and in telecommunications.

The uses of the Internet are dependent not only on connectivity, but on the quality of the connection. Standard telephone lines are not sufficient to carry and distribute the potential of Internet-based communication. Market competition, and deregulation have created extraordinary differences between cities and within cities around the world in the ability to network efficiently. Fiber-optic grids and advanced telecommunication systems have become a necessary condition for cities to compete in the global economy. Thus, around the world, key business areas are being equipped with state-of-the-art telecommunications gear, forming what Graham and Marvin call "glocal nodes;" that is, specific areas that link up throughout the planet with equivalent areas anywhere, while being loosely integrated, or not integrated at all, with their surrounding hinterland. They cite the case of Bangkok's "new towns in town" development enclaves, as well as the multimedia super corridor in Malaysia. I could add myself the development of Nova Faria Lima on the periphery of São Paulo, taking over as Brazil's global node from the decaying downtown and the old business concentration along Avenida Paulista. Or the development of Pudong, across the river from downtown Shanghai, a gigantic business complex organized around advanced telecommunication systems, largely isolated from much of the activity taking place in the bustling Chinese metropolis.

Yet this glocality is not confined to the industrializing world. Graham and Marvin describe how the City of London has been installing in recent years the most advanced telecommunications infrastructure in Europe, with at least six overlaid, fiber-optic grids superimposed on the City. Or else, Lima's new global business center, in the San Andres area, whose determinant role and segregating impact on Lima's metropolitan growth has been documented by Miriam Chion (2000). As for Graham and Marvin (2001), their analysis of one of these telecommunication networks in the City of London, operated by COLT, shows the concentration of its carrying capacity in the financial district, with broader grain extensions reaching to the West End and to the new business spaces in the Docklands. Another London network, built by WorldCom, with only 180 km of optic fiber within the City of London, had already secured by 1998, 20 percent of the whole UK international telecommunications traffic. Schiller (1999) documents similar developments in the UK and in the US, and Kiselyova and Castells (2000) find an analogous pattern in the restructuring of Russian telecommunications in the 1990s.

Overall, there is a global trend toward building dedicated telecommunication infrastructures that bypass the general telephone system, and link up directly the major business centers that generate and consume the overwhelming proportion of data traffic over the Internet. Internet networks also segment cities in terms of the purchasing power assigned to each area by market research. In the United States, by mid-1999, about 86 percent of Internet delivery capacity were concentrated in the affluent suburbs and business centers of the twenty largest cities.

Splintering networks accentuate the global trends toward increasing socio-spatial segregation in cities around the world whose extreme manifestation is the explosion of gated communities in many countries of the world, from California to Cairo, from Johannesburg to Bogotá (Blakely and Snyder, 1997). Indeed, Douglas Massey (1996) has shown that the increase of spatial segregation in the 1990s is mainly due to chosen spatial separation by affluent groups, which leave the city they fear. In this context, the Internet allows segregated, affluent enclaves to remain in contact with each other, and with the world, while severing their ties with their uncontrolled, surrounding environment. The backwardness of devalued spaces in their telecommunications infrastructure reinforces their isolation and digs the trenches of their place-based existence. A new urban dualism is emerging from the opposition between the space of flows and the space of places: the space of flows that links places at a distance on the basis of their market value, their social selection, and their infrastructural superiority; the space of places that isolates people in their neighborhoods as a result of their diminished chances to access a better locality (because of price barriers), as well as the globality (because of lack of adequate connectivity). However, this is only a structural tendency because people do react against their exclusion, and assert their rights, and their values, often using the Internet for their resistance and in support of their alternative projects, as I analyzed in Chapter 6. Yet, in the absence of social mobilization, and policies guided by the public interest, the splintering networks resulting from unfettered deregulation of telecommunications and the Internet, threaten to contribute to a new, and fundamental, social cleavage: the global digital divide.

Appendix: Methodology and sources for constructing the maps of Internet domains and Internet users

The maps of Internet users and Internet domains have been researched, developed, and plotted by Matthew Zook, as part of his PhD dissertation at the University of California, Berkeley (Zook, 2001a). These maps are reproduced in this book with the consent and support of Matthew Zook. My deepest thanks to him for his collegial generosity.

Maps of domains

The .com, .org, .net and .edu domain name data set for the maps is based on a tabulation conducted by Matthew Zook in July 2000. It uses an Internet utility program known as "whois" which returns contact information for a particular domain. Included in this information is a mailing address, contact names with phone numbers and e-mails, the date the domain name was registered, the last time it was updated, and the name servers responsible for the domain.

Geocoding domains to cities outside the US is done by matching country–city pairs in a global database of cities. Locating a domain to a specific country is almost 100 percent successful and locating it in a specific city is about 60 percent successful. This lower success rate is largely due to an incomplete world city database. Geocoding domains to US metropolitan areas was based on zip codes and the use of a zip code to MSA translation table.

The July 2000 survey was based on a randomly selected sample of 4 percent of all domain names (sample size = ~ 750,000). The sample is obtained by querying randomly selected three-digit combinations, e.g. def or sx1, and then randomly selecting 15 percent of the domains that start with this combination. Because three-digit combinations are not geographically biased, this provides a random selection for determining the geographical location of domains. Because these figures are based on samples there is a degree of error associated with these figures. However, given the large sample size, this error is less than 0.1 percent.

The counts for country code domains is based on statistics posted on each country code registrar's home page and supplemented by data from DomainStats (http://www.domainstats.com/). More information, analysis, and recent data on the geography of domain names are available at Matthew Zook's website (http://www.zooknic.com/).

Maps of users

NUA's estimation of the number of Internet users worldwide is based upon the aggregation of surveys by a variety of sources worldwide. See http://www.nua.ie/surveys/how_many_online/methodology.html for more details.

Reading Links

Abramson, B. D. (2000) "Internet globalization indicators," *Telecommunications Policy*, 24: 69–74.

Audretsch, David B. and Feldman, Maryann P. (2000) "The telecommunications revolution and the geography of innovation," in James Wheeler, Yuko Aoyama, and Barney Warf (eds), *Cities in the Telecommunications Age: The Fracturing of Geographies*. London: Routledge.

Baldassare, Mark (2000) *California in the New Millennium: The Changing Social and Political Landscape.* Berkeley, CA: University of California Press.

Blakely, Edward J. and Snyder, Mary G. (1997) *Fortress America: Gated Communities in the United States.* Washington, DC: The Brookings Institution.

Borja, Jordi and Castells, Manuel (1997) *Local and Global: The Management of Cities in the Information Age.* London: Earthscan.

Castells, Manuel (1989) *The Informational City.* Oxford: Blackwell.

—— (1996/2000) *The Rise of the Network Society.* Oxford: Blackwell.

—— and Hall, Peter (1994) *Technopoles of the World: The Making of Twenty-first Century Industrial Complexes.* London: Routledge.

Chion, Miriam (2000) "Globalization and localization in the transformation of metropolitan Lima in the 1990s," unpublished PhD dissertation, University of California, Department of City and Regional Planning, Berkeley, California.

Cukier, K. N. (1999) "Bandwidth colonialism? The implications of Internet infrastructure on international e-commerce," paper presented at the INET '99 Conference, June 22–25, San Jose, California.

Daniels, Peter W. (1993) *Service Industries in the World Economy.* Oxford: Blackwell.

Dodge, Martin and Shiode, Narushige (2000) "Where on earth is the Internet? An empirical investigation of the geography of the Internet real estate?," in James Wheeler, Yuko Aoyama, and Barney Warf (eds), *Cities in the Telecommunications Age: The Fracturing of Geographies,* pp. 42–53. London: Routledge.

Freire, Mila and Stren, Richard (eds) (2001) *The Challenge of Urban Government: Policies and Practices.* Washington, DC: The World Bank Institute.

Garreau, Joel (1991) *Edge City: Life on the New Frontier.* New York: Doubleday.

Gillespie, Andrew and Richardson, Ronald (2000) "Teleworking and the city: myths of workplace transcendence and travel reduction," in James Wheeler, Yuko Aoyama, and Barney Warf (eds), *Cities in the Telecommunications Age: The Fracturing of Geographies,* pp. 228–48. London: Routledge.

Graham, Stephen and Marvin, Simon (1996) *Telecommunications and the City.* London: Routledge.

—— and —— (2001) *Splintering Urbanism: Networked Infrastructures, Technological Mobilities, and the Urban Condition.* London: Routledge.

Gupta, Anil K. and Sapienza, Harry J. (1992) "Determinants of venture capital firms' preferences regarding the industry diversity and geographic scope of their investments," *Journal of Business Venturing*, 7: 347–62.

Gupta, Udayan (ed.) (2000) *Done Deals: Venture Capitalists Tell their Stories*. Boston, MA: Harvard Business School Press.

Hall, Peter (1997) *Megacities in Europe*. Amsterdam: University of Amsterdam, Center for Metropolitan Studies, Megacities Lectures Series.

—— (1998) *Cities in Civilization*. New York: Pantheon.

Harvard Design Magazine (2000) *Sprawl and Spectacle*, special issue. Cambridge, MA: Harvard Graduate School of Design.

Hochschild, Arlene R. (1997) *The Time Bind: When Work Becomes Home and Home Becomes Work*. New York: Metropolitan Books.

Horan, Thomas A. (2000) *Digital Places: Building our City of Bits*. Washington, DC: The Urban Land Institute.

Kiselyova, Emma and Castells, Manuel (2000) "Russia in the Information Age," in Victoria Bonnell and George Breslauer (eds), *Russia in the New Century*, pp. 126–57. Boulder, CO: Westview Press.

Kopomoa, Timo (2000) *The City in your Pocket: Birth of the Mobile Information Society*. Helsinki: Gaudeamus.

Kotkin, Joel (2000) *The New Geography: How the Digital Revolution is Reshaping the American Landscape*. New York: Random House.

Kuntsler, James H. (1993) *The Geography of Nowhere*. New York: Simon and Schuster.

Leyshon, Andrew and Thrift, Nigel (1997) *Money/Space: Geographies of Monetary Transformation*. London: Routledge.

Lo, Fu-chen and Yeung, Yue-man (eds) (1996) *Emerging World Cities in the Pacific Asia*. Tokyo: United Nations University Press.

Massey, Douglas (1996) "The age of extremes: concentrated affluence and poverty in the twentieth century," *Demography*, 33(4): 395–41.

Michelson, Ronald L. and Wheeler, James O. (1994) "The flow of information in a global economy: the role of the American urban system in 1990," *Annals of the Association of American Geographers*, 84 (1): 87–107.

Mitchell, William J. (1995) *City of Bits*. Cambridge, MA: MIT Press.

—— (1999) *E-topia*. Cambridge, MA: MIT Press.

Mohktarian, Patricia L. (1991) "Telecommuting and travel: state of practice, state of the art," *Transportation*, 18 (4): 319–42.

—— (1992) "Telecommuting in the United States: letting our fingers do the commuting," *Telecommuting Review: The Gordon Report*, 9 (5).

——, Handy, S.L., and Salomon, I. (1995) "Methodological issues in the estimation of the travel, energy, and air quality impacts of telecommuting," *Transportation Research*, 29A (4): 283–302.

Moss, Mitchell L. and Townsend, Anthony (2000) "How telecommunications systems are transforming urban spaces," in James Wheeler, Yuko Aoyama and Barney Warf (eds), *Cities in the Telecommunications Age: The Fracturing of Geographies*, pp. 228–48. London: Routledge.

Quarterman, J. (1997) "Is .'com' primarily US or international?," *Matrix News*, 7: 8–10.

Sassen, Saskia (1991) *The Global City: London, Tokyo, New York*. Princeton, NJ: Princeton University Press.

Saxenian, Anna Lee (1994) *Regional Advantage*. Cambridge, MA: Harvard University Press.

Schiller, Dan (1999) *Digital Capitalism: Networking the Global Market System*. Cambridge, MA: MIT Press.

Scott, Allen and Soja, Edward (eds) (1998) *The City of Los Angeles and Urban Theory at the End of the Twentieth Century*. Berkeley, CA: University of California Press.

Townsend, A. (2001) "Networked cities and the global structure of the Internet," *American Behavioral Scientist*, 44(10) (June).

Waldinger, Roger (ed.) (forthcoming) *The New Urban Immigrants*.

Wheeler, James, Aoyama, Yuko, and Warf, Barney (eds) (2000) *Cities in the Telecommunications Age: The Fracturing of Geographies*. London: Routledge.

Zayas, Madeleine (2000) "Telecommuting: myths and realities," Berkeley, CA: University of California, unpublished research paper for seminar CP 229.

Zook, M. A. (2000*a*) "Internet metrics: using hosts and domain counts to map the Internet globally," *Telecommunications Policy*, 24 (6/7).

—— (2000*b*) "The web of production: the economic geography of commercial Internet content production in the United States," *Environment and Planning A*, 32: 411–26.

—— (2001*a*) "The geography of the Internet industry: venture capital, Internet start-ups, and regional development," unpublished PhD disertation, University of California, Department of City and Regional Planning, Berkeley, California.

—— (2001*b*) "Old hierarchies or new networks of centrality?: the global geography of the Internet content market," *American Behavioral Scientist*, 44(10).

e-Links

Cheswick, Bill and Burch, Hal (2000) "The geography of cyberspace directory: mapping the Internet," at www.cybergeography.org/mapping. html
Major mapping projects of the Internet.

Dodge, M. (1998–2001) *Atlas of Cyberspace*, at <http://www.cybergeography.org/atlas/>

Telegeography (2000) *Hubs and Spokes: A Telegeography Internet Reader.* Washington, DC: Telegeography Inc., at <www.telegeography.com>

www.zooknic.com
Matthew Zook's continuing research on the geography of the Internet industry.

www.domainstats.com
Updates on the growth of country code domain names.

www.cybergeography.com
Maps of cyberspace.

www.alexa.com
Monthly ranking of the web's 1,000 most visited websites.

www.mediametrix.com
Monthly ranking of websites.

www.nua.ie/surveys/how_many_online/index.html
Statistical estimates of Internet users worldwide.

Chapter 9

The Digital Divide in a Global Perspective

The centrality of the Internet in many areas of social, economic, and political activity is tantamount to marginality for those without, or with only limited, access to the Internet, as well as for those unable to use it effectively. Thus, it is little wonder that the heralding of the Internet's potential as a means of freedom, productivity, and communication comes hand in hand with the denunciation of "the digital divide" induced by inequality on the Internet. The differentiation between Internet-haves and have-nots adds a fundamental cleavage to existing sources of inequality and social exclusion in a complex interaction that appears to increase the gap between the promise of the Information Age and its bleak reality for many people around the world. Yet, the apparent simplicity of the issue becomes complicated on closer examination. Is it really true that people and countries become excluded because they are disconnected from Internet-based networks? Or, rather, it is because of their connection that they become dependent on economies and cultures in which they have little chance of finding their own path of material well-being and cultural identity?

Under what conditions, and for what purposes, does inclusion/exclusion in/from Internet-based networks translate into better opportunities or greater inequality? And what are the factors that underlie the differential pace of access to the Internet, and the diversity of its uses? I will try to tackle these questions under two different headings. First, I will examine the various meanings of the digital divide, and their interaction with social sources of inequality. I will do so by referring to available information on the United States, albeit attempting to use this information to support broader analytical implications. Secondly, I will examine the digital divide in a global perspective, since the differences in Internet access between countries and regions in the planet as a whole are so considerable that they actually modify the meaning of the digital divide and the kind of issues to be discussed.

Dimensions of the Digital Divide

The usual meaning of "the digital divide" refers to inequality of access to the Internet. As I discuss below, access alone does not solve the problem, but it is a prerequisite for overcoming inequality in a society whose dominant functions and social groups are increasingly organized around the Internet.

I will illustrate this analysis with US data because there is a good statistical source that has analyzed differential access to the Internet since 1995: the survey of a representative sample of the US population conducted by the US Commerce Department's National Telecommunications and Information Administration (NTIA) (four reports in 1995, 1998, 1999, 2000; see NTIA, 1999, 2000). In August 2000, for the population aged 3 and older, 41.5 percent of households and 44.4 percent of individuals in the United States had access to the Internet, with 51 percent of households having computers at home. Yet, there were still considerable differences in Internet access for various social groups. I will use the data on individuals, unless otherwise stated, because given current technological trends toward ubiquitous Internet access individuals are the key accounting unit for future uses of the Internet.

In terms of income, while 70.1 percent of people earning 75,000 dollars and above had Internet access, the percentage was 18.9 percent for those with less than 15,000, 18.4 percent for those between 15,000 and 24,999, and 25.3 percent for those between 25,000 and 34,999. Education also matters: among people with a bachelor's degree or higher, 74.5 percent had access to the Internet, but the proportion fell to 30.6 percent among high-school graduates, and to 21.7 percent among those not having graduated from high school. There was also an age divide: only 29.6 percent of people over 50 years had access, in contrast to 55.4 percent for the age group 25–49, 56.8 percent for the group 18–24, and 53.4 percent for the group 9–17. Thus teenagers, as a group, had almost twice as much access as individuals over 50. Not being in the labor force was also a major discriminating factor in lowering access to the Internet: 29 percent in contrast to employed individuals at 56.7 percent.

The ethnic digital divide continued to be indicative of the fact that the Information Ages is not blind to color, in spite of optimistic statements: 50.3 percent of whites and 49.4 percent of Asian-Americans had access to the Internet, but only 29.3 percent of African-Americans and 23.7 percent of Hispanics did. It must be noted here that data for households show similar unequal access to those for individuals, but African-American households have an even lower access threshold than individuals (at 23.5 percent), the reason being that African-Americans had some degree of access at work. On the other hand, Asian households had the highest percentage of Internet access, at 56.8 percent, well above the 46.1 percent for white households. Furthermore, even for households with incomes below 15,000 dollars, over 33 percent of Asian-Americans were connected to the Internet, above white households, and in sharp contrast to African-Americans (6.4 percent) and Hispanics (5.2 percent) in the same income group. Household composition, and a strong emphasis on children's education by Asian-American families, may be factors accounting for this differential. Highly educated minority households, and those in the higher-income groups, have much greater levels of access (70.9 percent for African-Americans and 63.7 percent for Hispanics), but still less than similar groups of whites and Asian-Americans. The gap between Asian-Americans and whites, on the one hand, and African-Americans and Hispanics on the other, holds at all levels of income and education. Thus, after adjusting for education and income, about half of the gap in access remains for African-Americans and Hispanics. As for the gender gap, by August 2000 it had all but disappeared in America in terms of access: among individuals, 44.6 percent of men and 44.2 percent of women were Internet users. In fact, other surveys indicate that in the United States in 2000 there were more women than men on the Internet, and women spent more time on-line than men.

Using household data, three other sources of differences in Internet access appear. One is family status: non-family households (single or unmarried) are the least likely to have Internet access (28.1 percent in contrast to 60.6 percent for married couples with children), although female-headed households with children are also at a disadvantage (30 percent). The second source of division refers to geography: urban areas are more likely to have Internet access, in contrast with futurologists' predictions concerning the electronic cottage: 38.9 percent of rural households had access in 2000, 2.6 percentage points below the national average. The third divide refers to disability. On the basis of a special survey conducted in 1999, the NTIA reported that, while 43.3 percent of people without disability had no Internet access (either from home or elsewhere), the proportion increased to 71.6 percent for people with some disability, to 78.9 percent with people with vision problems, and to 81.5 percent of those with walking problems. However, the disparity between those with and without disability declines when income levels rise, while increasing with age. Disabled women are also disadvantaged *vis-à-vis* men. In sum, in the absence of corrective, deliberate policies, disability seems to be an obstacle in access to the Internet, rather than being a condition which could benefit from the potential uses of the Internet to overcome physical barriers.

There is also a significant gap in access to the Internet for children from different income groups, and this could have considerable consequences for the future. According to a study released by the Packard Foundation in 2001 (reported by Lewin, 2001), the rate of diffusion of the Internet among American children was extraordinarily fast in the second half of the 1990s: in 1996, less than 50 percent of American households with children aged 2–17 had a computer at home, and only 15 percent had Internet access. In 2000, 70 percent of these households had computers and 52 percent were connected to the Internet; 20 percent of children between 8 and 16 years had computers in their bedrooms, and 11 percent had access to the Internet from that location. However, 91 percent of households with incomes over 75,000 dollars per year had computers in 2000, while the proportion dropped to 22 percent for children whose family income was less than 20,000 dollars. Moreover, low-income households were less likely to have Internet access, even when they had computers.

To understand the dynamics of differential access, it is necessary to see it in a time perspective: how access evolves over time for different groups. For reasons of statistical comparability, the 2000 NTIA report focuses on the changes that occurred between December 1998 and August 2000. Because this was a key period in the diffusion of Internet use (it increased from 32.7 to 44.4 percent of individuals, and from 26.2 to 41.5 percent of households) the observation is meaningful. The most important fact is that, with important exceptions, most gaps are being reduced. The growth rates in the use of the Internet are almost systematically inversely correlated to the level of penetration in each group in 1998. To be sure, the lower the starting-point the greater the statistical chances for a higher rate of growth, but if the trend is extrapolated, the penetration rates would converge for most categories. This is what has already happened for men and women (30 percent growth rate for men, 41 percent for women, leading to a similar level of Internet use in 2000). The lowest income group increased its use by 38 percent in contrast to 19 percent for the highest income group. Even the age gap, supposedly rooted in the inability of older generations to adapt to new technologies, is shrinking rapidly, the rate of growth in Internet use for individuals over 50 being 53 percent, way above the figure of 35 percent for the main age group (between 25 and 49 years), and twice as high as that for teenagers.

Furthermore, individuals over 50 were almost three times as likely to be Internet users if they were in the labor force. In other words, what increasingly matters in determining access to the Internet is less a question of age than the relationship of individuals to work, as the Internet becomes an indispensable professional tool. Other sources of differential access seem also to be waning. Thus, rural areas, after a slow start, are rapidly catching up, with rural households increasing their Internet access by 75 percent in 20 months. The proportion of single-parent households with Internet access is also increasing rapidly, and has equaled dual-parent households at higher-income levels. Connectivity among female-headed households doubled between 1998 and 2000.

Thus, overall, the general trend seems to be the closing of the gap in Internet access. But there is a major, and significant, exception to this trend: the widening ethnic gap. Thus, on the one hand, the rates of growth in use by ethnic groups were 54 percent for African-Americans, and 43 percent for Hispanics, in contrast with 34 percent for whites and 38 percent for Asian-Americans. As a result, both groups saw their diffusion rates for individuals increase substantially, from 19 to 29.3 percent for African-Americans and from 16.6 to 23.7 percent for Hispanics. Yet, in spite of this high rate of diffusion, the divide between African-American household Internet penetration rates and white households increased by 4 percentage points between 1998 and 2000, resulting in a difference of 22.6 points. The gap between white and Hispanic households increased by 5.3 percentage points. Thus, racial inequality continues to be the distinctive mark of America, and perhaps beyond, in the age of the Internet.

But how does racial inequality play out specifically in the differences in access to the Internet? Rather than going into an always suspect elaboration on cultural differences between races, available evidence comparing whites with African-Americans in the use of the Internet, suggests some hypotheses (Hoffman and Novak, 1999). Researchers have found no differences among white and African-American students in using the web when students have a home computer. Yet, white students without a computer at home were much more likely to use the web at other locations because they have a greater range of opportunities for access. For instance, predominantly white schools have better computer labs. Studies have also shown that African-Americans and Hispanics were less likely to own computers at home, once adjusting for income and education. Thus, less likelihood of owning a computer at home, and fewer access opportunities outside the home, translated into lower access to the Internet. If home ownership of a PC, and availability of computer use, were indeed the key factors underlying the ethnic digital divide, the trends could be changing soon, for two different reasons.

First, the differences in computer ownership between ethnic groups, while still considerable, seem to have stabilized between 1998 and 2000: for African-American households their differential with the national average showed a small decline from 18.9 percentage points to 18.4, and for Hispanics increased slightly from 16.6 percentage points to 17.3, in contrast to the widening gap experienced during the 1990s. And as computer prices fall, and more applications can be found on-line, minorities and low-income groups are likely to find greater incentives and fewer obstacles to owning a home computer (Spooner and Rainie, 2000). Secondly, the decline of the PC, the development of other technological means to access the Internet from portable devices, growing public access at schools, libraries, and community centers, and the widespread use of the Internet at work, are all trends that seem to point toward broader opportunities for access to a computer for minorities—a most obvious barrier for being on-line. Indeed, a Pew Internet and American Life Project survey in 2000, using its own sample of the American population, found a reduction in the gap of Internet access between whites and African-Americans: while in 1998, 23 percent of African-Americans and 42 percent of whites were on-line, the respective percentages in 2000 were 36 percent and 50 percent (Spooner and Rainie, 2000).

As for Hispanics, in addition to problems similar to those found by African-Americans, the language issue may be playing a role, particularly for those recent immigrants with limited knowledge of English, since 87 percent of global websites are in English only. On the other hand, cheap communication with their home countries, over the Internet, is an incentive for recent immigrants to be on-line. Language *per se* should not be a problem, since the Internet is global, and there is an abundance of surfing possibilities in Spanish (indeed, the number of web pages in Spanish is growing faster than the number of pages in English). Yet, studies show that minorities tend to use the Internet mainly for practical matters related to job search, education, health information, and the management of everyday life issues. Thus, for immigrants, the English language of the US websites that they really need for their life in America may be an obstacle. Nevertheless, as Hispanics grow in number, influence, and buying power, the spread of bilingual websites in the US Internet is only a matter of time (Cheskin Research, 2000).

In sum, as far as the US experience is concerned, the Internet started from a sharp digital divide in access, a divide that still remains, except in terms of gender, but the gap seems to be closing as rates of diffusion reach the majority of the population. With projected penetration rates of 63 percent of Americans on-line by 2003, and over three-quarters around 2005, the digital divide, in terms of access to the Internet, will be mainly the concern of the poorest, most discriminated segment of the population—thus furthering their marginality. But for most people, including most individuals from minority groups, access to the Internet is likely to become pervasive, as we see substantial pre-existing divides (between genders, between rural and urban areas, between age groups) either disappear or dwindle in just five years.

A similar process seems to be happening in other contexts. Just to cite one important case, the study by Kiselyova and Castells (2000) of the Russian Internet showed a significant divide in terms of age, class, gender, and territorial disparity—with Moscow and St Petersburg accounting for about two-thirds of Internet users in the mid-1990s. Yet, the trends in 1998–2000 seem to mirror those in the United States, albeit with much lower penetration rates, and with a slower pace in the reduction of inequalities. For instance, the diffusion of the Internet in the Russian regions was proceeding rapidly in 1998–2000, and Moscovites had lost their overwhelming dominance in the population of Internet users. Similarly, Russian women were making substantial strides in on-line presence, as access became more available and the range of applications broadened.

It must be noted, however, that as of November 2000, not only did the world trail the United States in the diffusion of the Internet (with the exceptions of Scandinavia, Canada, and Australia), but the digital divide, measured in terms of access, was broader in Europe than in North America (again with the exception of Nordic European countries). Thus, a survey conducted by the Pro Active Institute, and reported by NUA Surveys, showed an average of 25 percent of Europeans on-line in contrast with 53 percent for the US. But comparing the highest and the lowest income groups, the relative proportions for the US were 82 percent and 26 percent, while for Europe they were 51 percent and 7 percent. Also, age discriminates much more in Europe, with 44 percent of people in the 55–64-year age group being on-line in the US in contrast with only 12 percent for the same age group in Europe. Women were almost as likely as men to be on-line in the US (52 percent to 55 percent), while in Europe the gender gap remained, with women trailing men by 20 percent to 35 percent. In addition, there was a great national difference in the practice of on-line access between Northern and Southern Europe: the UK, Germany, and The Netherlands had a level of diffusion equivalent to two-thirds that of the US, while France, Italy, and Spain had less than one-third of the US level.

The fact that the rise of the Internet took place in conditions of social inequality in access everywhere may have lasting consequences on the structure and content of the medium, in ways that we still cannot fully comprehend. This is because users shape the Internet to an even greater extent than any other technology because of the speed of transmission of their feedback, and the flexibility of the technology. Thus, first users may have shaped the Internet for the latecomers, both in terms of content and of technology, in the same way that the pioneers of the Internet shaped the technology for the masses of users in the 1990s. As the technology of access becomes more complex with more sophisticated technologies (for example, graphic user interface), it may slow down the rate of adoption among less-educated groups. However, while the libertarian strand that created the Internet provided a world wide web of opportunity (albeit at the price of some cultural elitism), it could be that the largely commercialized uses of the Internet in the late 1990s, following a model of consumption and social organization anchored in the affluent groups of the most advanced Western societies, may have biased the practice of the Internet in specific ways, still to be revealed by future investigation.

The New Technological Divide

As soon as one source of technological inequality seems to be diminishing, another one emerges: differential access to high-speed broadband service (currently using technologies such as integrated services digital network (ISDN), digital subscriber line (DSL), cable modems, and, in the near future, wireless-based Internet access (WAP), which, by the way, is most often narrowband at the time of writing). Speed and bandwidth are, of course, essential for fulfilling the promise of the Internet. All projected services and applications that people will really need for their work and lives depend on access to these new transmission technologies. Thus, it could well happen that while the huddled masses finally have access to the phone-line Internet, the global elites will have already escaped into a higher circle of cyberspace. The NTIA 2000 report included for the first time in its annual survey of the Internet, data on access to broadband services. In August 2000, only 10.7 percent of on-line households (representing 4.5 percent of all US households) had broadband access, with the remaining on-line households connecting to the Internet by regular phone line service. Most broadband-connected households used cable modems (50.8 percent) or DSL (33.7 percent), while wireless and satellite only accounted for 4.6 percent. Diffusion of broadband access was, in general terms, sharply differentiated by income, education, and ethnicity. Thus, while 13.8 percent of the most affluent households on-line have broadband access, the penetration rate was only 7.7 percent for the poorest group. Asian-Americans had the highest rate (11.7 percent) followed by whites (10.8 percent), African-Americans (9.8 percent), and Hispanics (8.9 percent).

Two interesting observations deserve comment. The lowest income bracket (under 5,000 dollars) exhibited a relatively high percentage of broadband access (9.9 percent). According to NTIA, this may reflect the importance of broadband for students, usually at a low level of income, emphasizing the critical role of broadband access for education, although other analysts suspect that this is probably related to "peer-to-peer" on-line sharing of music files (Dutton, personal communication, 2001). The other point concerns the fact that non-family households exceeded the national average of broadband penetration by a full-point (11.7 percent) in contrast with the relatively low ranking of this category in terms of Internet access *vis-à-vis* family households. This may reflect the fact that non-family households include both elderly people, less likely to be connected to the Internet, and younger, single persons who, if connected to the Internet, are interested in the new, expanding range of services for which broadband is needed.

Lower cost and the greater technological choice of broadband access are likely to increase the proportion of households with broadband access in the years to come: projections for the United States put at one-third the proportion of American households with fast Internet access, in their different forms, by 2005.

Furthermore, technologies of Internet access, both via DSL and (in Europe) by UMTS (universal mobile telecommunication systems) may develop on the basis of asymmetry between emission and reception. That is, access from the users to the service providers could be fast but the response could be slow. Rather than horizontal interactivity, it would result in an updated form of broadcasting (Bernard Benhamou and Patrice Riemens, personal communications, 2001). Differential speeds could be allocated to different uses and users on the basis of new Internet protocols, such as lvp6, allowing for the technological discrimination of various forms of traffic. The more the technology of delivery becomes flexible, the more price-based differentiation can be implemented, extending the scope of Internet-based inequality.

The head start that a minority of affluent households is enjoying in the uses and services provided by the Internet may prove a major source of cultural and social inequality in the future, as children of the first Internet generation grow up in very different technological environments.

The Knowledge Gap

Let us go one step further in exploring less obvious dimensions of the digital divide. If there is a consensus about the societal consequences of increased access to information it is that education and life-long learning become essential resources for work achievement and personal development. While learning is broader than education, schools still have a great deal to do with the learning process. In advanced societies, schools are rapidly becoming connected to the Internet. In the US, the percentage of public schools connected to the Internet increased from 35 percent in 1994 to 95 percent in 1999, and to almost 100 percent in 2001. More significantly, while in 1994 only 3 percent of public school instructional rooms were connected to the Internet, in 1999 the figure was 63 percent. In other words, the Internet was being rapidly included as an educational tool throughout the school system, and it can be safely assumed that in advanced societies it will soon be as pervasive as computers in the classroom (in 1999, in the US, the ratio of students per instructional computer in public schools was approximately six). However, Bolt and Crawford (2000), in their documented study on this subject, have shown that Internet use, and educational technology in general, are only as good as the teachers who use it. In this regard, in the US as in the world in general, there is considerable retardation between investment in technology hardware and on-line connectivity on the one hand, and investment in teacher training and school staffing for technology, on the other hand. And yet, in the US, a 1997 study of the US Department of Education showed that most teachers had not had education or training in using technology in their teaching, and only 15 percent reported having had at least 9 hours' training in education technology in 1994.

Furthermore, Internet-based learning is not only a matter of technological proficiency: it changes the kind of education that is required both to work on the Internet and to develop learning ability in an Internet-based economy and society. The critical matter is to shift from learning to learning-to-learn, as most information is on-line, and what is really required is the skill to decide what to look for, how to retrieve it, how to process it, and how to use it for the specific task that prompted the search for information. In other words, the new learning is oriented toward the development of the educational capacity to transform information into knowledge and knowledge into action (Dutton, 1999). The school system as a whole, both in the US and in the world at large, is, by all accounts, woefully inadequate in the use of this new learning methodology. Even if it has the technology, it lacks teachers able to use it effectively, and it lacks the pedagogy and institutional organization to induce new learning skills.

How does this educational imbalance relate to the digital divide? Basically, at four levels. First, because schools are territorially and institutionally (public/private) differentiated by class and race, there is a substantial cleavage in terms of technology among schools. Secondly, Internet access requires better teachers, and yet the quality of the teachers (in spite of their individual motivation, often very high in the poorest schools) is unevenly distributed among schools. Thirdly, the differential pedagogy of schools contrasts those systems that focus on the intellectual and personal development of the child with those essentially preoccupied with the ability to maintain discipline, warehouse children, and process them through their graduation. And these opposing pedagogical styles tend to correlate with the school's social status, and with the cultural and economic ability of the parents to put pressure on the schools. To be sure, authoritarian school systems, such as some traditional French schools (particularly those exported to foreign countries), do not fare any better than lower-class school districts when it comes to suppressing children's initiative, regardless of the dose of "high culture" they dispense. Yet, overall, upper and middle-class schools tend to be more attentive to the opening of the mind than schools in low-income areas. Fourthly, in the absence of adequate training of teachers, and pedagogic reform in the schools, families take over much of the responsibility for instructing their children, and helping them in the new technological world. Here the presence of Internet access at home, and of relatively educated parents with the cultural capacity to guide their children (often while learning the uses of the Internet themselves), makes a substantial difference.

The cumulative result of these different layers of inequality translates into vast differences in the effects of Internet use on educational performance. Although studies on the matter are scant and do not allow firm conclusions, it may well be that, in a context where the ability to process information on and with the Internet becomes crucial, children from disadvantaged families fall farther behind their class mates with greater information-processing skills that they obtain from their exposure to a better-educated home environment (Gordo, forthcoming). Differential learning capacities, under relatively similar intellectual and emotional conditions, are correlated with the cultural and educational level of the family. If these trends were to be confirmed, in the absence of corrective measures, the use of the Internet, both in school and in professional life, could amplify the social differences rooted in class, education, gender, and ethnicity. This may be the most fundamental dimension of the digital divide emerging at the dawn of the Internet Age.

The Global Digital Divide

The rapid diffusion of the Internet is proceeding unevenly throughout the planet. In September 2000, of a total of about 378 million Internet users (representing 6.2 percent of the world's population) North America's share stood at 42.6 percent, and Western Europe at 23.8 percent, while Asia represented 20.6 percent of the total (including Japan), Latin America 4 percent, Eastern Europe 4.7 percent, the Middle East 1.3 percent, and Africa a meager 0.6 percent (with most users being in South Africa) (NUA on-line surveys, 2000). This is, of course, in sharp contrast with the share in each region of the world's population. The level of Internet penetration for individual countries was incomparably lower in the developing world: thus India, for all the hype about its high-technology industry, and of substantial growth of users in 2000, still counted only 1.5 million people on-line, accounting for a meager 0.16 percent of the population, in contrast to 41.5 percent of households in the US, 30.8 percent in the UK, and 24.7 percent in Germany. In absolute numbers, the US, with 139.6 million people having on-line access from home, and Japan, with 26.3 million, were the largest contributors to the Internet society. So, the world, the global economy, and the networks of communication are being transformed with and around the Internet, while ignoring for the time being the overwhelming proportion of the population of the planet—over 93 percent in the year 2000. Indeed, in 1999, over half the people on the planet had never made or received a telephone call, although this is changing fast.

However, if we consider the trends over time a more complex picture arises. Between January 1997 and August 2000, the number of Internet users worldwide increased by a factor of four, and the shares of each region of the world changed substantially. North America's share plummeted, in spite of the rapid diffusion of the Internet in the US and Canada, from 62.1 percent of the world total to 42.6 percent. Most other regions displayed impressive gains, both in absolute numbers and in their relative share: Asia increased from 14.2 to 20.6 percent of the world total, and is on its way to reach the level of the European Union in absolute numbers of users, in spite of the growth of Europe's share from 15.8 to 23.8 percent. Eastern Europe has exceeded the growth rate of all other regions, increasing its share from 1.8 to 4.7 percent. Australia increased its share moderately, from 2 to 2.4 percent, with one of the highest penetration rates in the world in proportion to its population. The Middle East increased from 0.8 to 1.3 percent, and Latin America almost doubled its relative share, going from 2.3 to 4 percent, for a total number of over 15 million users. And while India only counted about 1.5 million users by the end of 2000, this figure has to be contrasted with just about 270,000 users in 1999. Africa, in spite of multiplying by three the number of its users, from 700,000 to 2,124,800, saw its share slightly decline from 0.9 to 0.6 percent, underscoring the fact that at this speed of change in the

world's technological paradigm, the laggard countries are compelled to outperform the most advanced societies in order to
improve their lot: if they stay where they are, they will go back-
wards. Furthermore, the key figure for Africa is that South Africa
accounts for 1.8 million users in this total, leaving a meager
325,000 users for the rest of the continent, although this latter
figure is probably underestimated since other reports put
the total number of Africa's Internet users at 3.1 million, with 1.3
million for Africa outside South Africa. It should also be noted that
in developing areas, and particularly in Africa, access points to the
Internet (even if they are counted as individual users) are collectively shared among groups of related people, so standard surveys
may not provide an accurate picture of the actual diffusion of the
Internet in Africa and other low-income areas.

Overall, measured in terms of access, it is likely that we will see
fast diffusion of the Internet around most of the globe in the
coming years. The bulk of new users will certainly come from
developing countries, simply because it is where over 80 percent of
the population of the world live. East Asia is the fastest growing
area in the world in terms of use of the Internet. By the end of
2000, South Korea was the leading country, with 42 percent of the
population on-line, including 25 percent of users with high-speed
Internet connection from home. Taiwan's penetration rate was
over 36 percent, and almost 30 percent for Hong Kong. Beijing
accounts for one-third of Internet users in China.

However, the conditions under which the Internet is diffusing in
most countries are creating a deeper digital divide. Key urban
centers, globalized activities, and the higher-educated social groups
are being included in the Internet-based global networks, while
most regions and most people are switched off. For instance, in
South Africa, Internet use is growing very fast: the number of users
jumped from half a million to 1.82 million between October 1999
and October 2000 (NUA Surveys, 2000). Yet, the large majority of
the users were younger than 25 years and from higher-income
groups. Indeed, in 2000, from the 9 million households in South
Africa, 5.9 million did not have a wireline telephone, and 2.1
million remained without access to telephones within 5 kilometers

of their homes. Less than 1 percent of rural households had telephones; 90 percent of white households had a telephone, but only 11 percent of black households (Gillwald, 2000). In Chile, where the Internet is diffusing rapidly, this expansion is socially and territorially limited: Santiago (where 40 percent of the population live) accounts for 57 percent of the phone lines and 50 percent of Internet users. The 26 percent of Chileans in the higher-income groups represent 70 percent of Internet connections. In Bolivia, where Internet development started in the late 1990s, only 2 percent of the population had Internet access from home at the end of 1999, but the bulk of these homes were in La Paz, and the gap in dial-up Internet use between La Paz residents and the rest of the country was increasing (Laserna, Morales Anaya, and Gomez, 2000).

This differential use of the Internet in the developing world is being driven by the huge gap in telecommunications infrastructure, Internet service providers, and Internet content providers, as well as by the strategies being used to deal with this gap. First, faced with the imperatives of global communication, key activities in each country (financial institutions, media, international business, high-level government institutions, the military, international hotels, transportation systems, and the like) cannot wait for the costly and lengthy revamping of the entire telecommunications system, often proceeding through a necessary, but slow, and conflictive process of privatization and deregulation. Thus, dedicated systems, often via satellite transmission connected to sophisticated local area networks, cater to the needs of preferential clients. The study by Kiselyova and Castells (2000) on the Russian Internet documents how Russian banks and foreign international business linked the main Russian centers to the world with specific telecommunications links, largely bypassing the obsolete Russian telecommunications infrastructure. Secondly, Internet service providers tend to be dependent on the US or European Internet backbones, increasing cost, and complexity, as well as creating intractable problems in the design and maintenance of the network. Thirdly, as shown by the worldwide mapping of Internet domains by Matthew Zook (see Chapter 8), Internet content providers are very much concentrated in a few metropolitan areas of the developed world (for instance, London has more Internet domains than the whole of Africa). This concentration considerably biases the usefulness and appropriateness of Internet use for much of the world. It certainly starts with language, as 78 percent of websites are in English only, thus creating a substantial barrier for most people in the world (other sources estimate a higher figure for this percentage). But it is also related to the kind of content that users can find on the Internet, and to the difficulty for people without sufficient education, knowledge, and skills to appropriate the technology for their own interests and values. Of course, all these obstacles are not cast in stone, and the flexibility of the Internet allows alternative uses, and adaptation to the users under proper technological, institutional, educational, and cultural conditions. But this is exactly the heart of the matter. More precisely, how does the Internet, and the digital divide currently associated with its differential, worldwide expansion, relate to the process of global development?

During the 1990s, coinciding with the explosion of the information-technology revolution, the rise of the new economy, and the diffusion of the Internet, the world experienced a substantial increase in income inequality, polarization, poverty, and social exclusion, as documented, among other sources, by the annual *Human Development Reports* elaborated by the United Nations Development Programme (UNDP, 1999, 2000, 2001). To be sure, trends differ by countries and areas. For instance, China and Chile have seen a substantial reduction in the proportion of the population living in poverty. And the industrialization of a few countries, and of the major metropolitan areas in others, have substantially improved the living standards for tens of millions of Chinese, Indians, Koreans, Malaysians, Brazilians, Argentinians, Chileans, and others in scattered areas around the world. Yet, on the other hand, the collapse of the transitional economies, the hardship imposed by financial crises in Mexico, Brazil, Argentina, Ecuador, Indonesia, Thailand, South Korea, and other Asian countries, the lingering economic and social crisis in Africa and the Middle East, and the patterns of social exclusion in most countries in the world, have swelled the legions of doom and survival. At the turn of the millennium, close to 50 percent of the world's population was trying to get by on less than 2 dollars a day, in a sharp increase in the proportion of people in a similar condition one decade earlier. On the other hand, 20 percent of the people disposed of 86 percent of the wealth. Inequality is even more accentuated for young people, since four-fifths of people under 20 live in developing countries. And women continue to bear the burden of poverty, illiteracy, and health problems, while being in charge of managing everyday survival for their families.

Overall, the gap in productivity, technology, income, social benefits, and living standards between the developed and the developing world increased during the 1990s, in spite of spectacular strides in economic growth in China's coastal areas, India's high-tech industries, Brazilian and Mexican manufacturing exports, Argentina's food exports, and Chilean sales of wine, fish, and fruits. Environmental conditions deteriorated, both in terms of natural resources, and in the mushrooming cities of developing countries, projected to be home for half of their population in the next 25 years.

Naturally, correlation is not causality, so it could well be that all these social and environmental problems are independent of the process of globalization and Internet-led economic development. It could be, but it's not. It can be argued instead that, under the current social and institutional conditions prevailing in our world, the new techno-economic system seems to induce uneven development, simultaneously increasing wealth and poverty, productivity and social exclusion, with its effects being differentially distributed in various areas of the world and in various social groups. And because the Internet is at the heart of the new socio-technical pattern of organization, this global process of uneven development is perhaps the most dramatic expression of the digital divide. Here is the argument.

(1) The extreme social unevenness of the development process is linked to the networking logic and global reach of the new economy. If everything and everyone that can be a source of value can be easily connected, and as soon as he/she/it ceases to be valuable can be equally easily disconnected, then the global production

system is composed simultaneously of highly valuable and productive people and places, and by those who are not so, or not any longer, while still being there. Because of the dynamism and competitiveness of the new economy, other forms of production become destructured, and ultimately phased out—or else transformed in informal economies, dependent on their uncertain connection to the dynamic, global system. The mobility of resources, and the flexibility of the management system, allow the global system to be largely independent of specific locales—where people live.

(2) Education, information, science, and technology become the critical sources of value creation in the Internet-based economy. Educational, informational, and technological resources are characterized by extremely uneven distribution throughout the world (UNESCO, 1999). While enrollment in schools has substantially increased in the developing world, most education is tantamount to the warehousing of children, as many teachers do not have education themselves, and are underpaid and overworked. Furthermore, the education system in most countries is technologically backward and institutionally bureaucratized. While telecommunication systems have improved lately in much of the world, there is still a substantial gap between countries, and between regions within countries, both in the quality of the infrastructure and in teledensity. Satellite transmission and wireless telephony could allow leapfrogging of the gradual lay-out of the traditional technological infrastructure, but the financial and human resources for such developmental investment are missing in most of the world. Lack of education and lack of informational infrastructure leaves most of the world dependent on the performance of a few, globalized segments of their economies. Since most of the population cannot be employed in this sector, because it lacks the skills, occupational and social structures become increasingly dualized. For instance, in South Africa, in 2000, while the unemployment rate was above 35 percent of the labor force, the demand for tens of thousands of jobs requiring a college degree could not be met by supply: in 1995–9 the demand for this kind of job soared by 325 percent. At the same time, many professional workers were

leaving the country, unable or unwilling to endure the arduous adjustment to the new social and political conditions.

(3) This developmental connection to the global economy is increasingly vulnerable to the whirlwind of global financial flows, on which national currencies and the valuation of national stock markets ultimately depend. In a period of systemic financial volatility, financial crises, of variable intensity, are recurrent. Every crisis wastes labor resources, devaluing people who are hardly able to get back on track. They end up withdrawing to the back alleys of survival that constitute the informal economy.

(4) As new technologies, new production systems, new global markets, and the new institutional structure of world trade eliminate traditional agriculture (still employing about half of the working people of the world) a rural exodus of gigantic dimensions is being induced, particularly in Asia, with hundreds of millions of new migrants destined to be painfully absorbed in the survival economy of overcrowded metropolitan areas already on the edge of ecological catastrophe (Roy, forthcoming).

(5) Governments are increasingly constrained by global flows of capital and information, disciplined by the enforcers of freedom of circulation of these flows (such as the International Monetary Fund), and limited by the supranational institutions that they built as defensive devices to survive globalization. The ensuing crisis of governance leads to the breakdown of regulations, and even their underdeveloped welfare states come under attack. The social contract between various social groups, wherever it existed, is challenged. Labor becomes individualized, and the old system of industrial relations, built on collective bargaining between business and labor, takes refuge in the public sector, creating a new social cleavage between the few protected workers, using their bargaining power to siphon resources from the rest of society, and the mass of unorganized workers, often employed in the informal economy.

(6) In the wake of crisis, and with large segments of the population unable to participate in the productive, competitive sector of the economy, some try a new form of globalization: the global criminal economy, made up of transnational networks engaging in

any kind of illicit trade that could yield a profit—often with the help of the Internet—and practicing electronic money-laundering in the financial markets. The global criminal economy penetrates politics and institutions, destabilizes societies, corrupts and disorganizes states in many countries—and not just in the case of the usual suspects.

(7) Subjected to extraordinary pressures from above and from below, and with a decreasing margin of maneuver in a globalized system, governments suffer a widespread crisis of legitimacy. Thus, according to a global opinion poll conducted by Gallup for the United Nations in 1999, two-thirds of respondents thought that their country was not governed by the will of the people (Annan, 2000). The weakening of political institutions diminishes the ability of societies to adjust and correct the negative shocks induced by the transition to a new techno-economic system, thus amplifying these shocks.

(8) In the extreme cases of the crisis of legitimacy, and political disintegration, large-scale banditry and civil wars develop, sometimes leading to mass massacres, to the exodus of hundreds of thousands, to famine, and to epidemics. This is the case in Africa, but, at the time of writing, a country as important as Colombia was suffering what appears to be an endless civil war between different factions, Peru and Ecuador were shaken by the collapse of their political regimes (hopefully for the better), Indonesia was on the edge of all-out regional wars, and the elected president of the Philippines was ousted after he turned out to be "the lord of gambling lords."

It would seem that all this has little to do with the digital divide and, for that matter, with the Internet. And yet, this is precisely the point I want to make. The ability of the Internet-based economy, and of the Internet-based information system, to network segments of societies around the world articulates the key nodes in a dynamic, planetary system, while discarding those segments of societies and those locales that offer little interest from the point of view of value-making. But these discarded elements have the ability to control people and local resources in their countries, as well as their political institutions. Therefore, the elites try to use the leverage of their power over people and territory to provide the global networks of money and power with access to whatever is still valuable in the country, in exchange for the elites' subordinate participation in these global networks. As for the people marginalized in the process, they tend to use a variety of strategies, not necessarily incompatible. They survive in the informal economy at the local level. They try to compete globally on the basis of the networks of the criminal economy. They mobilize to obtain resources from the globalized local elites, putting pressure on these elites to share the benefits obtained from their incorporation into the global networks. Or they mobilize to build their own agency of intermediation with the global system, by challenging the state—either through separation or through succession.

The fundamental digital divide is not measured by the number of connections to the Internet, but by the consequences of both connection and lack of connection. Because the Internet, as shown in this book, is not just a technology. It is the techological tool and organizational form that distributes information power, knowledge generation, and networking capacity in all realms of activity. Thus, developing countries are caught in a tangled web. On the one hand, being disconnected, or superficially connected, to the Internet is tantamount to marginalization in the global, networked system. Development without the Internet would be the equivalent of industrialization without electricity in the industrial era. This is why the often-heard statement concerning the need to start with "the real problems of the Third World"—meaning health, education, water, electricity, and the like—before coming to the Internet reveals a profound misunderstanding of the current issues in development. Because, without an Internet-based economy and management system, there is little chance for any country to generate the resources necessary to cover its developmental needs, on a sustainable ground—meaning economically sustainable, socially sustainable, and environmentally sustainable.

In the absence of global economic and technological integration of countries around the world, it would have been reasonable to consider alternative models of development, less technology-intensive, probably with lower productivity yields and slower material improvement, yet closer to the history, culture, and natural conditions of each country, and perhaps more satisfying for the majority of its people. However, it is too late to afford this kind of serene reflection. The Internet-based economy and information system, proceeding at Internet speed, has locked in the developmental trajectories within a narrow range. Barring a global catastrophe, it is unlikely that societies around the world would engage freely in non-technological forms of development—among other reasons, because the interests and ideology of their elites are deeply rooted in the current model of development. And once the option is taken to part of the global networks, the Internet-based logic of production, competition, and management is a prerequisite for prosperity, freedom, and autonomy.

But it can also be a recipe for crisis and marginalization, as the argument I presented above suggests. Indeed, the experience of the first years of the Internet Age points in this direction. This is not the consequence of the Internet *per se*, but of the digital divide. That is, the divide created between those individuals, firms, institutions, regions, and societies that have the material and cultural conditions to operate in the digital world, and those who cannot, or cannot adapt to the speed of change. Under such conditions, the networking logic of the Internet-based global system scans the planet for opportunities, and links up what it needs for its programmed goals—and only what it needs. There follows the fragmentation of societies and institutions, in parallel with the dynamic networking of valuable firms, triumphant individuals, and surviving organizations.

Of course, these processes are ultimately dependent on human action, so they can be reversed or modified. Yet it is not only a matter of knowledge and political will, although these are indispensable conditions for any alternative course of action. It depends on the extent of the digital divide in each country. It depends on the ability to generate a process of social learning, in parallel with the building of an information and communication technology infrastructure. It depends on the managerial capacity of the economy, on the quality of the labor force, on the existence of social consensus, based on social redistribution, and on the emergence of legitimate political institutions rooted in the local and able to manage the global. And it depends on the ability of countries and social actors to adapt to Internet speed in the process of change. More of the same leads to the broadening of the digital divide, a divide that may ultimately engulf the world in a series of multi-dimensional crises. The new model of development requires leap-frogging over the planetary digital divide. It calls for an Internet-based economy, powered by learning and knowledge-generation capacity, able to operate within the global networks of value, and supported by legitimate, efficient political institutions. It is in the shared interest of humankind that such a model emerges while there is still time.

Reading Links

Annan, Kofi (2000) *Report to the Millennium Assembly of the United Nations.* New York: United Nations.

Bolt, D. and Crawford, R. (2000) *Digital Divide: Computers and our Children's Future.* New York: TV Books.

Castells, Manuel (2000*a*) "Information technology and global development," Keynote address to the Economic and Social Council of the United Nations, New York, United Nations, ECOSOC, May 2000.

—— (2000*b*) *End of Millennium,* 2nd edn. Oxford: Blackwell.

Cheskin Research (2000) *The Digital World of the US Hispanic.* Redwood Shores, CA: Cheskin Research Report.

Dutton, William (1999) *Society on the Line: Information Politics in the Digital Age.* Oxford: Oxford University Press.

Evans, Peter (ed.) (forthcoming), *Liveable Cities? The Politics of Urban Livelihood and Sustainability.* Berkeley, CA: University of California Press.

Gillwald, Alison (2000) "Building Castells in the ether? Lessons for South Africa's information and communication sector," paper delivered at the Seminar on Globalization, Development, and Technology organized by the Center for Higher Education Transformation, Pretoria, June 20, 2000.

Gordo, Blanca (forthcoming) "Overcoming the digital divide: community technology training centers in California," unpublished PhD dissertation, University of California, Department of City and Regional Planning, Berkeley, California.

Guimaraes de Castro, Maria Helena (1999) *Education for the Twenty-first Century: The Challenge of Quality and Equity*. Brasilia: Instituto Nacional de Estudos e Pesquisas Educacionais.

Hamelink, Cees (1999) "ICT and social development: the global policy context," Geneva: United Nations Research Institute for Social Development, discussion paper 116.

Hoffman, Donna L. and Novak, Thomas P. (1999) "The evolution of the digital divide: examining the relationships of race to Internet access and usage over time," Nashville, Vanderbilt University: Owen School of Graduate Management, Project 2000, research paper (published on-line).

Kiselyova, Emma and Castells, Manuel (2000) "Russia in the Information Age," in Victoria Bonnell and George Breslauer (eds), *Russia in the New Century*, pp. 126–57. Boulder, CO: Westview Press.

Laserna, Roberto, Morales Anaya, Rolando, and Gomez, Gonzalo (2000) *Mundos urbanos*. La Paz, Bolivia: Programa de Naciones Unidas para el Desarrollo.

Lewin, Tamar (2001) "Children's computer use grows, but gaps persist, study says," *The New York Times*, January 22: A11.

Lin, Marcia C. (1999) *Computers, Teachers, and Peers: Science Learning Partners*. Hillsdale, NJ: Lawrence Erlbaum.

Loader, Brian D. (ed.) (1998) *Cyberspace Divide: Equality, Agency, and Policy in the Information Society*. London: Routledge.

Mansell, Robin and Wenn, Uta (eds) (1998) *Knowledge Societies. Information Technology for Sustainable Development*, Oxford: Oxford University Press.

Muller, Johen, Cloete, Nico, and Badat, Shireen (eds) (2001) *The Challenges of Globalization: South African Debates with Manuel Castells*. Pretoria: Center for Higher Education Transformation/Longman.

National Science Board (2000) *Science and Engineering Indicators – 2000*. Arlington, VA: National Science Foundation.

NTIA (1999) *Falling Through the Net: Defining the Digital Divide: A Report on the Telecommunications and Information Technology Gap in America*. Washington, DC: US Department of Commerce.

—— (2000) *Falling Through the Net: Toward Digital Inclusion*. Washington, DC: US Department of Commerce.

Presidencia de la Republica de Chile (1999) *Chile hacia la sociedad de la informacion*. Santiago de Chile: Informe al Presidente de la Republica.

Roy, Ananya (forthcoming) *Squatters, Politics, and Gender: The Domestication of Calcutta*. Minneapolis, MN: University of Minnesota Press.

Servon, Lisa (forthcoming) *Bridging the Digital Divide*. Oxford: Blackwell.

Spooner, Tom and Rainie, Lee (2000) "African-Americans and the Internet," Washington, DC: Pew Internet and American Life Project, on-line Life Report, posted October 22.

UNESCO (1999) *World Communication and Information Report, 1999–2000*. Paris: UNESCO.

UK Department of Trade and Industry (2000) *Closing the Digital Divide: Information and Communication Technologies in Deprived Areas*. London: HMSO.

United Nations Development Programme (1996–2001) *Human Development Report*, annual reports. New York: United Nations and Oxford University Press.

US Department of Commerce, Office of Technology Policy, Technology Administration (1999) *The Digital Work Force: Building Infotech Skills at the Speed of Innovation*. Washington, DC: US Department of Commerce.

US Department of Commerce, Economics and Statistics Administration (2000) *Digital Economy 2000*. Washington, DC: US Department of Commerce.

US Department of Education, Office of Educational Research and Improvement, National Center for Education Statistics (2000) *Internet Access in US Public Schools and Classroom: 1994–99*. Washington, DC: US Department of Education.

Zook, Matthew (2001) "The geography of the Internet industry: venture capital, Internet start-ups, and regional development," unpublished PhD dissertation, University of California, Department of City and Regional Planning, Berkeley, California.

e-Links

www.ntia.doc.gov/ntiahome/digitaldivide
The US National Telecommunications and Information Agency annual reports on the digital divide in America.

http://wbLn0018.worldbank.org/external/lac/lac/lac.nsf/sectors/inftelecoms/175blefOe678f649852569ad00018365?opendocument
World Bank database on the digital divide in a global perspective.

The Digital Divide

www.oecd.org/dsti/sti/prod/digitaldivide.pdf
The OECD reports on the digital divide in an international perspective.

www.digitaldivide.gov/
Clearing house on data about the digital divide in the US.

www.childrenspartnership.org.pub low income/introduction.html
www.ovum.com/presoffice/pressreleases/default.asp?wp=WAP.htm
Policy Information Center–The Educational Testing Service Network (PIC–ETS) (1999) "Computer and classrooms: the state of technology in US schools," published on-line: www.ETS.org
Data and analyses on the educational dimension of the digital divide.

www.ctcnet.org
The network of community technology training centers.

www.pluggedin.org/
One of the most innovative experiences in community technology training, located in East Palo Alto, on the other side of Silicon Valley.

www.urbantech.org
A non-profit corporation addressing its resources to diffuse technological know-how in low-income communities around the US.

Conclusion

The Challenges of the Network Society

The Internet Galaxy is a new communication environment. Because communication is the essence of human activity, all domains of social life are being modified by the pervasive uses of the Internet, as this book has documented. A new social form, the network society, is being constituted around the planet, albeit in a diversity of shapes, and with considerable differences in its consequences for people's lives, depending on history, culture, and institutions. As with previous instances of structural change, this transformation offers as many opportunities as it raises challenges. Its future outcome is largely undetermined, and it is subjected to the contradictory dynamics between our dark side and our sources of hope. That is, to the perennial opposition between renewed attempts at domination and exploitation and people's defense of their right to live and to search for the meaning of life.

The Internet is indeed a technology of freedom—but it can free the powerful to oppress the uninformed, it may lead to the exclusion of the devalued by the conquerors of value. In this general sense, society has not changed much. But our lives are not determined by general, transcendent truths, but by the concrete ways in which we live, work, prosper, suffer, and dream. So, to act upon ourselves, individually and collectively, to be able to harness the wonders of the technology we have created, find meaning in our lives, better society, and respect nature, we need to place our action in the specific context of domination and liberation where we live: the network society, built around the communication networks of the Internet.

At the onset of the Information Age, we can perceive around the world an extraordinary feeling of uneasiness with the current process of technology-led change that threatens to generate a widespread backlash. Unless we address this feeling, its exacerbation may well wreck the promises of this new economy and society springing from technological ingenuity and cultural creativity.

This feeling is sometimes collectively expressed, as in the protests against globalization, the code word for the new technological, economic, and social order. These protests represent mainly the view of an active minority, and include interest groups with a very narrow vision of the state of the world—for instance, the defenders of rich countries' protectionism to keep their privileges against competition from the developing world. Yet, except for the excesses of their violent fringe, many of the issues raised by the anti-globalization protesters are a legitimate matter for debate, and they have found an echo in public opinion, as the growing attention paid to this debate by governments and international institutions seems to indicate.

Beyond the realm of radical protests, there is also fear among many citizens about what this new society, of which the Internet is a symbol, will bring about in terms of employment, education, social protection, and lifestyles. Some of these criticisms are objectively founded—in the deterioration of the natural environment, in job insecurity, or in the growth of poverty and inequality in many areas—not always in the developing world. For instance, in Silicon Valley, considering the whole decade of the 1990s, average real wages declined, in spite of the extraordinary growth in income of the top one-third of households—such was the extent of inequality. But there is something less objective, less quantifiable, but equally powerful in its potential effects. It is a personal feeling of lack of control, of acceleration of our lives, of an endless race toward unknown goals—or to goals whose meaning evaporates on close inspection. This feeling encompasses many of the actors of the new economy, in the moments when the thrill of innovation lapses, and prosperity appears to be fragile. While the fear of change is an historical constant in human experience (paradoxically, together with the urge for innovation from the most daring people), I believe that much of the resistance to, and dissatisfaction with, the Internet-led, networked world can be related to a number of unmet challenges.

The first one is freedom itself. The Internet networks provide global, free communication that becomes essential for everything. But the infrastructure of the networks can be owned, access to them can be controlled, and their uses can be biased, if not monopolized, by commercial, ideological, and political interests. As the Internet becomes the pervasive infrastructure of our lives, who owns and controls access to this infrastructure becomes an essential battle for freedom.

The second challenge is the opposite: exclusion from the networks. In a global economy, and in a network society where most things that matter are dependent on these Internet-based networks, to be switched off is to be sentenced to marginality—or compelled to find an alternative principle of centrality. As argued in Chapter 9, this exclusion may proceed by different mechanisms: lack of technological infrastructure; economic or institutional obstacles to access the networks; insufficient educational and cultural capacity to use the Internet in a self-determined manner; disadvantage in the production of the content communicated through the networks. The cumulative effects of these mechanisms of exclusion divide people around the planet, but no longer along the North/South cleavage, but between those connected in the global networks of value-making, around nodes unevenly dotting the world, and those switched off from these networks.

The third major challenge is the installation of information-processing and knowledge-generation capacity in every one of us—and particularly in every child. By this I obviously do not mean literacy in using the Internet in its evolving forms (this is presupposed). I mean education. But in its broader, fundamental sense; that is, to acquire the intellectual capacity of learning to learn throughout one's whole life, retrieving the information that is digitally stored, recombining it, and using it to produce knowledge for whatever purpose we want. This simple statement calls into question the entire education system developed during the industrial era. There is no more fundamental restructuring. And very few countries and institutions are truly addressing it because before we start changing the technology, rebuilding the schools, and re-training the teachers, we need a new pedagogy, based on interactivity, personalization, and the development of autonomous capacity of learning and thinking. While, at the same time, strengthening the character and securing the personality. And this is uncharted terrain.

The emergence of the network enterprise, and the individualization of employment patterns, raise another major challenge, this time to the system of labor relations constructed in the industrial society. Furthermore, since the welfare state was built on these systems of industrial relations and stable employment, it also comes under stress. The mechanisms of social protection on which social peace, working partnership, and personal security were based need to be redefined in the new socio-economic context. This is not an impossible task. After all, the most welfare state-oriented societies in the world, the Scandinavian democracies, are also the most advanced Internet-based, new economies in Europe. But, even in these societies, tensions between the logic of individual competition and the logic of social solidarity are rising, trade-offs will have to be found, and new forms of social contract will have to be negotiated, and perhaps fought over. On the other hand, the excesses of a purely liberal order of individual self-contracting, as epitomized by California, may lead to a search for some institutional form of personal security as soon as the fantasy world of endless, uninterrupted economic prosperity dissipates under the acid test of historical reality.

The new economy is overdue for new, flexible procedures of institutional regulation. There is no such thing as a purely free market. Markets are based on institutions, on laws, on courts, on supervision, on due process, and, ultimately, on the authority of the democratic state. When they are not, when economies engage in experiments of total de-institutionalization, as post-Communist Russia did in the early 1990s, under the impulse of Yeltsin's reformers supported by the International Monetary Fund, what emerges is not the market, but economic chaos, in which oligarchies are formed by the forceful appropriation of public wealth. Western capitalism prospered, even with crises and social struggles, by building institutions of social bargaining and economic regulation. The shift to computerized global networks as the organizational form of capital, production, trade, and management has largely undermined the regulatory capacity of both national governments and existing international institutions, starting with the increasing difficulty of collecting corporate taxes and controlling monetary policy. Systemic volatility of global financial markets and vast disparities in the utilization of human resources require new forms of regulation, adapted to the new technology and to the new market economy. It will not be easy. Particularly, it will not be easy to enact effective, dynamic regulation of global financial markets, for the reasons presented in this book. Yet, since no one has really tried, we actually do not know. It would be wise to find sensitive ways of channeling global finance before a major crisis forces us to do it under more strenuous conditions. Indeed, computer networks offer new technological tools of reasonable regulation that, powered by political will, could harness the dynamics of the market while preventing excessive disequilibrium.

Environmental degradation represents a critical challenge to be reckoned with. But its relationship to the Internet-based world is a double-edged process. On the one hand, because the network-powered economy relentlessly scans the planet for opportunities to make money, there is a process of accelerated exploitation of natural resources, as well as of environmentally damaging economic growth. To put it bluntly: if we include in the same model of growth the half of the population of the planet which is currently excluded, the model of industrial production and consumption that we have created is not ecologically sustainable. On the other hand, the Internet-based management of information introduces two counter-trends into the model of economic growth. First, we can substantially increase our knowledge of what is environmentally suitable and what is not, and we can factor this knowledge into our production system, given adequate institutional regulation and consumer information, along the lines suggested by the proponents of the "natural capitalism" school of thinking. Secondly, as argued in Chapter 5, the Internet has become a major organizing and mobilizing tool for environmentalists around the world, raising people's consciousness about alternative ways of living, and building the political force to make it happen. If we put together the two trends, it seems plausible that a redefinition of the model of economic growth, leading to a comprehensive sustainable development strategy, could be gradually established in time for the incorporation of the entire planet into this truly new economy. But this is only one possibility. Current trends, when taken into a global perspective, point in the opposite direction: extensive economic growth, mixed with destructive poverty, thus continuing the dilapidation of our natural heritage.

The greatest fear for people, however, is the oldest fear of humankind: fear of the technological monsters we can create. This is particularly the case with genetic engineering, but given the convergence between micro-electronics and biology, and the potential development of ubiquituous sensors and nanotechnology, this primary biological fear extends to the entire realm of technological discovery. One of the creators of networking technology, Bill Joy, has articulated this discourse on the dangers of uncontrolled technological ingenuity. He strikes a deep chord in our collective psyche because he is pin-pointing the most significant contradiction in the rise of the network society: the one between our technological over-development and our institutional and social under-development.

This is indeed the most fundamental challenge: the absence of the actors and institutions able and willing to take on these challenges. I have been referring to "we." But who are "we?" In terms of those affected by these trends, I mean all of us, humans. Yet, it is not the same to live in California (or for that matter in Barcelona) as in Cochabamba. And it is not the same in California to live in

Palo Alto as in East Palo Alto. You perceive the world analyzed in this book very differently if you are an Internet entrepreneur or a school teacher. Our professional, social, ethnic, gender, geographical, cultural differences lead to very different consequences in the relationship of each one of us to the network society. Yet, I contend that the challenges I have outlined affect all of us in a very fundamental way. But who should reckon with these challenges? Who are "we" in this case? Who are the actors in charge of managing our transition to the Information Age?

In democracy, it used to be governments, acting on behalf of the public interest. I still think they are the ones. But I say this with great difficulty because I am fully aware—as should be obvious from reading this book—of the crisis of legitimacy and efficiency that characterizes governments in our world. Not that they were great before our time. But we knew less about them, and they could do more—for or against us. How can we trust with the lives of our children governments controlled by parties that usually operate in systemic corruption (illegal financing), entirely dependent on image politics, led by professional politicians only accountable at election time, managing insulated bureaucracies, technologically outdated, and generally out of touch with the real life of their citizens? And, yet, what is the alternative?

Corporate business is displaying lately much greater social responsibility than people credit it for, but businesses are the main creators of our wealth, not the solvers of our problems—and most people would not trust such a corporate-dominated world. NGOs? These are to my taste the most innovative, dynamic, and representative forms of aggregation of social interests. But I have a tendency to consider them "neo-governmental organizations," rather than non-governmental organizations, because in many instances they are directly or indirectly subsidized by governments, and ultimately represent a form of political decentralization rather than an alternative form of democracy. They are part of the emerging, network state, with its variable geometry of institutional levels and political constituencies. Besides, while they represent legitimate interests, they can hardly substitute for the expression of the public good, and regulate or guide the network society on behalf of all of us.

The Challenges of the Network Society

"We" could still be *we*, the people, you and me. Building on our individual responsibility, as informed human beings, conscious of our duties, confident in our projects. Indeed, only if you and I, and all the others, are responsible for what we do, and feel responsible for what happens around us, can our society control and guide this unprecedented technological creativity.

However, we still need institutions, we still need political representation, participatory democracy, consensus-building procedures, and effective public policy. This starts with responsible, truly democratic governments. I believe that, in most societies, the practice of these principles is in a shambles, and a large proportion of citizens do not count on it. This is the weak link in the network society. Until we rebuild, both from the bottom up and from the top down, our institutions of governance and democracy, we will not be able to stand up to the fundamental challenges we are facing. And if democratic, political institutions cannot do it, no one else will or can. So, either we enact political change (whatever that means, in its various forms) or you and I will have to take care of reconfiguring the networks of our world around the projects of our lives.

Maybe there is another option. I imagine one could say: "Why don't you leave me alone?! I want no part of your Internet, of your technological civilization, of your network society! I just want to live my life!" Well, if this is your position, I have bad news for you. If you do not care about the networks, the networks will care about you, anyway. For as long as you want to live in society, at this time and in this place, you will have to deal with the network society. Because we live in the Internet Galaxy.

Index

Index

Index

Index

Index

path dependency 100, 101
PDP–11 computers 43
peer review 40, 46
performancebike.com 75
Pittman, Bob 190
political causes 53, 137
  citizen networks 144–55
  informational politics 155–8
  networked social movements
    138–43
political control 164, 169, 170
  mutual trusts 184–5
  regulation of the Internet 184–5
  surveillance technologies 170–3,
    177–82
    privacy protection technologies
      182–4
political disintegration 268–9, 281–2
political instability 107
political sabotage 51, 139, 158–64,
  177
Polman, Michael 149
pornography 196
  see also sex-oriented systems
Postel, Jon 11, 18, 24, 31
privacy 170
  consumers 174–5, 184
  e-mail 175–6
  employees 173
  surveillance technologies 170–3,
    175–82
    privacy protection technologies
      182–4
privatization 30
PRNET 11
Prodigy 25
productivity 96–100
protocols 26–7, 30, 38
Public Electronic Network 144
public key encryption 172
Putnam, Robert 121, 141

Quaterman, John 208
Quicktime 195

racial inequality 249–50, 252–4
radio broadcasting 191, 197
Rai, Shirin M. 140, 143
Rainie, Lee 121

Raymond, Eric 41, 44, 45, 46
Real Networks 175
Realplayer 195
Red Hat 101
Redfield, Robert 125
regulation 184–5
requests for comment (RFCs) 29, 30
Rheingold, Howard 52, 54, 119
Rice, Ronald, E. 120, 124
Richardson, Ronald 232, 233, 234
Riemans, Patrice 123, 148, 153
Ritchie, Dennis 42
Roberts, Lawrence (Larry) 18, 22
Robinson, John P. 117, 121, 124
Rodriguez, Felipe 149
role-playing 118–19
Ronfeldt, David 158, 160, 162, 163
Rosen, Jeffrey 175
Russia 254–5, 263, 279
  see also Soviet Union
Rustema, Reinder 153

Salomon, I. 232, 233
satellite broadcasting 191
SATNET 11
Saxenian, Anna 94
scalability 76
Scantlebury, Roger 17
Schiller, Dan 240
Schuler, Douglas 53, 144
Seattle Community Network 144
secure socket layer (SSL) 171
security issues 158–64, 177
segregation 238–41
self-programmable labor 91, 92, 95,
  103
service providers 12
sex-oriented systems 52–3, 54, 169–70,
  179, 180, 196
Shiller, Robert 87
Sichel, Daniel 97
Singapore 164
skilled workers 93–4, 103–4
social exclusion 3, 238, 247–8, 277
  see also digital divide
social outcomes 4–5
  business practices, *see* e-business
  civic involvement and social
    interaction 120–5

HIGHLINE COLLEGE LIBRARY

Index